HERITAGE OF YEARS

Kaleidoscopic Memories

BY

FRANCES M. WOLCOTT

1851–1889

ILLUSTRATED

MINTON, BALCH & COMPANY
NEW YORK   1932

Copyright, 1932, by
FRANCES M. WOLCOTT

All rights reserved. This book, or parts thereof, must not be reproduced in any form without permission.

Printed in the United States of America by
THE KNICKERBOCKER PRESS, NEW ROCHELLE, N. Y.

FRANCES METCALFE BASS, LONDON, 1875

FOR MY SON

This is a chronicle of my youth and the influence surrounding my once-upon-a-time little boy; he who pulled his own hair and bit his hand in passionate protest of being thwarted. At three years of age, being swept off my seven-eighths thoroughbred by a clothes-line, near the stable, he picked himself up, wiped the gravel from his bleeding cheek, and beseeched to be remounted. His request was granted by the hard-shelled Baptist coachman, with whom he at times went to meeting, and who promised not to tell his mother.

At three years of age he was given liberty of choice. The best and wisest course was always pointed out to him, but he was left to take the consequence of his own decisions. He best knows, now that he has wilful descendants, whether such personal responsibility should be given by parents. Shielding children from care and responsibility is an occupation with those who make maternity an amiable vice, and fathers who would save their children from the pitfalls into which they themselves once fell.

Character and efficiency are forged by the individuals, who in truth walk alone from the cradle to the grave. The generous promise of my lovable little boy as to gentleness has been fulfilled in his manhood. Would he care to know that the father of his maternal great-grandfather, Thomas Metcalfe, was killed in the Tory army at the Battle of Bunker Hill, and that Thomas Metcalfe was taken by his mother to Virginia, where later he freed his Virginia-born slaves and trekked to Central New York?

He became a respected citizen, beloved of the children of the town. Perhaps a dash of the blood of the fighting Metcalfes of Yorkshire, who went out on white horses, three hundred strong, to battle for Prince Charlie, is still operative.

The blend of ancestral blood of his forebears may have given him hatred of defeat, and lust of battle, whether on the football field or in courts of law.

His cry was always for the open. His delight in adventure has often been the trailing of big game,—killing of bear, mountain goat or sheep. Thomas Metcalfe, too, liked the open. He could follow a bee from the fields to its secret store of honey in a hollow tree in the then virginal forests. He loved every weed, wild flower and tree, as well as all flying birds, growing things and the four-footed animals of the wood.

Perhaps the urge of the itching foot to wander on the world's highway, shown in his descendants, is but his call of the wild, but in my son's veins is the calmer strain of John Alden, whose daughter Ruth on December 3, 1657, married John Bass, from whom my son is in direct line of descent.

We should have a larger charity for others and ourselves had we the knowledge of inherited tendencies when we weigh humanity in the balance of judgment.

PROLOGUE

WHEN I came to the peak of eighty years, a gala week, a début into senility, lifted me on a rising tide of affection and friendship which possibly has the brilliancy of the setting sun against the lengthening shadows of days lived and loved.

If there be but two passions that survive old age—gambling and gardening—the first I have never tasted, but the making of gardens has still a beckoning hand. It has the cult of beauty, the mystery of birth, growth, sleep, death and resurrection, a place of hopes and a place of graves.

I think it was in the year 1920, when I was in England on a curious mission, that John Buchan urged me to dictate my memoirs. I said I could not remember my past, and he asked, "What is your first memory?" I replied, "A wildcat in a tree on a farm in Genesee County." "A good beginning for your book," quoth he.

While the wildcat may not be the totem of my tribe, the subtlety and grace of the cat family, whether the kitten on the hearth or the black panther in the zoo, or the wild puma in the Rockies, are still a contributing interest to life. Perhaps it accounts for the fact that I believe to enhance life one must envisage death; that a spice of danger is the flavor of real vitality.

I still hold that emotion which comes around the corner

unexpectedly is the crown sheaf of experience. Thought lifts one's soul, but emotion makes us one with the human race.

Returning not long ago under the full moon of a June night from a poetic party in a garden overlooking Long Island Sound, where Barrere's golden magic flute hidden among the trees awoke the sylvan call of Pan and Romance, my companion, who seemed to have a monopoly of this world's blessings—years under thirty, good looks, magnetism, wealth, power, and a beautiful wife and two sons—suddenly exclaimed that after mounting with the bombing squad to greet the sun, haunted by the fear of pursuing death, to destroy the enemy from above the clouds, all else was anti-climax and dull.

Of my frontier days I now recall with a thrill the rides over the Veta Pass through the Grand Canyon on the cow-catcher of a locomotive, shot like a catapult through the high walls of the Canyon, lighted only by the early rising stars.

Who can forget the ecstasy of the moment when the hounds give tongue and a spirited horse springs to follow? Joy and danger ahead! Pursuit! The spice of a bright morning!

To enjoy life one should have five keen senses. One should relish good food, the bouquet of fine wine, the song of a bird or a symphony, the sight of towns, the vastness of the golden sands of the desert, the green world and the melancholy romance of a hurdy-gurdy playing at twilight a block away.

The old know that nothing lasts; that no unrequited love or love fulfilled endures; that heartache, like joy, has self-limitations, and one forgets and forgives.

Those sitting on the sidelines of life, having the sophistication of past living, can look the world between the eyes and say,

PROLOGUE

"Come Sorrow, come Joy, Living is worth it, and one is sharing with one's kind."

The privileges of my life have been great, including the acquaintance of distinguished persons of three continents, audiences with Popes and Kings, intercourse with soldiers, artists, musicians and writers. Those who have attracted me most are those who have had great dreams and striven to make them reality. One has infinite sympathy for those on the threshold of life, and living alone can make that sympathy deep.

Many there are who long for the divine companion of the road, possibly the poet in tatters who eagerly climbs towards the light upon the mountain; but the perfect comrade, like the flawless hour, is the treasure at the end of the rainbow.

One must throw aside the personal yardstick of measurement at any age in trying to enter into the universal; one must sit reverently at the feet of Gamaliel and bask in the simplicity of great natures; must understand the point of view of the Indian and the white man of whatever clime, reckoning that though the super-Englishman may be the most delightful of civilized beings, the man who turns the potter's wheel in India or the American Indian who uses his potter's thumb in Arizona, or the native black man who bears the white man's burden as he treks in the jungle, has knowledge of which we are ignorant, which can enlarge our vision. Those of long life must be astonished at nothing; must love gossip of their time, for it is history in the making. There is no greater wit than that of the man of the street and no more bleeding slices of life than one gets from taxi drivers when held up by traffic. I once asked a clever Frenchman to define an interesting person. He replied, "An interested one, alive with intellectual curiosity." For to an illuminated mind there is nothing great or small; all is harmonious in the mosaic of one's days.

Many years ago "H. H." (Helen Hunt) said to me that next to the real thing, love, flirtation was the most interesting of the give and take of human experience. Without hypocrisy, she stated the truth that women love power even as men do. When they rise above petty tyranny and are unable to give the color of their souls in song or verse, with paint brush or model of clay in creative art, they call for one another. The exercise of power of men over women or women over men has been the seed of romance and tragedy since Lilith, before Eve, shared the duality of Adam's heart in the Garden of Eden.

The rich pattern of my life includes, in my childhood, looking from my nursery window at night at the soldiers passing to the station in the Civil War, playing "Marching through Georgia," then the fevered days of the Spanish War when those I loved served at the Front; the excitement and my delight when in the Great War I crossed on the *Lusitania,* lying off the Irish Coast seven hours and passing through St. George's Channel without a pilot, pursued by submarines, as we were loaded with "bully beef" between the decks, and food supplies of all sorts; soldiers returning to their colors from every land; later walking the hospitals of wounded men; the adventurous day spent on the battlefield of the Marne in 1915; the French Army on Bastille Day coming through the Arc de Triomphe, which had been closed to them for thirty years, followed by Pershing's best; watching the English troops and our stalwart Americans and the depleted Black Watch marching with pipers playing under Admiralty Arch in London; the floating colors of the Italian

PROLOGUE

Peace Festival in the Square of Victor Emmanuel at Rome. They make a brilliant panorama of War and Peace.

Many parades have come and gone, touching our hearts and lifting our ideals and our patriotism toward the struggle for the rise of humanity, but what edification and admiration stirred the blood and lit enthusiasm when the parade of the New York police passed up Fifth Avenue last spring. What order! What chic! An amalgamate of more than one race, though I murmured, "God bless the Irish." An organization with the faults and virtues of the human family, but on the whole wearing the badge of courage. In this melting pot of Manhattan, of the criminal class, the upper ten and the submerged tenth, the police make life fairly safe for the decent citizen. How can any paranoiacal, self-seeking reformer, who hunts rabbits with a brass band, smirch them one and all? To have lived behind the curtain of politics for half a century and to have superficially watched the political life of more than one foreign nation, one knows that not all honest men are able, nor all able men honest. Solomon knew the psychology of men better than any equipped modern politician or the head of Scotland Yard. Modified by environment and education, human nature remains inviolate and unchanged, though the temperament of an individual is his fate. The pageant of one's past informs one's present, now and again sending a ray like a searchlight into the future. At eighty one waits for morning coffee and the newspaper, whose bulletin embraces the earth from pole to pole, and the value of the front page takes zest, knowledge and a genius for living to know its value.

In Rostand's poetic drama, "La Princesse Lointaine," Rudell, the troubadour, embarking from the shore of France to see the face of the lady of his dreams in Tripoli before death closed his eyes, asks his companion, the poet, "What is the greatest thing in the world?" "Enthusiasm" was the poet's answer. Whether it be football, original research or the winning of battles, they are one and all kindled by that selfsame torch.

When in the long shadows of the evening of life one may still love the tellers of great stories, the undaunted thought of the real aristocrat and of the fearless man of the gutter, for they understand one another and care naught for the Joneses.

One must believe work, and achievement through it, is a blessing, not a curse; for the idle must, in dancing, sport and hunting, sweat to be sane and healthy as the laborer sweats to till the field.

In this age of worship of the God of Speed we cry for madder music and stronger wine to free our craving for excitement. For the thinker there is still solitude and love of woods, fields and sky to give clear call above the roar of cities and the rush of motors and airplanes.

Younger eyes there are at eighty than at eighteen, for we old ones have ceased to stumble over our emotions and our eyes are no longer blinded with the dust of desire. We value the moment which youth wastes as a spendthrift flinging away his gold.

The banner of the Lend-A-Hand Club holds the secret of rich philosophy—"Look up, not down, look out and not in, look forward and not backward, and lend a hand."

The old know that in their personal lives the younger people have no interest, but the young are swift to recognize one who has laughed, who has danced until morning, who has walked with Pain and Sorrow as a friend. They seek sympathy, and the finding of it makes their friendship become, for those to whom it is given, a mine of gold.

Richard Le Gallienne once sent me a gift of a novel of his with a letter saying, "This goes to you because you understand. Next to Creation comes Understanding. The heart loves not more the heart that loves it, than the brain loves the brain that comprehends it."

Old and young may be spellbound by oratory or lifted by the compelling influence of a great artist, whether actor, singer or speaker of winged words; may feel the stride and rhythm of marching humanity, but all we really can hold beyond the moment are blessed memories. There is nothing, when maturity enriches the mind, to equal the value of friendship, the interchange of talk by the blaze of an applewood fire, a tale of high adventure, or to watch the day die or the sun rise as on the first day of the world. The theater, the world of music, one's book, one's bed and a light over one's shoulder, the love of form and color, the association of informing minds, to love and to give—this is the ageless cycle of life. Man's prerogative is adventure. To woman to be the mother of a son is the only moment of life which equals its anticipation.

It is a privilege to live in this great age, when the dream of men to fly as birds is realized and has become a mechanism of commercial highways girding seas and mountains, to live when men strive to free the atom that can destroy the world, and who make war and build for peace.

F. M. W.

January, 1932

CONTENTS

		PAGE
Prologue		vii
Chapter I.	A Childhood in Buffalo	3
Chapter II.	Other Days in Buffalo	15
Chapter III.	School Days	28
Chapter IV.	Introduction to Washington	41
Chapter V.	The Grand Tour	50
Chapter VI.	Colorado Springs	65
Chapter VII.	A Frontier Colony	85
Chapter VIII.	Berthe Pourtalès	102
Chapter IX.	"H. H." and Others	112
Chapter X.	Politics and Mormons	125
Chapter XI.	New York in the 'Eighties	140
Chapter XII.	Cairo	158
Chapter XIII.	The Nile—and Tanta	172
Chapter XIV.	Asia Minor and Constantinople	191
Chapter XV.	Greece	208

CONTENTS

		PAGE
Chapter XVI.	Venice	217
Chapter XVII.	Paris	229
Chapter XVIII.	A London Season	248
Chapter XIX.	The Closing of a Book	268
	Index	279

ILLUSTRATIONS

	FACING PAGE
Frances Metcalfe Bass, London, 1875	*Frontispiece*
Girlhood Home of Frances Metcalfe in Buffalo	4
A Vignette of Frances Metcalfe, aged 13	18
Frances Metcalfe in 1874	42
Manitou Park Hotel	78
Colorado Springs in 1877—Tejon Street and Cheyenne Mountain	78
Berthe Pourtalès	102
The Terrace, Glumbowitz	108
Glumbowitz	108
Lyman Metcalfe Bass at Edgeplain	270
Edgeplain	270

HERITAGE OF YEARS

CHAPTER ONE

A CHILDHOOD IN BUFFALO

JULY, 1931, found me in what in common parlance is called one's "Home Town," Buffalo—the loveliest summer city in the United States. I had a charming apartment which overlooked the property once owned by my family where, in a large and spacious house, my girlhood was spent; a house which had the record France demands to make a home:—a marriage, a birth, a death. When we moved there a large cemetery with lichen-covered headstones stretched towards the town and made me shiver and look over my shoulder as I scuttled home when darkness was coming on.

Looking out on the panorama of 1931, on the harbor lighthouses, I see the dominating Rand Building whose scarlet light is a flaming beacon for airships. It was built by a loving son in honor of his father, who was killed in an airplane accident en route to present a monument to be erected on the battlefield at Verdun. The gleaming windows of buildings among the elms were magical, but my mind's eye turned to the old mansion built by Aaron Rumsey, the head of a ruling family, and purchased by my father,—its graperies and pines, the lot where our cow was pastured, the house where I became the wife of Lyman K. Bass, where my son was born, where my father died, and where the body of my youngest brother was brought followed by a group of weeping children of the neighborhood who had seen him drown as he fell from a canal bridge. The huge porte-cochère with its sitting-room deck, where in warm weather the family and friends gathered, so impressed James G. Blaine when he came with Mrs. Blaine to see us, that in parting he said, "If I ever build a house, it shall have a porte-cochère." He kept his word in the vast mansion which he erected in Du Pont Circle at Washington.

My thoughts were not held by the life my mother presided over—a brilliant center—first in the old house, which was sold at my father's death, and then in the first house in Buffalo planned and erected by McKim, Mead & White, for which John La Farge made the glass which filled the transoms in the dining-room. It was built on a part of my father's original holding.

But farther back still my thoughts went to the Buffalo of my childhood, the later 'fifties and 'sixties. We then had a delightful, commodious house on Swan Street, one door from Michigan. Next door lived the City Surveyor, Lovejoy, who had a benign, Pickwickian face, and wore dark goggles and a welcoming smile as he drove his discouraged sorrowful horse harnessed to a shaky buckboard which carried his surveyor's instruments. His mother had been scalped by the Indians when Buffalo was burned. His two spinster daughters, gentlewomen both, always welcomed me, and let me repose at ease on a long sofa with rockers called a "rockee," which I suppose was made in earlier times when babies were many and servants few, for two or three children could be rocked at one time. They made me delicious currant jelly tarts and gave me "Godey's Lady's Book" to look at. The

GIRLHOOD HOME OF FRANCES METCALFE IN BUFFALO

plates were like the toilettes of my dainty mother, whose smooth dark hair, looped over her ears, her rustling crinolines and flowing sleeves, her bare, pretty shoulders, form a charming picture in my memory. She had what was called a Cheney silk long gown of green satin stripes alternated with bright roses in brocade. I must have been fifteen before I ever wore a high-neck dress; and all babies wore long dresses, had bare arms and necks. I coveted that dress of hers, and one afternoon when she was driving with my father, I arrayed myself in it, took her parasol and flowered bonnet, and stepped with royal grace upon the street, unmindful of dirty sidewalks. I remember the sting of a freshly cut switch of a tree in the yard which was the reward of that escapade. The switch was put over the mirror in the library. Later I climbed up and viciously burned it.

From Michigan Street to Main Street there were houses set far back from the street in ample grounds where a child could have a swing or a teeter beneath the trees. There were at least two hitching posts before every house, with iron chains where a farmer bringing produce could hitch his team, or a visitor in a buggy hitch his horse. Oh! those delightful gutters where a heavy rainfall invited the imagination to build bridges of stray bricks, unmindful of wet feet or clothes.

One of the numerous Pratt family lived opposite in an old house whose brick cellars and high basement opened on an old-fashioned garden with the rose-covered summer house where we crowned the Queen of the May. A shack at the back enabled the children to play mother, housekeeping, and to build bonfires and roast potatoes in the ashes.

Every house had a large stable and there were fine horses and equipages, and the hay-mows were a source of endless excitement. One of my brothers seemed always to be falling from the loft or from the old tree of blue plums where our raccoon was chained.

My father must have loved animals, for he indulged us in dogs and cats, and once gave me a bear-cub which was chained in the stable. Crowds of children came to see him, and all went well until a boy vendor of popcorn balls, apples and candies approached too near, and baby Bruin, with a quick grab of his paw, tipped over the basket and ate its contents, growling to prevent the interruption of his meal.

Oh! that lazy gray pigeon with the sly glamorous glances from her pink eyes, enticing her suitors,—the fantail who spread his tail feathers until they must have ached, and the pouter pigeon who blew up his pouch until it was like to burst. Those demure ladies in gray are always ardently followed.

Never were there more entrancing stories than those told by basket beggars who went from door to door begging for cold "vittles" (loathsome word). They said their fathers were drowned at sea and their mothers were dying. I gave away all of the food I could get from the larder and my shoes and clothes, until my shrewd father solved the mystery and captured a Munchausen in tatters. He could not remember his yarn despite all my promptings, and so he disappeared from my small tellers of large tales.

We had a large library where in cold days a fire always burned, and, nearby, a lounge where my father took his forty winks. The tall bookcases had plaster busts of Goethe, Schiller and Shakespeare, and there my mother read aloud with a simplicity and charm unequaled by any one I have since known. There I listened to most of Dickens's and Thackeray's novels as they came out; there, pitied Rasselas who was bored with his "Happy Valley"; thrilled under the recountings of Fanny Burney's writing of the novel "Evelina," or shivered at "The Mysteries of Udolpho." There we made friends with Madame Piozzi, Sir

Joshua Reynolds, and all of the circle of Dr. Johnson so graphically described by Boswell.

Years after, when Dr. Leonard, a Professor from Columbia who taught at Mrs. Macauley's School, asked me how I was so familiar with eighteenth century literature, I was struck dumb. I did not know what he meant. But it was an education to live even with the backs of books, or to lie on the floor looking over Flaxman's drawings or Lavater's plates, and the brilliant illustrations of Froissart's Chronicles, though my steady diet was Grimm's Fairy Tales, the Franconia Books and the Rollo Books.

There was an enticing blacksmith shop not far away where we children watched the kindly blacksmith shoe the incoming farmers' horses. There was the town crier on an unkempt black horse, ringing a dinner bell and telling the age, size and clothes of lost children, whose agonized parents employed him. There were soldiers going to War, marching to the New York Central Station at the foot of Michigan Street.

There was a railway ditch into which I walked in quest of polliwogs, wearing an embroidered dress which had taken my mother months to make, and to which she had added blue kid shoes and a sash to perfect the toilette of a nice girl. I only thought of how cunning the polliwogs were as I came home holding them in the skirt of my dress. My mother burst into tears when she saw me. I was threatened with a leather dress and with having my curls cut off, all of which seemed a glorious relief. All my childhood someone said "Don't."

I never liked dolls, but when a fat girl stole mine, it became valuable to me, and I firmly believed that when my black pony, whose left flank bore a brutal brand, bucked her off, it was just retribution provoked by divine wrath. Such are the comforts of religion a Hebraic tradition can bring.

My father liked my companionship until he faced the loss of my first teeth. He then permitted my ugliness to go with my stern grandfather to Illinois. What excitement to wear my mother's blue veil and ride face forward on the train! Children were usually riding backward facing their elders and betters.

The night of my arrival at my aunt's peach farm, I, who had been taken to the circus by my nurse and ridden proudly on an elephant, faced fear for the first time. A baby cousin was in a rocking hooded cradle covered with a mosquito netting, and an army of revolting June bugs invaded the lighted room. Snatching up the baby from his bed, I handed him to my aunt and took his place in the cradle, an arrant coward.

There were no children to play with. The hired man John, who looked like Bluebeard, tried to teach me to milk cows. He did succeed in teaching me to wring chickens by the neck with one fling, pluck them and singe their pin feathers with flaming newspaper, then take them to the hired girls with their hearts, livers and gizzards neatly tucked under their shorn wings. This art served me well later in my frontier days. But, alas, my pet white rooster which followed me everywhere! I had brought him in a yellow basket from a distant farm where I had driven with my grandfather over the black deep earth of the prairies carpeted with wild flowers. But the tragedy came, for Bluebeard John, in a fit of drunkenness, killed my rooster. There were long avenues beneath the peach trees where I ran in my chemise during the warm summer showers, or sat in the notch of a tree looking at the illustrations in Frank Leslie's Magazine.

Finally, my grandfather took me to Cairo to see my grandmother. The sidewheel steamers with their ear-splitting steam driven music of calliopes announced their arrival before tying up by the levees which protected the country from the inundations of the Mississippi and Ohio Rivers. One night the burning of a cotton-laden boat called out the population to the banks of the levee and we went, as did scores of people in skiffs, to try to recover, if possible, a valuable bale or two of cotton. The heavens were lighted with the conflagration and from the hundreds of bales on the water we brought one to shore. I still recall the harmonious singing of the negro boat hands.

My grandfather sank a fortune in real estate in Cairo believing that at the joining of two great waterways of trade would rise a large city. His expectations were never realized. My grandmother, whose regal pose of head was acquired in early life by walking an hour a day with the Holy Bible on her head, had a classical beauty inherited by none of her descendants. She sat in her house on a bluff above the muddy flow of rivers. She was fanciful and proud, an expert needlewoman. She was born within the sound of the sea on the shore of Rhode Island. Her father was a well-to-do manufacturer of woolens, and she dreamed always of again seeing the Ocean. But she lived and died in Illinois.

My grandfather was cruel, though he must have had a soft spot in his makeup, for he lent money without ever collecting it. He read Tom Paine's writings with approving conviction and such extracts of Voltaire as were within his reach. He hated hypocrisy and the "unco good." He reviled camp meetings and revivals as being too immoral for a woman of his family to attend. I believe he was a born agnostic. I fancy it may have been a trial to him to have to wife a beautiful and romantic woman. The impressions of early childhood ripened into the late conviction that the pain of longings defeated and beautiful dreams ruthlessly shattered, poison the arteries of happiness, and the pain of a broken leg would be far easier to heal and forget. As a little child, watching my grandmother, the foundations of my present convictions were laid.

My grandfather bought me a chestnut gelding which had formerly been used in the United States Cavalry. It ran away miles of prairie with me but did not throw me. My grandfather, who had been driving in a buggy, caught the horse, and on our return informed me that it would be sold. I insisted on remounting and he protested, and standing on the sill of the barn doorway, he looked at me, saying, "You have the will of a man and that is a damn sight too strong for a woman."

And then I went back to Buffalo.

To the housewife of today, if housewives there be, with fresh vegetables and fruits, giant apples from the West, and delicacies from all parts of the world, the markets of earlier days are a contrast.

There was venison of various types, grouse, quail, prairie chicken, wild turkey, wild ducks and geese, and when the spring came, delicious pink-fleshed brook trout, speckled with red, from nearby streams. Oysters came from the Atlantic seaboard, frozen in small wooden kegs, and from the age of two, I climbed to thrust a greedy finger to pull out a luscious bivalve. There were baskets of delicious peaches from lake and river orchards, and no Western apple, however colored or polished, has the tang and flavor of the Spitzenburg, Pippin, Greening and Russet apples grown in New York State. There are no better grapes than the Hamburg and Niagara vines yield.

Our breakfasts had no international coffee and toast standards. Chops, steaks, eggs, corn beef hash, corn bread, yellow and white, sausages with buckwheat cakes and maple syrup. Nobody talked of vitamins and indigestion. As I read Frances Kemble's description of her French mother's storeroom, I recalled the days in our spacious summer kitchen where my mother directed the women preserving fruits and jellies and the making of condiments, catsups and mangoes; where melon rinds and green peppers were filled with mustard seeds, chopped cabbage and tiny onions. My mother's achievements were highly praised. Then the baking days, when chocolate, cocoanut and cream layer cakes were in evidence, with spiced cake and plain Kate Stewart cake, which was made to be broken, not cut. All housekeepers vied with one another in making mincemeat and plum puddings.

It was the era of real lace and fine India shawls. Machine imitations were not esteemed at that period. The making of an expected baby's outfit was an occupation and delight to the prospective mother.

There was no training school for nurses. Hospitals, insane asylums, old ladies' homes and orphan asylums were maintained, but the sick were nursed in their own families. The doctor was a family friend and counselor. These general practitioners knew the psychology of their patients and in my childhood I believed the doctor was omnipotent, master of life and death, and that all clergymen were sinless, and Boston a spotless town.

Dime novels were plentiful, but crime less in evidence. One read occasionally of a great bank robbery. I sat entranced on a hassock as Francis Tyler, one of the greatest detectives in the United States, related to my father the tracking of expert English and American cracksmen, often quietly following and running them down after a year or two's pursuit.

In the 'sixties and 'seventies there was a large population of southern Germans towards the east in Buffalo and the whole length of Genesee Street had second-story windows filled with fuchsias and brilliant geraniums—the expression of the nostalgia for Vaterland of German women. There were reputable beer saloons where fathers of families played pinochle and dominoes, and pumpernickel and strong cheese were served. The whole town turned out to hear the first mechanical organ in a clean, large, beer saloon where it played the overtures, "Zampa," "Freischutz" and "William Tell." Today Buffalo has more Poles than the capital of Poland, more Italians than many of the larger cities of Italy, as well as a powerful section of Irish citizens. Those who frequented law courts recognized that the first generation born of foreign parents was lawless. They despised the orderly handicrafts and traditions of their parents, and had not fully accepted the privileges of our country founded on individual freedom within the law.

For years St. John's gray stone church on the corner of Swan and Washington Streets had as Rector the Reverend Orlando Witherspoon, father of the former basso of the Metropolitan Opera Company. In the square pew on the left-hand side, well to the front, my seat commanded the pulpit, the chancel and the high-set choir at the back. It is a blessing, only to be realized at the end of a life, to have heard the sonorous English of King James' Version of the Bible read in a rich voice with clear utterance. In the frequent attendance at service in the Lenten Season one unconsciously learned by heart the ritual, in noble language, of the Book of Common Prayer. I watched what seemed to me romantic flirtations in the choir.

I had a poor opinion of the humanity and integrity of the patriarchs, Abraham's attitude toward Isaac, and the inhuman cruelties to Hagar and Ishmael roused my indignation. Bible stories I had learned through the line engravings of a child's edition of the Old and New Testament. I so visualized God the Father, that in 1912 and 1913, when in the night I passed through the Red Sea beneath Mount Sinai, I had an instinctive feeling that, had it been day, I would have seen the flowing beard of the Most Hight, blown in the wind, as He handed the Tables of the Ten Commandments to Moses. The dishonesty of Jacob revolted me then more than that of Al Capone does today. Those records of Esther, Joseph and his Brethren, and Miriam sounding her cymbals as she sang of victory, enthralled me. The revised edition of the Modern Bible where Joseph's coat of many colors is accurately stated as being his tunic with long sleeves, the garment of the male reaching the age of puberty, is a dull affair compared with the blood-stained coat of many colors as I recall it. I wept then at the sorrowful turning back of Moses from the Promised Land, as I did last winter at the tragic setting of Robert Edmond Jones of Moses' Farewell in "The Green Pastures." My eldest brother was wont to say, "Sister, you quote the Bible for the devil's uses."

The Church was a social center with strawberry festivals and Christmas trees marked by the type of amusement I presume obtaining in all inland cities.

In a house near the church, formerly occupied by the family of S. V. R. Watson, lived a Jewish Rabbi named Cohen. His rich flowing black robe, silken, well-kept beard, and cap, marked him as a Sephardim Jew of royal or sacerdotal tribe. His two stately daughters of Oriental beauty seemed to me of the same blood as Rebecca in "Ivanhoe." It was whispered that in the family of Cohen should come the Second Messiah. Socially, in that era, the Jew had no place in Buffalo.

Soon came the morning when I found my family plunged in gloom before the library fire and tears in every eye. Lincoln had been assassinated. Every possible bit of news of the scene in Ford's Theater in Washington, the flight of Booth, the trial and execution of Mrs. Surratt, was freely discussed before us children. When President Lincoln's body lay in state at the Buffalo Rink, I held my father's hand in the crowd until he lifted me that I might look on the dead face of the great martyr.

My father had been in sympathy with the South. His father and mother had come on horseback from Louisville, Kentucky, on the way from Virginia to Bath, Steuben County, New York. My father, the ninth child in the family of twelve, was born in his full time the week after his mother reached Bath. The deep-breasted black woman, a child of a slave my grandfather freed, nursed me when I had the measles. From time to time, in a darkened room, my mother, shading a candle with her hand, read aloud Charles Kingsley's "Heroes." Those tales sowed the seed of my love for Greece and all things Greek.

CHAPTER TWO

OTHER DAYS IN BUFFALO

GOVERNMENT statistics acclaim Buffalo one of the storm centers of the world. There were no clouds of black smoke in old Buffalo from the Lackawanna and the great furnaces which have made for the advancement of today's prosperity. Where now the lake shore is lined with fine residences and clubs, where gardens are protected by windbreaks or coniferæ, there was a stretch of bare sand where my father used to take us sometimes on a free Sunday, to wade and paddle in Lake Erie. Godly people thought to stay at home and eat cold food on the Sabbath was a form of religious devotion.

The soil about Buffalo is clay and hard as Pharaoh's heart. The natural first growth of trees had little charm. Poor things, bent and crippled by bitter winter winds, and the orchards of the occasional farmers, are all turned to the east by the prevailing gales. Spring was late in Buffalo, for all the ice of the upper Lake region packed above the mouth of the Niagara River, and the great grain ships beat against the ice, vessels waiting for navigation to open and the ice to break and plunge down the river to the rapids and over the Falls at Niagara. The sap flows earlier in Detroit.

Dark clouds boiled up from the west, but on the clear snows of winter there were sunny days when sleigh bells made music and affluent men drove their standard-bred horses to race on what was then called "Delaware Street." Graceful, large sleighs filled with those eager to see the sport and covered from the bitter cold by rich robes of black bear, beaver and mink, lined Delaware Avenue. Buffalo robes were then but twenty-five dollars each, and were used equally by rich and poor. There was no park in which to drive. Forest Lawn Cemetery had good roads, and there shy lovers proposed to willing maidens.

When Dean Richmond, of Batavia, built the New York Central Railroad, Pullman cars were not invented. The nights of our earliest trips to New York were passed in day cars, in which we found comfort as best we could. I slept well covered by my mother with a Scotch plaid shawl. The fathers of my friends told me eminent citizens, in haste, had been accustomed to go to the Atlantic seaboard by express canal boat, which landed them in New York in ten days.

All grain from the West came by boat, to be stored in the elevators on the docks at the foot of Main Street, and re-shipped by canal to the coast. The Erie Canal had a life of its own. In the forecastle, at the front of the boat, lived the wives and children of the drivers, cooking, washing and stretching their clothes-lines along the decks. The men on the towpath, with revolting profanity, urged their mules and horses to pull their heavily-laden boat. To say a woman had been a cook on a canal boat barred her from service in any decent family.

A tolling and ringing of bells summoned the fire department, the engines horse-drawn, the hose-carts manned by volunteer companies, who themselves pulled their carts through the streets. Hose House No. 1 was manned by the young bloods of fashion who, in the upper story of their Hose House, had a meeting room in which they occasionally gave small exclusive dances. In a blizzard, when St. James Hall was burned, three of their number sacrificed their lives.

In the early days of Swan Street, the gayety of New Year's Day included covered sleighs or livery hacks, drawn by long-tailed horses, in which gentlemen in full dress, white gloves and tall hats, went calling to be received by richly-dressed hostesses and pretty girls. Inherited recipes for making eggnog, Tom and Jerry, and Cherry Bounce made for delicious beverages and a headache the following morning.

In my family papers I found specimens of two cards tied with a small white satin bow, inscribed with the names of the gallants making the round of calls together.

Until I was in middle life I never saw a girl or woman smoke. It was not considered respectful for men to smoke in the presence of women and nearly every home included a smoking room.

The vignette taken when I was thirteen years of age belongs to a vague romance of my adolescence. An ingratiating young man in the late twenties, secretary to my uncle in New York, brought important business documents to my father in Buffalo. His name was William Nestelle, a relative of Miss Wolfe, whose legacy to the Metropolitan Museum included both good and bad art. Half his blood was French. His large dark eyes, olive skin, quick movement and easy manners bespoke the Latin. He doubtless discovered my spelling was as faulty as my punctuation, and before taking his leave, he asked if I would not write him every Sunday, and if there were faults in my letters, he would correct and return them. Alas! To this day I should not be able to take a prize at a village spelling bee, and as to that hall-mark of a cultivated Englishman, the proper use of a semicolon, my ignorance is as dense as that of a Zulu.

Each spring, after the strain of a hard winter in that storm center, Buffalo, I was sent to visit my aunt and uncle, living in Thirty-seventh Street in New York. I was vain of my cooking, and young Nestelle being invited to luncheon, I insisted on going to the kitchen to prepare corn-starch blanc-mange. In haste and pride, I put four times as much corn-starch into the milk as the recipe required. It produced a dessert that could have been thrown at the Walls of Jericho and made a breach. Vainly the young man tried to swallow what could not have been forced down his throat with a ramrod, but he was amiable and uncritical.

Until I went to Mrs. Macauley's School, we corresponded. During my visits to New York my uncle permitted him to take me to afternoon theatrical performances, to see pictures, and to go one night to his birthday party at his father's large house near Harlem. I remember seeing a pretty young woman who seemed petulant and annoyed that William Nestelle was taking me home. Later I learned that William Nestelle was pledged to marry that girl when he first came to Buffalo.

During our long rides in horse-drawn street cars, to places of entertainment, he gave me advice to which I listened and paid more or less heed, which I would have brushed aside if given by one of my relatives. His epigrams were, "Never allow any man to hold your hand. It is a short jump from the hand to the lips." At that moment he was reassuring me by holding my hand beneath my cape, on a long excursion to a fairy pantomime at Niblo's Garden. Another injunction, "Never kiss any man until Prince Charming comes who will be your husband."

On my seventeenth birthday, William Nestelle died of typhus fever. On my return to school in the autumn, I received a note from his father saying he was not well and asking me to come to see him. My uncle left me at his house, to call for me on his

A VIGNETTE OF FRANCES METCALFE, AGED 13

return from his afternoon drive. I found the aged father sitting alone in his library, eager to talk of his boy. At the end of our interview, he handed me a package of my illiterate letters and the little photograph of myself which had been taken for his son, framed in mother-of-pearl. At parting, shaken with the loss of his only son, he said, "He loved you. The frame on your picture stood to him for your purity. I had hoped that you might be my daughter. Will you come again?" I never returned, and the experience now is but a sad, romantic dream.

When I was fifteen I went to Cincinnati to visit the sister of the poetesses Phoebe and Alice Cary. On the return journey to Buffalo I was in the care of polished, fascinating General Dick Taylor, brother-in-law of Jefferson Davis. His flattering interest in what I studied, read and what amused me most in life, won my heart. His question before he took leave of me, "Have you a sweetheart?" astonished me, for in my lexicon of youth, "sweetheart" was as yet unwritten.

One is glad for every recollection of the Civil War. From time to time, through the whole of my life, at long or short intervals, the Civil War seemed to touch me on the shoulder.

The sight of reckless General Custer, massacred in 1876, standing twenty feet away, raising his soft military hat to greet his friends, the sun touching his yellow hair as he bent to speak to a lady in a box at a race meeting, his hand on his hip, was a military vignette. He had the halo of romantic record of his bravery at the capture of Lee's army. From Mrs. Custer's book, "Boots and Saddles," I only remember her protests against reckless waste of water, for she stated that in the crossing of the alkaline plains of the American Desert, she could be clean with a bath from a tumbler of water, and she felt that no one could be a great traveler who could not sleep on the ground with the sun shining full in his face.

On one of our long short journeys to New York, General Kirkpatrick, too ill to leave his berth, accepted a tidbit from our lunch basket. The young hate to be talked down to, and as I sat upon his berth in my untried youth, I had that premonition of love and death which gives understanding sympathy. Poor Kirkpatrick poured out his loneliness at the loss of his wife and showed me her miniature in a locket hung on a chain beneath his army shirt. He answered courteously my eager questions and later wrote me a letter to say he was none the worse for his journey.

One must not forget the white and gilt auditorium of the Academy of Music. When I was a small child I often accompanied my father and mother to the play. There was the pantomime "Aladdin's Lamp" with the joyous pelting of stupid heads with gay bladders at the Feast of Lanterns. My father took some of my playmates with me to see "East Lynne" one afternoon in a box. The crowd of children was so great that he could see nothing and so he slept on the floor at the back of the box, while we stained the red plush of the rail with our tears. That theater still exists, an inferior movie house in the business center. What a record of glory could come from its walls: Mary Anderson playing "Ion." But there was a fly in the ointment of Katharine Cornell's handsome grandfather, for Mary Anderson wore the wrong sex of calves, a technique of the theater only recognized by one as professional in criticism as he. Douglas Cornell knew the theater.

Daly's Company used to have a Buffalo season of a fortnight each year. There the loveliest of all women, Agnes Ethel, played

"Frou-Frou" and "Divorce" and was taken from her career by the impetuous wooing of Frank Tracy, rich and of a leading Buffalo family. All who saw her loved her. To the Academy came Adelaide Neilson as Juliet; Janauschek as Lady Dedlock in "Bleak House"; Charlotte Cushman at the end of her days as Lady Macbeth and Meg Merrilies; then the reading of Frances Kemble, when she was old, which needed no stage setting but a chair and table to make one visualize Catherine of Aragon, Wolsey and a score of characters in Shakespeare's plays; Jefferson as Rip Van Winkle; E. A. Sothern as Lord Dundreary and David Garrick, and all the merry antics of Francis Wilson; Henry Dixey as Adonis, Forrest as King Lear, crowded the theater.

From the swiftly flowing waters of the River of Time come the voices of tragediennes and comedians, including the spell of Ellen Terry and Henry Irving. One must not forget the negro minstrels who brought song and clog dancing, endmen and "Brother Bones," to the joy of the period.

The relations between New York and Buffalo have plied a busy shuttle. The polo teams of Long Island, internationally triumphant both at home and in England, were fed from the parent stock of Buffalo's first team. George and Devereux Milburn were born here. They put the United States on the map by winning the Oxford Boat Race and changing the attitude of England and the University toward students from our land.

I fancy children of Carys, Rumseys, Watsons, Spragues, Nortons, Goodyears, Glennys, and other leading families, have a persistence of individual vitality in their descendants. Being a breeder of dogs and horses, reading human nature by retrospective flashes of decades, I believe in persistence of race individual qualities, whether by the bar sinister or by marriages so often not made in heaven. In the "Popular Science Monthly" of long ago it was stated that the wild broncho, with golden chestnut coat, who showed the white of his eye, hard to conquer, like the thoroughbred race horse of like color, had in his veins the blood of ancient war horses, brought to this Continent when Cortez conquered Mexico.

Buffalo has contributed a large share to New York in the making. Conger Goodyear, a great citizen, in his youth made the first Polish Survey of Buffalo. He is now at the head of the Museum of Modern Art in New York, an art collector and critic. John Milburn, who became the leader of the New York bar and came from the north of England, lived in Buffalo many years, winning all hearts with his charm of voice and manner. He had an exuberance of life and in his face a touch of the gods of Greece.

The tide of prosperity changed the character of Swan Street and carried many families to more modern habitations on Delaware Street.

S. V. R. Watson built the home now occupied by the Buffalo Club. The ballroom and perfectly equipped theater on the third story were a background for an accomplished circle. Mrs. Watson's influence and her familiarity with Europe led her to educate three pretty daughters to grace the world. Gertrude was an equipped and sympathetic player of the piano. She had the skill of a professional.

Bronson Rumsey built a noble dwelling with its high ceilings, large hall and rooms for comfort and entertainment. There was no better landscaped garden than that of the park on which the terrace at the back gave, a place of beautiful trees bordering a lake which made for beauty in the summer and merry skating parties in the winter. Bronson Rumsey dreamed of a patriarchal life and that his two sons and two daughters should have houses grouped about the park. He was a man of vision and brought from England the first large herd of Hereford cattle, which was a spur to breeding of fine stock in this country. The transmission of his spark of vital spirit was seen in the sculpture of Charles Cary Rumsey, whose collection of animal sculpture, now in the Brooklyn Museum, will be in the grounds of the Art School, the combined gift of his wife, Mary Harriman Rumsey, and his aunt, Evelyn Rumsey Cary.

Dr. Walter Cary, coming from Batavia, built at 184 Delaware Avenue, the house which has been occupied by four generations of his family. With the coming of his children he was forced to add a mansard roof. In that house the same standard of hospitality has obtained for seventy-five years. His wife, Julia Love, was, throughout all her years, a striking individual and a great lady. Her sisters, Maria and Elizabeth, were members of the household. Miss Maria Love carried on the standard of living in this home after the death of Dr. and Mrs. Cary. It was a house where people of note naturally came. Saints met recognition and sinners were helped, not condemned.

Miss Love, who recently died at 92 years, was the most eminent citizen of Buffalo. On her return from a European trip and visit to Belgium, she founded the Crêche, which until this day is a help to working mothers and their children.

Dr. Walter Cary was the most picturesque character in Buffalo. He took his whole family the length and breadth of Europe in a four-in-hand coach, and his six boys, by their untrammeled charm and sense of justice, pride of manner and the inheritance of his own fiery temper, at some time or other had a lodging for a night in a prison in nearly every European capital. Three of the boys saw the Germans come under the Arc de Triomphe after the defeat of Napoleon the Third. Dr. Charles Cary, alert and gay at nineteen, after six years of European education, returned to Buffalo. He had studied in Brussels, Bonn University, and in Paris. Charles, the polo player, became a beloved physician. His friends recall his singing of the Evening Star from "Tannhäuser," and all the wives, widows and maids were thrilled and moved by his music and audacity. Dr. Walter Cary, white of beard and keen of eye in his later years, a world traveler and the kindest of neighbors, driving four-in-hand to sleigh or coach, filled with young and old, was a familiar picture. He and Mrs. Cary and his six sons and daughter were always notes of joy in all our gaieties. Three of his sons were members of the second polo team in the United States. The first team was that of Newport. In the match of 1877, James Gordon Bennett, Herman Oelrichs and August Belmont were on the opposing team. Lawrence and Bert Rumsey were on the original Buffalo team, and their descendants have been players on Long Island and in international games. George Cary designed the building for the home of the Historical Museum overlooking the Lake and Park, which Olmsted considered, of all the parks he created, his *chef d'œuvre*.

Later John J. Albright gave a superb building of Greek type to be a Temple of Art, commanding the same panorama.

The young ladies of Buffalo were sent abroad to study the piano and learn French and German. I have heard fierce discussions as to whether the method taught at Leipsig or Stuttgart was the better. Some of the young men studied at the Beaux Arts in Paris or took a degree at Oxford.

There were women of rare beauty in Western New York. Not only the Wadsworth sisters who married titles in Great

Britain, but the loveliest face I ever saw was that of elegant Marian Strong, who married Horace White of Syracuse. Her three talented granddaughters, Mmes. Fuller, Burden and Coward, stand today for charm, culture and beauty in the inner circles of New York. Buffalo was enriched by the fascination of that great lady, Mrs. Augustus Porter of Niagara Falls, and her radiant daughters. There was a highly intelligent group of men of affairs, writers and great lawyers in Buffalo. John Ganson, a handsome man, in the plenitude of success, standing before the Court as he had just finished a lawsuit, raised his hand and dropped dead. Death, I Salute You! A supreme way to end a useful life on the high tide of achievement.

The day of Lindbergh's welcome in New York, a graduate of Harvard, a pleasant young man belonging to the Four Hundred, who had probably never been west of Albany, said, as we watched the pilot of the sky,—"Yet he comes from the West." I could have quoted—"Not by eastern windows only . . . comes in the light . . . but westward, look, the land is bright." The entrenched New Yorker perhaps fails to perceive that the blood, energy and dollars which make the commercial aristocracy of New York, are not wholly furnished by those born on the rock of Manhattan.

Artists were born in Buffalo. Bierstadt, painter of the plains peopled with buffalo against the complementary line of the Rocky Mountains, first showed me the background of a life in the sunshine which I loved for a quarter of a century. The American man, perhaps through necessity, has been short of vision and ruthless of hand. The western canyons have rivulets instead of singing waterfalls, for man has slaughtered the forest which held the snow. Gone are the migrating herds of buffalo and the free grazing on buffalo grass of gentle-eyed antelope.

Neither painter nor herder can restore that life. Bierstadt painted as well the laughter-provoking canvas, in two sections—"If it rains when the sun shines the Devil is beating his wife,"—above, a showery landscape, below, the Devil with trident making it hot for his spouse. Another of Bierstadt's paintings is of Indians, ear to the ground, listening to the rumble of the first train on the new railroad that linked East to West.

In the wake of the Civil War came a crop of new sects under the banner of Christ. The vanity, ambition and credulity of men in the nineteenth century in the United States alone, I have read, created communities and religious sects well over a hundred. As one notes the revenue of imposters and fakirs that the law is now trying to curtail and suppress, one must suppose, from the beginning of time, that the human race loved to be fooled, whether one looks back to Pharaoh or enjoys Alexander Dumas' account of Cagliostro and Cardinal de Rohan in "The Queen's Necklace." Mormonism thrived. Robert Louis Stevenson's "Dynamiters," picture of that sect, is bloodcurdling, and "Saints and Sinners" by Phil Robinson, less terrifying, filled a Gentile with fear.

All wars, no doubt, make mourning hearts open to the clairvoyant and spiritualistic mediums, and manipulators of the Ouija Board, to probe the mystery beyond the grave. Joseph Smith, born of a neurotic and epileptic stock, master of trances and visions, made the power of the Mormon Church strong through the practical genius of Brigham Young. Virginia Woodhull, a flaming siren of a psychic family, lit an unsatisfied society with her audacious lectures on free love as being both for health and happiness. She practiced what she preached. Men of business and culture consulted her as to their affairs, and loved her. Susan

B. Anthony, the flag bearer of women's suffrage, became her friend. Mesmerism, phrenology, crystal-gazing and the far-reaching power of the Fox Sisters of Rochester as spiritualistic mediums, had followers in all walks of life. My father investigated the Fox Sisters, who preached the materialization of spirits, the interchange of messages with the dead, reunion in another world, and the doctrine of affinities, including a certain latitude in triangular relations for the unhappily married in this world. My father's remark, when he had satisfied his curiosity, was, "I have known no good to come from it, and infinite evil."

CHAPTER THREE

SCHOOL DAYS

IT was time that I should make ready to be sent to New York to school. Most of my clothes were made in the sewing room and I departed with great anticipation and excitement. Two high-stooped brownstone houses, on the corner of Fortieth Street and Madison Avenue, served not only as a Day School, but as the home of seventy girls in residence at Mrs. Macauley's School. With a governess, two by two, from Fortieth Street to Madison Square, we walked. We passed the old Knickerbocker Club, often filled with observant men. This made for our health and delight. Sometimes, on Saturday afternoon, my uncle took me, behind a pair of standard-bred horses, to drive in Central Park where Commodore Vanderbilt, white hair flying, was in evidence speeding his fine team. Among our French teachers were the distinguished French emigrés, Monsieur and Madame d'Orémieux, parents of Mrs. West Roosevelt, which enabled me, in my later Washington life, to indulge in ungrammatical conversation with diplomats.

We looked forward to the four-in-hand meets at the entrance of Central Park, the coaches filled with beautifully dressed women. On one occasion there was great delay in starting, the horses were restless and the drivers evidently annoyed. Years afterwards Fred Beach told me, in Colorado, that the cause of that delay was that he had arranged to have one of the most beautiful of Southern girls occupy the box seat of the leading carriage. When she arrived at the entrance of the Park, he discovered she was wearing a pair of pea-green kid gloves. Enticing her to a bench, he engaged her in conversation until an emissary could procure a modest pair of gray ones, she unconscious that she had given the slightest trouble. She afterward married a man of title in England and is, as Lady Bingham, to this day one of the most admired hostesses of London.

There was talk among my schoolmates of August Belmont, founder of that family in this country. He had, in his young manhood, represented the banking house of Rothschild in Naples, under the Bourbons, without whose consent European nations could not make war. Living in a palace and maintaining almost royal state, he was vital, autocratic, as short of temper as he was long of purse. The schoolgirls believed he had been wounded in a romantic duel, as he limped a little as he walked. At all events, we knew he had introduced the great style of living and a European social code and standard. I used to argue that whatever "balm of Gilead" there might be for a man wounded in a duel, the woman for whom the duel was fought, innocent or guilty, radiated a miasma of dishonor from her name.

In my girlhood there was one other duel, in speaking of which our elders and betters lowered their voices and tried to keep us in ignorance. It rocked the foundations of influential New York families and stirred a well of bitterness. The man and woman who followed the flowery path of dalliance, believing that "all for love and the world well lost" was their destiny, broke the hearts of the guiltless and in the end faced disillusion, pain, tragedy, death. So one rejoices that in the march of modernity, the dueling pistols and swords, like the blunderbuss, have been relegated to the dustbin for all time.

It takes a pot of money for a man to put a woman with elegance on wheels. Perhaps it takes more to enclose her in a Rolls-Royce than it did at that time when August Belmont set the high-water mark for his ladies, framed by graceful Victorias, high C-spring-swung barouches and coaches. August Belmont radiated power. I used to say I believed he had his hat nailed to his skull. He wore it at an angle of forty-five degrees. His colors were well worn by the jockeys of his racing stables, his numerous household flunkies and footmen. The crowd believed he maintained a *valet de pied* to give his dogs their airing.

All pedestrians enjoyed the sight of equipages with high-stepping horses driving up and down Fifth Avenue. Women dressed to drive,—feathers, lace parasols,—and they could walk, thinly shod, from their doors to their carriages, as red velvet carpets were rolled down by their footmen. One can hardly realize that in that era, a lady in a passing Victoria bowed to a member of her own coterie, bending gracefully from the waist, giving to an acquaintance a cordial bow, to an inferior a nod.

August Belmont made a wise marriage when he won the hand of the beautiful daughter of Admiral Perry, who opened Japan to the United States. As a girl, I watched Mrs. Belmont in her proscenium box at the opera, ermine and sables slipping from her shoulders, her slender throat wearing a string of pearls, the largest known in this Republic, and every opera-glass in the house turned upon her. One wondered how any mollusc or oyster of an oriental fishery ever produced pearls of such splendor.

To my friend, Mrs. Sam Howland, the daughter of August Belmont, was left the famous string of pearls on the death of Mrs. Belmont, but they had the threat of death upon them. Perhaps they had been too long closed from light in the vault of a bank. The tradition is that to restore vitality to a pearl, it should be worn by a healthy woman. I doubt if all the milkmaids who sported with the young Buddha upon the hills could have restored the Orient to those pearls. In 1915, in the restaurant of the Ritz Hotel in London, the second wife of Sam Howland set the world in a flutter as she entered the room wearing the renowned pearls. As I last saw them, they stood for me as great tears shed at the debacle of a ruling family.

August Belmont, for himself and his children, had the attitude of contact with foreign lands. People laughingly said he and many others held that the best accent, German, Italian or French, for a lovely woman, could only come from association with titled foreign lovers. One rebuke of August Belmont to me, in the house of a friend, should have added a word of life wisdom to my pilgrim scrip. I made a snippy, ill-advised criticism, founded on venomous rumor. Mr. Belmont turned to me, saying, "The private life of any man or woman is none of your affair. If you can manage your own wisely, you will be doing better than most of the human race."

How thankful I am that part of the education at Mrs. Macauley's School was inclusive of seeing all Shakespeare's plays which Booth presented. He and Adams alternated in taking the rôles of Iago and Othello, and at that time, Lawrence Barrett was considered in diction, subtlety and the perfection of the folds of his toga, to be a perfect Cassius.

We went to the play in charge of a governess called Miss Harrington. We were taught to commit to memory large portions of the text of the plays that we were to see. I had recited with such fervor that I brought tears to the eyes of my schoolmates,

> Speak of me as I am; nothing extenuate,
> Nor set down aught in malice: then must you speak
> Of one that loved not wisely, but too well.

I was held up to ridicule for the remainder of my stay at Mrs. Macauley's, because when Booth started to smother Desdemona, I had gripped Miss Harrington's arm and said, "Oh! he will not kill her, will he?" Until today, as I sit before the footlights, my instinct is to impersonate every character in a drama.

On Friday evenings at the school, family and friends were invited, and the girls were expected to play four hands or solos impromptu at the piano. Sometimes we had a play, and I always felt to see one's friends do professional things in an unprofessional way was akin to the shame one had had when a brother's halting performance in recitation, on the last day of school, made one wish to sink under a chair.

At that time there was the forbidden play, "The Black Crook," and we heard that Pauline Markham had the beauty of the Venus de Milo with her arms restored. It was the day of Offenbach's operas, Schneider singing the "Grand Duchesse." Ristori revealed to us the genius of a great actress in "Marie Antoinette" and "Sor Thérèse." Richard Hoffman, famed pianist, father of Malvina Hoffman, came to teach and often to play on Friday evenings.

Some of my schoolmates are still my friends, among them Mrs. E. H. Harriman and Mrs. Trumbull Cary, née Alabama Tomlinson, of Batavia.

In the early 'seventies, stages and street cars were drawn by horses. Delmonico's Restaurant was in Fourteenth Street, where we spent our last cent to eat entrecôte with marrow, or vanilla ice cream flavored with the real bean. Tiffany's, Jewelers and Silversmiths, were sought at their establishment in Union Square. Lower Fifth Avenue and Stuyvesant and Gramercy Parks were the homes of the leading conservative families of the city. The Academy of Music was the home of the Opera. The Astor Hotel was an esteemed hostelry, and Niblo's Garden produced pantomimes and ballets. Union Square was the theater center and Lester Wallack was in his prime. Joseph Fagnani painted "The Nine Muses," for which all the models were fashionable beauties. The gifts of generous citizens were the nucleus of the present Metropolitan Museum. The water supply was from the Reservoir on Fifth Avenue reaching from Fortieth to Forty-second Streets. The present crowded quarter of Harlem and the north of the city was filled with squatter sovereigns, whose shanties were among the goats which grazed the rocks. The beautiful architectural dreams of French châteaux on Fifth Avenue, of the Vanderbilt family, were to be realized and already have been demolished.

Is the time near when no man will care to erect a palatial home within the city limits, so fast is the pace of commerce, and the crumbling touch of time, which drive them to the roofs of apartment buildings and skyscrapers?

We were sent to all of the symphonic concerts and rehearsals of Theodore Thomas's magnificent orchestra, to hear for the first time, the Pastoral and Fifth Symphonies of Beethoven, the earlier ones of Mozart, and the divine waltzes of Strauss.

Three years I spent at Mrs. Macauley's, where, to my surprise, I took a prize for Logic and English Composition. Dr. St. John never had a bad recitation from me in Astronomy or Chemistry, not one word of which he ever made intelligible, but beloved Dr. Leonard, of Columbia, taught us and stimulated our interest in what was then called "Moral and Mental Philosophy and Literature." Miss Macintosh, in a brown poke-bonnet, taught us Rhetoric and Composition, and that greatest of all striking women, Mrs. Macauley, in rustling black silk frocks, white hair pompadour, made me love Roman and Greek History and Mythology and the power of the stage.

Returning home from New York for my school vacation in the early summer, the talk was all of the Buffalo Races. A grandstand had been erected, on the upper story of which the élite of society, in their best bibs and tuckers, watched the horses or looked to the back to see the carts, barouches or four-in-hands, drawn by fine horses, arriving,—a day of parasols and floating veils.

From the mansion of William G. Fargo, the founder of the Wells-Fargo Express Company, came a score of guests, including General Phil Sheridan, whom he suggested to me as a fitting husband. His short, stumpy figure, red face and limping gait, banished the illusion of a dreaming girl of a Great Hero, whose Ride to Winchester she declaimed with passion.

We were often early at the race-course to see the drivers work the horses, speeding like brilliant spiders, round and round the track. With the races came the gypsies, their gaudily painted wagons and bonfires. They camped on the outskirts of the town. Foxy-faced men wore, like the women, bright kerchiefs and gold chains, their red waistcoats affording a note of gaiety. They were as keen on barter and bargain as their ancestors in the Far East. Illy kept children, women with nursing babies, and barking mongrel dogs, thronged about us. The old women and young women found their way among the prosperous residences, and with whining, wheedling voices, coaxed silver from the romantic and curious with which to cross their palms that they might lift the curtains of the future.

Among the pretty immigrant Irish girls of that time who

served us, were those with blue eyes and golden hair, and also those who might have been of the strain of Dido, who brought the sparkling eye of the Orient, as well as its arts, to the shores of Ireland. Tea was always steeping at the back of the kitchen range, and the flexible wrists of the nimble-witted Irish girls swung the tea grounds in their cups to tell their mates whether the red-haired policeman or the black-haired plumber was likely to drop in with a gold ring in his pocket and a proposal on the tip of his tongue. They were not far in spirit from the daughters of Romany. The tales of children stolen by the gypsies added a touch of fear to the pleasure.

With the present fierce drive of steam and electricity one sometimes doubts if, in the real values and grace of living and in great gain, there has not been grave loss of charm and fancy.

The year that Mr. and Mrs. Samuel Clemens came to live in Buffalo, I do not know, but on one of my vacations my mother took me to a small elegant reception in their house a square or so from ours. There was a secret on everyone's tongue in Buffalo; namely, Mark Twain, during his engagement to Miss Langdon, had faced the catastrophe and anxiety of his fiancée's total loss of memory, both of speech and of the printed word, after typhoid fever. His patience and devotion did not restore her memory, but gave her speech and a new education. This romance filled my mind.

On entering the Clemens drawing-room, we were greeted with cordiality: Mrs. Clemens, a dainty woman, replete with intelligence and charm, and he speaking with a slow drawl that I thought he used to perform for me. I burst into unholy laughter which shocked everyone. When I reached my father's roof I realized it were better to commit murder than to be stupid.

In 1912 I found in India all educated natives, whether Mohammedan or Hindu, quoting Mark Twain, above all, the epigram that "for the first time he saw a man trying to split a rock with a shirt." We who have seen our best underwear in tatters in the land of the washerman, who pounds the clothes on a rock by a sacred lake, can appreciate the irony.

Mrs. Clemens' brother, Mr. Langdon, lived in Buffalo. It was he who gave to Buffalo the bronze replica of Michael Angelo's Young David, standing on a knoll in the Park, reflected in the Lake.

The end of the summer school term found me visiting a roommate whose house overlooked the Mohawk Valley. To one born on the flats who dreamed of hills, the vistas of windings of the river and across fertile farms to distant hills presented a panorama of loveliness.

There was in the house party a Yale graduate who was to be a Presbyterian clergyman. Why Presbyterians talk of being much more religious, and more aristocratic than other people, was then, as now, a mystery to me. This young man, with flirtatious eyes, and the laudable desire to work my reformation, dearly loved the younger of his two sisters, and their cloying demonstrations of affection were repellent to me, brought up in the jeering frankness of merciless fraternal banter. However, this young man had recently been received into the cryptic fold of Skull and Bones fraternity at New Haven. I asked what his pin meant, but was seized and taken to the garden and told in whispers by the sister, that no one ever spoke, in the presence of one of its members, of that honorable Society; that the night before their brother was tapped had been one of strain and agony for them.

He wished to pray with me. Failing that, he asked that I be prayed for. The incense of sisterly adulation and that of susceptible girls fed a male vanity. He could not dance and there were gay hops and good music at the nearby hotel, and I never missed tripping to every note.

The fact that the elder brother in the family I was visiting rode and gave me a good mount, and was a skilled whip and took me, in his stylish trap, over the hills and far away, was a convincing proof of my worldliness. In spite of that fact, the divinity student still put at my plate each morning a bunch of pansies. I read him as an open book.

All this preamble brings me to the fact that the intellectual elder brother read aloud to us "Innocents Abroad," Mark Twain's skit on the agent for sale of lightning rods, and other humorous articles, until I crumpled up with laughter and tears. The traveled, cultured, faultlessly-attired brother tried to open my mind to Emerson's Essays and the Victorian poets, and I am still grateful to him. His ideas on marriage were, that a man should take a wife who could support him in the style to which he was accustomed, or a washerwoman who could keep his linen clean and earn enough to feed him.

Finally the embryonic clergyman made me promise to hear him preach his first sermon. I said I would, but that if he looked at me I should wink,—which I did when he later gave a bromidic sermon in Buffalo, and walked back to take luncheon with my family.

From spring until autumn the gathering place of fashion was at the Parade Ground of Fort Porter, overlooking the treacherous Niagara River,—a gay scene, carriages filled with well-dressed people, where gentlemen walked from group to group paying their respects. The Regimental Band played. A cavalcade of young men and women on horseback listened to the music, heard the sunset gun, and watched the lowering of the flag, the western sky often making cloud pictures worthy of the home of all storms.

At the Post were stationed men who had served in the Civil War, and one who had been in New Orleans during the plague of yellow fever, where each night, during the mess dinner, as the ranks grew thinner, a toast was given "to the next man who dies."

Once a week there was a dance given by the officers,—jolly and simple. The Commandant received in the Castle and the dancing went on in the adjoining building. There was a halo of romance about the handsome lieutenants, whose pay was fourteen hundred dollars a year and perquisites. Parents pricked the bubble of budding romance. No belle of Buffalo was known to have married in the army. Photographs taken, wearing a soldier's cap and cape, were a compliment much coveted by romantic girls.

What gay parties we had in the great rooms of Mrs. Watson's house! Her three lovely daughters and their children carry on the tradition of a great hostess and a collector of *objets d'art*.

My impression is that the society of Buffalo in my youth was a distinguished one. With New York a far cry, the life of people of culture was intensive in a small town. There was a renowned amateur theatrical club of ladies and gentlemen, where "The Rivals" and "Richelieu" had a production and standard of excellence rarely attained by professional actors. The grace and diction of Maria Love in those plays has not been forgotten, and George Lovering impersonated Richelieu as well as Booth. As my parents were in Europe, when I was asked to take a leading part in the play "Richelieu," I cabled my father for permission. I received the laconic answer, "No."

The seven bachelors of Buffalo, a group which included Grover Cleveland and Lyman K. Bass, wishing to return their indebtedness, commandeered the Tifft House, the largest and best hotel in Buffalo, and gave an entertainment, the beauty and gaiety of which was talked of for years after.

Between the night when Buffalo's privileged class thronged the old Buffalo Club, corner of Chippewa and Delaware, at a ball given in honor of Grand Duke Alexis, and today, stands the tragedy of the Romanoffs and the elimination of eighty Grand Dukes.

Statuesque Jane Wells, who sang like a nightingale and looked as Empresses should, and rarely do, was an arresting figure. Alexis had the commanding height of his family and was young and slender. At the formal opening of the entertainment with the traditional quadrille, Jane Wells was the partner of the Grand Duke. Buffalo in beauty matched Russia in rank.

The gentlemen of the suite danced with exuberant vitality the varsoviana, the polka and mazurka and waltzed to the lovely music of Strauss. They spun like tops and never reversed. The girls of Buffalo were giddy when returned to their chaperons. Ruffled flounces of tarlatan, torn to shreds by the spurs of the Russian officers, were the fate of all good-looking girls.

Well-boned corsets beneath pointed bodices, hair puffed and curled, and the nuke, which the French have always considered the beauty of a woman's head, was emphasized in hairdressing; satin slippers peeped from the amplitude of tulle and tarlatan skirts. Dowagers wore rich fabrics and long trains. Not many of us who danced till dawn that night survive.

Years later I saw Alexis. He came to the Hotel Bristol, in Carlsbad, for the cure. We, who counted every crumb of prescribed diet of zwieback and schinken for supper, beheld the stuffing of Royalty. The manager of the hotel combed Europe for delicacies, providing oysters from France and crawfish, cooked with dripping brown sauce, which His Highness gobbled like a wolf. To an onlooker, it represented a death cure through gluttony. Some time later, at the gambling table at Aix les Bains, where an uncle of the Czar kept the bank, I watched Alexis. At his elbow sat an enchanting woman in a black dress, open at the throat about which was a king's ransom of pearls. She had soft dark eyes, luxuriant hair, a skin warm from the sun of Italy,— a woman to love and be loved. She met Alexis at the Russian frontier and always traveled with him in Europe. They have both joined the Great Majority.

CHAPTER FOUR

INTRODUCTION TO WASHINGTON

BUFFALO was the home of two Presidents,—Millard Fillmore and Grover Cleveland. The picturesque Fillmore house, a stucco-coated mansion in lower Delaware Street, added interest to what is now McKinley Circle. Fillmore, tall and dignified, looked the part of a President, and his pocket edition of a President's wife graced all festivities in the mode of the time when voluminous skirts, low-cut gowns and one-button gloves were the fashion.

Cleveland was political dealer of the Democratic Party, and suffered his only defeat when he ran for District Attorney against his friend, Lyman K. Bass, leader of the Republican Party of Erie County. Their friendship was never broken. It is amusing to note, that on the morning of the birth of his beautiful wife, Frances Folsom, he and Lyman Bass walked together to see the baby, the child of their dear friend, Oscar Folsom. When Lyman Bass went to the House of Representatives, Grover Cleveland became his law partner. The firm afterwards included Wilson S. Bissell, Postmaster-General under Cleveland. Grover Cleveland was an Executor of my father's estate and an old will of mine he wrote in his clear fine script. He was a past-master of perfect English.

In 1873 my father, to save his life, was sent to Europe, and he and my mother made the Grand Tour with Mr. and Mrs. Sherman S. Rogers and their children.

In their absence, on my young shoulders fell the care of a great establishment and twelve horses in the stable, with grooms and gardeners to direct. My four brothers, the youngest one three, and the governess were left with me. Malignant scarlet fever quarantined the house for three months, during which time I slept in day clothes. There were no trained nurses in those days. My father and mother returned in the spring of 1874.

Mr. J. N. Matthews, editor and owner of the Buffalo *Express*, a skilled writer and a devoted friend of my family, entertained distinguished people from all over the country. At his table I dined with Grant, Conkling and Blaine, and leaders of political thought.

I recall one brilliant dinner at which was present Kate Chase Sprague, supposed to be Senator Conkling's Egeria. She was a fine classical scholar and on that occasion filled out a Latin quotation over which Senator Conkling hesitated,—an assistance he would usually have resented, but he thanked her with courtesy. Conkling's sonorous sentences usually thundered out without hesitation. Every morning of his life from boyhood, he had committed to memory noble passages of great literature. We went after dinner to a mass meeting before Grant's second election, which filled the Rink with a surging crowd. We were suffocated in making for the platform. I saw fainting women passed lengthwise over the heads of the crowds.

Mr. Matthews, who in my childhood had taken me to hear the thrilling Adelina Patti as Violetta, and her sister, the wonderful coloratura concert singer, and Lucca in "Mignon," was always kind and included me in his excursions where men of note were asked. We went at the end of July with a group of Western Senators and Governors to Falconswood River Club. A celebrated oboe player from the band stirred the heart as his plaintive music

FRANCES METCALFE IN 1874

came from a skiff on that fast-running river. On that occasion I met Lyman K. Bass, and within a week, on the 4th of August, was engaged to him. We were married in November, at an improvised altar in the bay-window of my father's house. My four brothers, ranging from seven to eighteen years, were in attendance. As an indication of the fashion of the time, the glass of champagne which I drank as a returning toast, was the first time wine had ever passed my lips, although liquors, sherry and port were always on the sideboard of my father's dining-room.

Chauncey Depew sent his special car, and we set out for Washington. Rooms in the beautiful Annex of the Arlington Hotel, formerly the home of Senator Sumner and his striking wife, were waiting for us.

At the first breakfast in the large dining-room, Mr. Bass was eating what I thought might disagree with him and, pointing to a man at an adjoining table, I said, "If you continue such a diet, you will be as sick as that man." He said, "Well, then I will continue eating, as that is Senator Evarts, one of the greatest men in the country, and he never had a pain." Nearby were General and Mrs. Marcy, parents of Mrs. George McClellan, and later I listened to their accounts of earlier days when the carriages in Washington en route for dinners, had to be hauled out by oxen, and the women carried over the mire of mud to firm ground. Mrs. Marcy had a marmoset which she carried in a black satin bag to mill and to meeting. General Marcy said the only grain of sense it had was to close its eyes when he blew smoke in them. The pet died and its mistress did not come to table, mourning its death. In line of descent came Mrs. George McClellan and her son George, who was later Mayor of New York and a Tammany member of Congress.

Benjamin H. Bristow was Secretary of the Treasury, Hamilton Fish, Secretary of State, and General Belknap, Secretary of War. Mrs. Fish, seeing my youth, and wishing her state to stand for the order and elegance of a Capital, said, "You must always wear a low-cut gown at dinner or an evening reception at the White House."

An invitation from the President and Mrs. Grant was waiting for us. The night of the dinner of thirty-six covers in the then state dining-room, which barely held more than thirty-six people, fell at the time of a blizzard. I had a Worth gown of rich white satin and embroidered tulle in garlands of roses. My French evening wrap was left in the dressing-room. General and Mrs. Grant met me with cordial courtesy and a smile,—a friendliness that never failed while they lived. I heard that Senator Edmunds was cross, especially if he had dyspepsia, and my heart sank when that most eminent constitutional lawyer gave me his arm to go to dinner. Our seats were at the end, where a fierce cold draught swept from the serving-room. "Good God, child," said he, "you will take your death of cold," and he rose and went to fetch his wife's pink cashmere opera cloak, trimmed with swansdown, which had survived many a Washington season. All my French attire was hidden and I was muffled to my throat. But Senator Edmunds was very charming and fascinating and not condescending in his talk to me.

The perfect face and figure of Mrs. Potter Palmer, and her attractive sister, the bride of Fred Grant, graced the occasion,— faces that showed only kindness to me for many years.

At the corner of K and Fifteenth Streets was the spacious house occupied by Secretary and Mrs. Fish, which set a standard of stately dinners, beginning at a comparatively early hour and lasting never less than two hours. At the plate of each woman was a French favor, a bouquet of lilies of the valley or violets, and at least nine or ten glasses at each place, for different wines served with each course, liqueurs and fine champagne with the coffee. Mrs. Fish stood for high breeding and courtesy. Her daughter, Edith, afterwards married to Sir Stafford-Northcote, was always dressed in white.

At one dinner I saw, for the first time, the man who became General Francis V. Green. He was the cleverest and handsomest of West Point graduates, and just returned from the Turko-Russian War.

Mrs. Fish was insistent that every visit which was required of me should be made, and she called for me often in her carriage to take me with her. Senator and Mrs. Bayard were living at the Old Willard Hotel. We sent in our cards and the darky led us to a door which, on being opened, surprised the handsome Senator Bayard changing his shirt. Mrs. Bayard had left a few days earlier to return to Maryland. We beat a hasty retreat. The incident pleased me, as I hated paying visits.

It was an enlightenment to be included in the Sunday suppers of Mr. and Mrs. Blaine where Abigail Dodge (Gail Hamilton) seemed a permanent guest. These ladies were immensely interested in my French clothes, and kind and not adversely critical of my ignorance. They knew the Old and New Testament by heart, and interlarded all discussions with pertinent Biblical knowledge. James G. Blaine was the handsomest and the most magnetic of the line of Speakers of the House of Representatives. He was a prospective candidate for the nomination by the Republicans for the Presidency. The leading men of the press and politics of north, east, south and west flocked to the Blaine house on Fifteenth Street. I longed to have Blaine succeed to the Presidency after the second term of Grant.

On one occasion, hidden under the Speaker's desk when Blaine called the House to order, Jamie Blaine emerged, to the discomfiture of the entire House. He was but eight years old.

General Grant loved his friends and trusted them. He believed no evil. General Babcock, who sent us flowers from the White House Conservatory, was vilified. General Grant believed in him through all the destructive upheaval. Then came the terrifying scandal of General Belknap's wives, second and present, as to their receiving rebates by giving positions to army sutlers.

The Thursday night before the exposure, Mr. Bass and I dined with General and Mrs. Belknap. The table was sumptuous. Mrs. Belknap, tall and noticeably of the Kentucky corn-fed type of small hands and delicate feet, wore a satin pompadour dress of blue stripes and roses. I said to General Belknap, "How handsome your wife is." "Yes," said he, "I have had three wives, all beautiful." Eugene Hale of Maine, then in the House of Representatives and later United States Senator, with glossy black hair, slender and graceful, sat on Mrs. Belknap's left breathing adoration. Joe Blackburn, Representative from Kentucky, and Mrs. Blackburn were animated talkers. Blackburn, brother of the man of unsavory memory, said to have sent clothing infected with yellow fever across the Union lines to destroy the American soldiers, put an adverse question mark in my estimate of Joe Blackburn. On that night the accused sutler was secreted in the upper story of the Belknap house.

Mr. Bass was a member of the Military Committee of the Lower House. We lived in Fourteenth Street and the following night our house was besieged by newspaper reporters. Mr. Bass was called to counsel with the Committee before which General Belknap was summoned. Everyone liked General Belknap and when he was called before the Committee, he refused to incriminate his second and his present wife who were sisters, and only begged to shoulder all of the blame and shield them. To the day of his death, Mr. Bass believed General Belknap was ignorant of the dishonesty of those two women.

The scandal rocked Washington to its foundation. I went at once to the White House and found Mrs. Grant weeping, and, believing Mrs. Belknap maligned, begged for mercy for her. My visit to Mrs. Fish within the hour was of another order. She held for the justice which should be meted out to those who had besmirched high position, feeling in honesty and patriotism the personnel of their colleagues of the Cabinet had been insulted. Belknap resigned and his family were disgraced.

Then began large social experience because of the appreciation of my husband, who was a polished orator and the youngest Member of the House of Representatives, whose counsel was sought even by those who differed from him in politics. He had broken his health in his arduous work through the malarial summer weather, serving on the District of Columbia Investigation Committee.

Boss Shepherd was under fire, but in the last equation one must admit that the Washington of today owes a debt of gratitude to Shepherd. His house was renowned for rich entertainment. Finding the city with varying levels and with scores of negro squatters, he set order everywhere. Even to this time Washington has the ugliness of a child who has lost some of its first teeth, and has not acquired a regular set of second teeth.

Benjamin Bristow had the best cook in Washington. He was fighting the whiskey ring tooth and nail. His admired Kentucky wife presided over a table where good talk was the rule and distinction sat at meat. They included me in all their entertainments, I expect because, as my father once said, "Let her come, she has such a good time." And when Baron Alphonse de Rothschild and the Count de Turenne arrived on a financial mission, I dined with them, and after their return to Paris they sent a large bonbonnière of pink satin, painted with true lovers' knots, doves and garlands, and filled with luscious candy,—a graceful gesture of the gallantry of the Latin of old France to young America.

The New Year's reception at the White House was less formal and less crowded than those of today. The Naval and Army officers attended in full regalia. Mrs. Hale's father, formerly Secretary of the Interior; Zachariah Chandler, Western and kindly; Senator Conkling, prodding with brilliant satire Marshall Jewell, the Postmaster-General; Admiral Rogers, the Chesterfield of the Navy; Admiral Jewett, fearless runner of the Confederate Blockade, full of fun and story and gay gallantry. He had the passion of a sailor for horseback riding, and followed the pack of American hounds in Virginia, loving youth and feminine beauty. Mrs. Robeson, the wife of the Secretary of the Navy, a notable singer of professional standard, energetic and dominating, was an official hostess.

It was the day of Army and Navy cotillions and they were led by Woodbury Blair, a recently returned graduate of Harvard, who much resembled the portrait bust of young Emperor Augustus, and was the secret toast of every girl in town.

I was asked by Ulysses Grant, Jr., to dance with him. In those days girls were chaperoned, and I was asked to act in this capacity to the daughter of the Chief Justice. She was of a serious type and older than I, and when we reached the dressing-room and she saw me in a white tulle dress with festoons of morning glories, and my hair a mass of puffs and curls, she refused to go into the

INTRODUCTION TO WASHINGTON 49

ballroom with me. Mrs. Dennison, the wife of the former Governor of Ohio, acted as our chaperon. Mrs. Dennison was the attractive mother of beautiful daughters and handsome sons.

The members of the House, at that time, were fewer in number. Garfield was talked of as Presidential nominee. He spoke well. When Blaine and Garfield debated, the galleries were thronged.

General Morton, the War Governor of Indiana, spoke forcibly in the Senate, and Conkling, who hated Blaine and was pastmaster of brilliant invective, packed the Senators' galleries when he spoke. Mrs. Conkling, the sister of the beloved Governor Seymour of New York State, stood for dignity of race and bearing. Governor Seymour, the Democratic nominee for President, on the only occasion I heard him speak, said, "In my youth I valued heads above hearts; in my old age I value hearts above heads."

I was often asked to receive with Mrs. Grant. The informality with which she often called her husband "Lis" and brushed a stray lock of hair which he had forgotten to straighten, was a far cry from the scene in the Blue Room today. There were teas on the balcony at the back of the White House, facing the swamps and malarial flats beyond which the sluggish Potomac crept toward Chesapeake Bay. September was held in the Army medical reports as being the most dangerously unhealthy month of the year. A regimental band would play and well-known men of every branch of the Government made an exchange of pleasant intercourse, and I was loath even to go to Europe.

CHAPTER FIVE

THE GRAND TOUR

IN March of 1875 Mr. Bass and I embarked on a North German Lloyd steamship, the *Oder,* a staunch craft of four thousand five hundred tons, uncovered decks, and an overwhelming smell of bilge. Captain Willegerutte made the sailors construct a tarpaulin-covered bench, and he would carry me in his arms, a limp creature, half dead, saying, "Poor land rat." My brother, a Yale student, and a friend, made a quartette which disembarked at Southampton at two A.M. to take refuge in comfortable four-poster beds, sheltered from drafts by curtains. We ate our first sole for breakfast, drove in the sunshine to the picturesque ruins of Fountain Abbey, stopped to see Winchester Cathedral, and at luncheon watched a silver and gold pheasant strutting on the greensward in the garden as we sampled English cheese and bitter beer for the first time.

But London and England had short shriving, and with the intention of returning, we left to have a heartbreaking channel crossing, to reach the shelter of the tiny Hotel l'Amirauté, where my father and mother had lived for several months. We hastened to the boulevards, which seemed to us brilliantly lighted.

Washburne, the Ambassador, having been our representative during the siege of Paris, was an interesting friend. The pulling down of the Column Vendôme by the Communists was a matter of talk among our friends, and the starvation lines when cats, dogs, and all of the animals of the Jardin d'Acclimatation were eaten. I have today a curious menu given me by the celebrated restaurateur, Voisin, served at Christmas in those black days.

At that time no young woman cared to be without an escort or chaperon in the streets. One bright morning I left Monroe's Bank at nine A.M., with a wealth of assurance, to go to a dressmaker nearby. A stylish boulevardier raised his hat and spoke to me, and I fled running, to be called for at the dressmaker's. He was within his rights and I defying the conventions.

We went by one of the *mouches* on the Seine to the Fête de St. Cloud, escorted by a Buffalo bachelor, Edwin Movius, who had been educated in Europe. My new hat blew off and floated toward Havre, but I did not mind. We returned at midnight, after mingling with the hilarity of a French crowd.

We left Paris regretfully, stopping at Lyons en route to Marseilles, where we climbed to the sacred shrine of the Virgin, filled with the votive offerings of sailors. We drove on the Corniche along the brilliant Côte d'Azur from Marseilles to Cannes and Nice, along the coast. We saw gardens of jasmine, heliotrope and other flowers, cultivated to make essences for the perfumers of Paris.

At Nice we made arrangements for the traveling-carriage which was to take us to Italy. There was a high seat behind the driver, with an adjustable cover, where four people could sit with comfort. The main body was for luggage and servants.

We tasted our first green almonds and bought quantities of the, to us, unknown golden Mandarin oranges. The hotel put up our luncheon and we mounted, as a postillion cracked a whip, to wend our way along the Corniche Road to the Land of Heart's Desire. We crossed the frontier at Mentone, and the night at

Savona was full of street singing by rich Italian voices of folk songs of love.

One had time to drink in the theatrical beauty of the Apennines and the Mediterranean, as modern speed does not permit. I felt at home, repeating aloud the verses of Buchanan Read's "Drifting," the perfect picture by a lover of sea and shore.

We were bound for Genoa. The stupid boy who journeyed with us never sensed beauty, but dived, at every stop, into every hole in the hills in quest of robbers.

The carriage broke down after nightfall and we climbed to the Hotel de France at Porto Maurizio, carrying the robes. No rest was to be found there. The beds were filled with vermin, and the cooking flavored with garlic. My brother said he would try a boiled egg, as perhaps Italian hens did not eat onions.

The sapphire sea, bordered by towers erected as lookouts when the Saracens raided the maritime towns, was a lure to drive as far as Spezia. To the eyes of a foreigner the palace-crowned rocks overlooking the glorious harbor of Genoa, set in terraced gardens, stirred the inaccurate memories of one who had read many books and forgotten them.

The noble staircases led to glorious rooms built by the merchant princes, whose argosies from the Orient had brought gold for their coffers, followed by devastating plague to smite them, and who endeavored by the erection of churches of rich value, to arrest the flaying arrows of death. On the walls hung Van Dyck's masterpieces. Every stroke was painted by his own brush, portraits of the proud traders and stately wives, decked in velvets and rare laces and jewels.

Now these noble buildings house modern commercial firms, and the portraits have been sold to museums and art dealers.

I caught a glimpse of Verdi on the terrace of the Palace in

which he wrote some of his matchless operas. *Tout passe, tout lasse.*

We were bound for Rome and Naples before the heat set in, which was much talked of by English women in black dresses, white caps and colored bows, and whose shivering shoulders were covered with Shetland shawls. They came for winter sunshine and filled the reading parlors of the hotels, chiefly intent on reading the "Queen's Magazine" which reported the Court Calendar of English Royalty. They sniffed at Americans. We suffered their curiosity when sitting about the table d'hôte dinner, which was served on the stroke of the appointed hour.

We all had to travel with rubber or tin bathtubs and our own bath towels. Our book-bags were plump with Hare's "Walks," Murray's efficient Guide Books, "Childe Harold" and the Verses of Elizabeth Browning, and Grimm's "Life and Times of Michael Angelo," which I had forced my men friends to read in Buffalo, in their agony floored by unpronounceable Italian names, while I sewed a fine seam.

Then on to Rome!

Mr. Bass brought letters to the President of the American College from Bishop Timon of Buffalo, which paved the smooth path to a private audience with Pope Pius IX. Bishop Timon's name is marked in the marble pilaster at the right of the high altar of St. Peter's among those who, in 1870, fastened the doctrine of the Immaculate Conception and the Infallibility of the Pope as a tenet of faith of the Romish Church.

Thomas Bailey Aldrich and his wife with long golden hair were the guests of Mayor Pearce of Boston. Mr. Bass had arranged for them to share the private audience with the Pope. All three men insisted they would not kneel and kiss the Pope's hand, but on the following day they wore their dress suits, and Mrs. Aldrich and I in simple black frocks and veils, drove to the Court of the Damas at the Vatican, passing between ranks of the Swiss Guard, whose gay uniform was designed by Michael Angelo. Walking through noble rooms, we knelt in line, awaiting the arrival of the white-clad Pius IX, wearing red slippers and followed by his Cardinals clad in crimson mantles and soutanes. The head of the American College introduced us by name as we kissed the pontifical ring, and the Pope spoke to me in French of the piety and devotion of Bishop Timon, by whom I had been blessed as a child at a school of the Catholic sisters in Buffalo. The men of the party were humble and abject and kissed the Pope's ring with fervor.

Mr. Bass was an unprejudiced weigher of evidence, and he contended that the conservative influence of the Church of Rome was a power for good in the United States. I who had sat under the eloquent thunderings of the Episcopal Bishop Cox of the Western Diocese, had some prejudices to overcome, and to read that Pius IX believed in the use of the Inquisition in the early days of his pontificate at the last meeting of the tribunal, which was held in a building at the left of St. Peter's, where a Bishop from the Near East was tried and condemned, revolted me.

In 1875 Margarita was in the floodtide of her beauty and her bodyguard of tall officers wore her favorite flower, the violet. As she drove down the Corso in her open barouche, with her little son beside her, now the King of Italy, she was beloved by the populace. At that time the carriages of the Cardinals were still picturesque.

In 1870 were closed the main entrances of the palaces of the leading nobles of the Papal Party, as a protest against the Kingdom of United Italy. Even when I lived in Rome years after, the doors of the great houses were still closed, only to be opened for the passing to the tomb of the owner, whose body had lain stretched on the stone floor in the garb of a monk of an order of which he was a lay member, with candles lighted for the last offices of the Church.

Prince Humbert was often seen riding, in 1875, on a spirited horse. He was an ugly man with fierce mustachios that did not make him impressive, but his reputation was of one who loved art and the ladies. A great Roman lady once said to me, "I have known the House of Savoy, and they are all great lovers."

The Corso was the fashionable promenade and on fête days, rich banners and tapestries hung from every window, and medieval Rome met one at every corner. Flocks of goats came from the Campagna at dawn, driven by their herders, who mounted the stairs of high apartments and milked the animals at the door of rich and poor alike. There were lighted shrines at every corner before which, at Christmas, the shepherds from the Abruzzi Pieffere played their bagpipes in honor of the Virgin. The Forum still waited for the pick of archeological excavation. The Spanish steps were bright with flowers, for freesias and violets bloom in sheltered places in mid-winter. Gaily-dressed peasants from the mountains waited to be chosen as models by artists of all countries who worked in Rome.

We met writers and artists socially, climbed to the dome of St. Peter's, walked the tortuous paths of the catacombs, thrilled with the reading of Hawthorne's "Marble Faun," whose statue graces the Capitoline Museum, and we gazed at the flickering light in Hilda's Tower. Gone was the merriment of the Carnival and the horse races in the Corso. Liszt was the idol of Rome, and the guest of Cardinal Hohenlohe, owner of the Villa d'Este. A Jewish sculptor who lived in the ruined Baths of Diocletian was their friend and frequent guest. The three walked through ilex-shaded paths to the sound of plashing waters. Everyone, save me, was fatigued with the endless walking of museums and the Vatican Gallery of treasures.

Garibaldi, the red-shirted hero of the populace, Cavour, and Pazolini, supporters of United Italy in the First Ministry of Victor Emmanuel, made a fascinating society. The Court came from Florence to make Rome the capital. No young noble of the Black Party went to Court under pain of excommunication, a blow to their efficiency and loyalty to their country. The Pope, a self-made prisoner until recently, was behind the walls of the Vatican.

To an American, the indifference of Italian society as to any claim of an American to place of prestige, save that of personal charm, was a revelation. How can a society descended from those who have seen all power, pomp and prestige pass, and the panorama of ancient, medieval and modern Rome, sense the claim of an old family from Oshkosh, New Orleans or Boston?

On the occasion of the accession of the present King, when the Duke of Massimo paid his respects, he was driven from the portal of the Palazzo Massimo, a triumph of architecture whose curving front follows the line of the street. On his arrival he was honored by the question from the King, "You are a descendant of Ancus Martius, are you not?" "It has been, Sire, a popular superstition for thirteen hundred years," replied the Duke. Nevertheless, literary, artistic, cultivated Americans had entrée to the brilliant centers of Rome and ordered copies of the old masters to decorate their homes in the United States.

Charles Coleman, an associate of Elihu Vedder, lived in that street of studios, the Via Margutta. The flitting about of nude models from door to door in the Via Margutta, at the foot of the Pincian, was a shock to one born on the shores of Lake Erie.

In spite of the fact that Ambassador March was a friend of Mr. Bass, a man of culture and kindness, who made our presentation to Humbert and Margarita possible, we were eager to reach Naples, and we said good-bye to Rome.

The smoke of Vesuvius rose from her cone, since changed by many eruptions. Naples, city of beggars, fleas and filth, looked on a sapphire sea. The smells of the city were as unpleasant as those of famed Canton. The Chia was a fashionable drive. More than once I saw Victor Emmanuel driving his own horses in a vehicle akin to an English tilbury. On the road beneath the hill to the Citadel, along the Chia, were the caves filled with mendicants, where they were born and bred. At the foot of the hill were the aged, crippled and whining, midway were the mothers with nursing babies, and at the top, gamins turning cartwheels and handsprings in quest of coins.

During the cholera, when Humbert came to direct the work in Naples and risked his life, these pestilential haunts of vice and disease were cleaned and abolished. It was there that Dr. Munthe worked among the stricken described in his widely read book, "The Mourning City."

Across the Bay, beyond the terrible prison of St. Elmo, Capri rose with strong appeal. There were no steamers and the only way to see the Villa of Tiberius and the Blue Grotto was by sailboat. At dawn we embarked, where the sailors in red berets, open shirts and striped blue and white trousers revealing the bronze torso of the sailor man, hoisted white sails,—an alluring picture.

My brother had been urging an extension of our trip to Greece. We had luncheon in baskets and mandarins, and it was not long before I lay limp in the bottom of the sailboat whose sails were taut in what men call a "spanking breeze." My brother, who had become the color of jade, said, "I believe we have too little time to go to Greece." At last we reached the Blue Grotto and later arrived at the port Grand Marino, where black-eyed boys helped us to mount donkeys. There was not a carriage or cart in the town. At the left of the square was the Villa Bourbon, and the town had the architecture of the Arabs, with its white houses and pergolas.

Capri was the retreat of artists, archeologists, writers and illicit romance. Some found devoted mothers for their children. A few English scholars married and tried the experiment of taking to Great Britain women who had never worn a hat on their braided hair, round the coils of which they had silver pins like a cartwheel, but the descendants of the Greeks at Anacapri, or the Caprician settlers of the Island, could not find happiness in the fogs and social restrictions of England.

Returning a wreck at midnight under a glorious full moon, prone among the ropes, I little realized in later life I should make a villa in Capri my home for six months.

On the night after my return from Capri, on my right at the table d'hôte at the hotel sat Castelar, twice President of Spain. He did not look his forty-five years and was then in the early days of his self-imposed banishment from Spain, after the restoration of the Bourbons. Liberal patriot, believer in a Republican form of government, from his sojourn in England able to speak as only a polished Englishman can, historian, and able writer on many subjects, he talked with me of English literature and of Lord Byron, whose life Castelar had brilliantly written. Disappointed in the overthrow of his dreams for his native land, he absented himself to embrace the career of a student and man of letters.

The urge to visit Pompeii sent us south in a traveling-carriage. Groves of oranges and lemons along the sea and inlets filled with the craft of fishermen, brought us to Salerno and on to spend the night at a picturesque convent. From the shaded terrace of pleached lime trees at Monte Cave, we descended to mount a rude cabriolet, escorted by an armed guard, to go to Pæstum, the road to which was unsafe. Even the peasants in the field had guns slung across their shoulders, whether to fight the bandits or to join with them, I never knew.

Not Greece, nor the far-famed temples of Sicily, ever filled my soul or gave the profound love for Greek architecture, as did three deserted ruined temples in the salt marshes by the sea at Pæstum.

We left Naples shortly afterwards for Florence, where I fell ill with a touch of fever. The valet told the English doctor he knew the cause of my sickness, that I not only bathed every day, but in cold water. Half delirious I drank bottled water and dreamed of cool springs that, when I stooped to drink, vanished and left me thirsty.

Florence, even now, seems fresh from the Thirteenth Century. The warring of religious orders had not defaced the convent walls, churches and palaces which reflect not only Fra Angelico, but all the great artists of the Florentine School. We arrived at Florence to find the iris and pink roses still blooming. We drove in the Cascini, where the ladies, in beautiful open carriages, were driving *d'Aumont*. The postillions, on their fine horses, were in light-colored satin liveries and top boots. Gallants paid court from one carriage to another.

Go we must to Pisa, not only for its Leaning Tower, and the epoch-making sculptures of the Baptistery, but in early morning to drive to the stretch of sand beyond Leghorn, where Shelley's funeral pyre was built by his friends, from which his burning heart was snatched.

Then on to Bologna, whose masterpiece, St. Cecilia, I could hardly see because of neuralgia, and whose shaded arches sent me shivering to the train.

We arrived at the Grand Hotel, in Venice, once a palace, in a gondola seemingly floating between two firmaments, the starry sky and the reflecting waters, to sleep in a grandiose bedroom with friezes of a painter of the time of Titian. From outside came the voices of impassioned singers from their barges on the Grand Canal. I then became a Venetian and until today a voyage to Europe which does not include Venice is incomplete.

Our gondolier, Pasquale d'Este, was head of the gondoliers and doubtless, by the bar sinister, a descendant of the great family of that name. He knew Tasso from cover to cover, and long extracts of Dante which it was music to hear him declaim. His knowledge of the traditions and history of Venice, its art and architecture, made him a brilliant cicerone and we reckoned him a friend. My son and his wife, on their wedding journey, were shown the glories of Venice under his guidance, and in the suffering of his old age, we climbed to pay him affectionate homage before he died.

Mr. and Mrs. Thatcher Adams joined us to go through the incomparable beauty of the Italian Lakes, and to cross by carriage the Simplon Pass. We arrived at Domo d'Ossolo at the foot of Mt. Cenis on a damp threatening evening, to leave the following morning. The stone steps of our hotel apartment were on the outside. As we mounted, we heard the beating of a drum and the notes of a flute. In the tiny square came a scene as from Pagliacci, a clown leading a fat white horse on which was mounted a pretty young woman in cotton tights and tarlatan ballet dress, Harlequin with his flute bringing up the rear with the announcement that there would be a performance in the evening. I was aflame

THE GRAND TOUR

with interest. Mr. Adams and Mr. Bass reluctantly consented to take me after dinner to the show. Mrs. Adams, more sensible, was disgusted with the idea. But we went. We found damp boards laid on chairs in a stable yard, and there this lovely girl, who had ridden standing as the clown gesticulated, descended to do the sword dance and the veritable egg dance with grace and skill, which is supposed to be given, but never is, in the opera "Mignon." A meager collection of coins ended this picture of strolling players.

In a fog we left for a safe crossing of the Pass, later to have a startling experience. After crossing the Tête Noir Pass we came to Badlands by carriage, and while we were at luncheon in a little hostelry, a small white-faced boy called at the door, "Le torrent, le torrent." The driver jumped to the box of the carriage, vigorously whipping the horses to a run. We dashed along as best we could, to reach a bridge which the villagers were taking up. The little boy stood on the bank pointing to a black spot which proved to be the head of a torrent fifteen or twenty feet high, carrying in its foaming power trees and débris. We mounted the carriage quickly to try to get beyond the incoming flood which desolated the plains for miles. We were swept down a swollen stream so swift that the carriage was nearly carried away, and we faced death, but finally the horses climbed the bank.

We wished to see the glacier and I walked down the Mauvais Pas in thin French morocco shoes.

Later from Geneva we made the excursion to Mont Brévent to see Mont Blanc. Our hearts gave out from the efforts and altitude. My husband nearly died. I threw myself down near a middle-aged Frenchman lying in the shade of a tree. He was taking a wedding journey with his nephew and his wife and, I think, paying for it. He said he should never climb again. He recalled the ascent of Mt. Etna in his youth, but now he would never leave Paris or even mount as high as the Tour St. Jacques.

We went with Mr. and Mrs. Abram S. Hewitt and their children to see the sunrise on the Rigi. We passed the night, but saw nothing, though it established a friendship which I enjoyed for years. Mrs. Hewitt was a daughter of Peter Cooper, and her distinguished husband I often saw in Washington, and enjoyed the hospitality of their great house which, by Sarah Hewitt's recent death, is closed forever. That house was for a lifetime renowned for its hospitality.

This constant journeying forced us to take a three weeks' rest at a German Spa. Then Heidelberg, where as we entered, among the ruins, a room where a gathering of students were singing in unison and drinking good beer, I found Edward Cramer, one of the handsomest and dearest friends of my girlhood. Mr. Bass removed me quickly. Then along the Rhine to Cologne, the river then unscarred by commerce, but the city living up to its reputation of bad smells, from whose Square I had my first sight of the Cathedral. The pure Gothic of the stern north was refreshing, after the bedecked churches of Italy. Standing alone in the ambulatory above the high altar, the tremendous harmonies of gray arches falling into line and rhythm submerged me with emotion and I wept, for it is akin to a Bach Chorale.

Holland with its procession of windmills came next, its wooden shoes, and its women all in the varied costumes of their provinces, spotless caps and odd gold earrings, but they are no longer in evidence. The food of Holland is the best. The paintings by the artists of the Low Countries were a stimulating contrast to the Virgins and Holy Families and Saints of Italy. Picturesque Ghent, Malines and the tower of Bruges, were quaint and endearing, but above all for me, were the cobblers who worked in a square tower which dominated Bruges, their light at night and in storms bringing migrating birds and attracting all of the feathered world to their windows. These cobblers became an authority on the migration of the birds,—self-taught scientific observers.

Motley's "Dutch Republic" and the "United Netherlands" made every bloodstained stone of Brussels alive, and in that unique square one paid homage to the statue of Egmont and recalled Beethoven's Overture.

Mr. Bass's letters had been the open sesame of all private collections, and Holland's hospitality was amazing as was its cleanliness. The Hollanders consider the Germans a dirty people living in unclean towns. The low skies and stretch of level country and waterways created an art which influenced Constable and English art and touched the spirit of the France of the 'forties.

Our time was growing short and the part of our journey from Brussels to Paris went like a flash. A brilliant man sitting in our compartment, whose name I never knew, was full of the story of Maximilian and Carlotta who were happy and had no desire to be rulers of Mexico. Hand in hand they walked from their white palace down the ilex paths and the marble steps to embark on the blue Adriatic from Miramar, he to face death from the firing squad, and she long days of anguish in a madhouse in Belgium, for she was the daughter of Leopold, Le Roi de Belge, lover of Cleo Merode, promoter of the cruelties of the Belgian Congo.

Our traveling companion had been an associate of Juarez who, according to him, did not die of apoplexy as the world was so informed, but was tricked and killed in the house of a woman whom he loved and who betrayed him. Juarez was a full-blooded

Indian, an honest, stubborn liberal, born in poverty, educated brilliantly by charity, and rocked in the cradle of revolutions. He became President before and after the reign of Maximilian; defeating the Imperial Party, he was seemingly victorious, but the shot that killed Maximilian killed Juarez's popularity.

Arriving in Paris where the ruins of the Tuileries stood untouched since the onslaught of the Commune, we wandered in the Palais Royale, under the arches of which were all of the great jewelers of Paris, and ate white truffles at Véfour's. We shopped and I came to know Worth, from whom my mother had ordered my coming-out dress of Valenciennes lace for eighty dollars. We saw the great actresses at the Theatre Français, the Opera and the Opera Comique, and at last made another terrific crossing to England. The Channel is, I believe, the secret of the liberty of England.

My father was very ill, and we were cabled to return home.

CHAPTER SIX

COLORADO SPRINGS

MY husband was no better for the eight months in Europe, but we hastened to Washington. It was a winter of dinners. The beginning of June, we were asked to the White House for an informal dinner of eighteen on Sunday night. I found myself on the President's right, and on his left was Mrs. Fred Grant, whose daughter, now the Princess Cantacuzene, was born, as was my son, a month later. On my right was General Sherman. General Thomas was seated at the extreme end of the table. At the opposite end of the table was aged Simon Cameron, formerly Secretary of War under Lincoln and father of Senator Donald Cameron. On his right hand sat Mrs. Paul, of Philadelphia, whose daughter later married Waldorf Astor, father of the present Viscount Astor. Whenever Simon Cameron spoke, Mrs. Paul called out to her daughter, who was sitting with young Ulysses B. Grant, "Listen, my dear. This is history."

General Sherman, tall, thin and gallant, an inveterate talker, kept the ball of conversation moving. The Sherman family were influential in public life, both on the bench and politically.

Lizzie Cameron, niece of General Sherman, was gloriously beautiful. Before she was eighteen, every waking hour was subdivided like a dentist's calendar with engagements with droves of men, young and old, who sought to pay her compliment. She later married Senator Donald Cameron, and her only daughter became the first wife of the English Secretary, Ronald Lindsay, now English Ambassador to the United States, and since her death, married to her cousin, Elizabeth Colgate Hoyt.

Sir Edward and Lady Thornton gave state dinners at the English Embassy. John Hay and Nicolay were intent on the "Life of Lincoln." George Bancroft had not completed his "History of America." Judge Bancroft Davis had the master hand in the etiquette of precedent, as to the place of the Supreme Court Justices, Senators and Cabinet officers at table. The Chief Justice, who administered the oath of office at the inauguration of the President, was always the chief guest. The Vice President, the Speaker of the House, then the Senators who ranked above the Cabinet, since they confirmed their appointments. Since then, all has been changed after wrangling for years. The right of succession in case of the death of a President now includes a long list.

The informality and home-like atmosphere which radiated from the President and Mrs. Grant were a fine form of republican simplicity.

In April, 1876, Mr. Bass went to attend, at Philadelphia, a judicial and legal gathering of the leading men of the country. The élite of the town entertained generously. Like all those who admired Benjamin Franklin, we went to the door of his aged and only relative, Mrs. Gillespie, upright and lean and of youthful mind, a forwarder of all patriotic and upstanding causes. John Cadwallader, forcible aristocrat and Democratic leader and lawyer, welcomed us, as did his kinsman, elegant, cultivated John Cadwallader of New York, and successful Samuel Dixon, who became our lifelong friend.

Cardinal Gibbons, behind whom we walked in the procession

to the Audience Hall, wore his Cardinal's mantle. Distinction marked him for a Prince of the Church. In the brief contact we had with him, he radiated vision, benignity and the saving grace of common sense and balance. Graceful, tall, slender in stature, he might have stepped from the canvas of a medieval painting. Oh, if his Encyclical Letter against Prohibition at the close of his noble life had been heeded, our country would not now be in the grip of crime with an impoverished treasury! His scholarly mind, rich in wisdom, knew the psychology of history and the conglomerate mind of society. Against the somber garb of republican simplicity of the legal fraternity, his colorful vestments shone like a ruby.

The first week of June, 1876, we went to the World's Exhibition at Philadelphia, and from a wheel-chair I saw all the art products, including triumphs in copper and brass, of coal scuttles and fixtures, wall papers and rich textiles from the work shop of William Morris. There we were introduced to the canvases of the pre-Raphaelites, Gabriel Rossetti's painting of "The Blessed Damozel," which framed the loveliness of the woman he afterward married, Burne-Jones and Watts. The Elgin marbles had inspired Watts and all painters.

Dr. Cary had brought his four-in-hand with his stalwart sons, and on the box seat of his coach I learned the beauty of the flowing Schuylkill and of the chestnut groves, then as umbrageous as those of Vallombrosa. Now no chestnut tree is standing.

I came back to Buffalo to have my husband sent to the Adirondacks, and in his absence my son was born. It was considered necessary for Mr. Bass to leave almost at once for Manitou Springs. I was to follow as soon as I was strong enough to travel.

Christmas promised to be a doleful affair, but it was resolved that the children in the neighborhood should give the metrical version of the play of "Cinderella" for a holiday fête. Among the actors were the children of Sherman S. Rogers: Fanny Rogers, who married Franklin McVeagh, now dead, but recently Ambassador to Japan; Robert Cameron Rogers, the poet who wrote "The Rosary," translated in many languages and set to music by more than one composer, and Lily, now the widow of Alex Sedgwick, living in Sedgwick Manor at Stockbridge.

At the end of December I was to leave for Colorado with a Scotch nurse and my baby. A delay in receiving our passes saved our lives. The friends who were to have gone with us were burned in the Ashtabula disaster, and there were but three links of a gold chain left of the lovely girl westward bound for balls and pleasure.

The night of our departure, my brother, James S. Metcalfe, a student at Yale, and later founder of "The Modern Age," and dramatic critic of "Life," found a classmate at the Lake Shore Station, a member of the Yale Glee Club, handsome and debonair. He bore our being often snowbound en route for Chicago with equanimity, and when we stood at an occasional station eating-house, he would remark, "When under nervous strain I always eat pork and beans," and so he did, valiant trencherman that he was.

My son may be said to have screamed with colic all of the time. Every man in the car walked miles with him, whether writer of novels or traveling butcher; all wished to help a woman and child.

In the wearing experience of the renewal of passes expired, only kindness was shown me in Chicago. A dear fellow in a railway office escorted us to the station and handed me a bunch of violets. At Omaha a cross man in his office roused enough anger for me to hold up my weary head when I asked for a renewal of transportation. Reaching the railway station at Cheyenne, I was seized with a chill. All nourishment for my child ceased. I went to the kind old man and woman at the lunch counter to ask for a can of Borden's Condensed Milk, and burst into tears. The good folk became parental at once, prepared sustenance for the child, and escorted me to the train for the branch line to Denver. Every male aboard had a gun. Soon the train was held up by an immense herd of antelope. Shots from every side from guns that were wanton, left many of those gentle creatures dead, and nothing was gained except that my child was nearly in convulsions.

Mr. Bass was at the Denver station. I had terror at my heart, for my boy was dangerously ill with croup. Finally, in a day car, at the Narrow Gauge Railroad to Colorado Springs, we followed the trail of John C. Frémont when he named Pike's Peak in passing, as he pushed on to the Pacific coast. At that time he wrote to his wife that further west the expedition found fly-bitten roan horses that could go, without exhaustion, eighty miles a day, up hill and down. No such horse as that met us at Colorado Springs, but a spring wagon with black rent curtains, ineffectual against seven degrees below zero over the frozen adobe road to Manitou Springs.

The motherly manager of the hotel, as we walked the long hall with small cubicle bedrooms, asked, "What room would you like?" I replied, "Any room with a bed in it."

Sore with fatigue I sank on my pillow for forty-eight hours' recuperation of soul and body and the strain of unindulged nerves. How far it all seemed from the familiar faces and happy voices of a large family!

On the morning of the third day, Mr. Bass took me, in an open buggy through blinding sunshine, to the Garden of the Gods.

Cold vanished, the glories of mountain mesa and distant plain caught me by the throat. What receding ocean of prehistoric days, what erosion and winds and suns of time, made the red bastions of the gateway of the Garden? Was it an old playground of the giants of a stature of which lesser folk never dream? I laid my heart that day at the feet of the Sun God of Colorado, and though I may never see it again, there are the garnered memories of joy and pain for a quarter of a century within the borders of that State.

Mr. Bass met the ennui of banishment in that country with a smile of noble indulgence. Some other exiles in quest of health played with him at cards for hours. I, who did not know the Jack of Spades from the King of Hearts, felt rebellion at tough meat and canned vegetables served in dismal soup dishes,—all was hateful.

A dapper elderly white-haired cosmopolitan named Conant from Dedham, Massachusetts, must have divined the truth. He had crossed the ocean under sail and steam thirty-five times. He had a smart cart and horse and took me to Colorado Springs. On the drive we passed a double frame house with the sign "To Let." We found the wealthy owner and his price for three months' occupancy. We then went to the second-hand stores where the ever-wandering people of the fluent West sold their belongings when they left the town. For under three hundred dollars, it was eventually proven, the tiny house could be made habitable. Mr. Bass rebelled at the idea, but finally yielded to my importunity.

Two small rooms opened into one another. Curtains were made of a pair of brown and yellow blankets. The jute carpet rugs, with gay border, filled in between a brown border on the floor, painted by an amateur wielder of a paint brush. The same artist painted and varnished two window-boxes, a cabinet for plates, and decorated the doors of a battered high-legged pine desk which cost two dollars—on one panel a red-winged blackbird on a branch, on the other a blackberry vine in fruit. The three large expenditures were twenty-seven dollars for the making of a comfortable divan, and a cast-iron stove which afforded the charm of an open fire, and twenty-five dollars for the smallest cooking stove devised by man. The beds on the second-story were roped and the mattresses needed Spartan courage.

The night we arrived "H. H.," Mrs. Jackson, whose house adjoined ours, sent us a tureen of oyster soup seasoned with mace, a flavor novel to me, and dainty tea biscuits with honey. Thus began a friendship with a glowing creative woman, a friend who was older than my mother, whose companionship opened for me many doors to understanding with a loving hand, until her great sad heart ceased to beat.

A boy from Buffalo, who inherited twenty thousand dollars and the desire to work in his old age and spend his money in his youth, arrived at our door. He was at all times the pink of neatness. He arrived wearing a long fleece overcoat with capacious pockets, all the luggage which he brought. He slept for a month on the divan in the living-room with our collie dog, made the fires and harnessed the horse. This same boy later became an architect and made the designs for my last home in the Genesee Valley. His name was William Lansing.

Our ranching friends would come to hitch their mustangs before our door after a day's journey of seventy miles on a broncho at a gentle fox-trot, and were willing to push the baby's perambulator to do the marketing. One often went twenty miles to get a chicken.

Gallant Mr. Conant would bring a brace of broilers with

pantalettes of letter paper, cut and fringed, their liver and lights coquettishly tucked under their arms as "the frog who would a-wooing go." We owned Warne's English Cook Book. A jack rabbit, someone said, might be as good as an English hare if properly prepared. We did not have three tumblers or plates that matched, but the winners of the West, men of science and eminence, dined and made merry at our little table. I procured the hare, Mr. Bass studied the Cook Book illustrations, where to put the carving knife in at A and bring it out at B, and we had a successful dinner.

We were asked to visit a ranch sixty miles away owned by two young men from Massachusetts. A motley caravan consisting of one surrey whose only dignity was its age, drawn by two mules, a covered buggy and pair of horses. The lumber wagons had the supplies and necessary bedding rolls, for all men carried individual rolls of blankets. Those for the women were roped and protected by buffalo skins. The battle to the death between cattle men and sheep men for pasturage on the plains was not yet active.

In the spring flocks of ewes were lambing, and one felt the poetry of the lonesome herder of sheep, whose only loved companion was his faithful collie. As in the world of women, so among the ewes were good mothers and those who disowned their offspring, and some large-hearted ewe by a shepherd's device suckled the deserted lamb.

Pre-irrigation days afforded dewless nights. The slow progress of miles gradually eats up a day from dawn to nightfall. At a distance, in passing, we saw the outlines of Dirty Woman's Ranch and Rattlesnake's Ranch, and now and again far-away bands of antelope. Only once the shimmering mystery of a mirage of lakes and hills deceived us. Patches of blue mertensias, yellow lupins and yellow and red painter's brush delighted us. The songs of meadow larks and the flitting of magpies against the blue heavens diverted us.

Jane Dennison, our guest, with dainty head and figure, her curls caught at the nape of her small neck with a black bow, and the come-hither glance of her eyes, would naturally captivate the simple heart of the man of the West, as she had done the beaux of Washington.

We made our first camp in time for the teamsters to prepare supper before bedtime. The hammock of my baby was strung between the wagons, and the women's blankets spread on the ground. Not a cloud from horizon to horizon. There is a thrill for the dwellers in towns on the first night spent beneath a star-filled firmament where, during a full moon, one could even read good print. There were night sounds and the bark and howl of the coyotes awoke but did not alarm us. The predatory curiosity of a field mouse seeking snug harbor alarmed our belle, and the camp was rent with her shrieks. I remembered the remark of a son of Dr. Leonard Bacon, President of Yale University, that his aversion to ranching was chiefly his dislike to have his hair tweaked, as he slept, by long-eared mice to line their nests. They were discriminating creatures, as he had the fine yellow hair of an over-civilized man.

The ranchman's friendly frying pan and the coffee pot were ready at dawn, and what coffee those men could make! Covering the ground coffee at night with cold water, letting it come to a boil on the coals in the morning, they would then turn a little cold water in the spout to settle it. We had perfect coffee. Evaporated and condensed milk were alone in use. Men who owned a thousand head of cattle used canned milk and never a cow was milked.

As the sun crept up like a ball of fire over the rim of the world, we saw the untouched wild roan stallion whom all of the cow punchers longed to lasso. Behind him, in rapid flight, streamed his cream-colored tail, as he led his wives and their young, and the flowing white plume of Henry of Navarre carried no greater standard of courage.

Count Otto Pourtalès was one of our escorts. We named him the "Mute Seraph." Good horseman and dancer, born lover, he carried a guitar on which he picked a few chords, singing a monotonous tale of unrequited passion as persistently melancholy as the call of a mourning dove.

As the sun went down we arrived at the long, low, rudely-constructed house of our kind host, who welcomed us with joyous glee. In the background were the herders and the Mexican greasers, sheep shearers and creosote dippers of flocks. There was a guest house of two rooms ready for our occupancy. One room for my husband and the other for the Scotch nurse, where a hammock for the baby was stretched from corner to corner.

We had a good supper prepared by a young man, the son of a shoe manufacturer in New England. He had been born in a house which cost eighty thousand dollars. One side of his face was crushed by the kick of a mule, a fact which sent him west. He had the art of bread-making and cooking vegetables from cans, which he learned in his mother's house, and our supper was a toothsome one.

We were escorted to the hay stacks, and my pretty friend and I climbed up to find our rolls spread, and we snuggled down to the luxury of fragrant hay beneath the stars. Before the ranch house was a long platform of rough boards on which all of the men, owners and herders, slept like sardines, side by side.

There were a pet lamb and a young antelope wandering about. Finally, when they gently stepped from the vitals of Puritan host to Catholic herders, the heavens were rent with English oaths and Spanish invectives which filled the midnight air.

The most necessary part of a woman's wardrobe in Colorado was a mountain dress to give her ease in a saddle or to climb mountains or walk rough paths. Jane Dennison, as we were to travel light, brought yards of pleated tarlatan ruching and red ribbon to cheer up her mountain dress. Alas, by the second morning after our arrival, the lamb and the antelope had explored her pack and eaten the seductive ruching and red ribbon.

That morning the sounds of shots roused us. A group of cowpunchers whose trousers were tucked in new high-heeled boots, fresh bandana handkerchiefs about the neck of their blue flannel shirts, wearing broad sombreros, some with the skin of a rattlesnake as a band, shouted, "Little Peaches, Little Peaches," and fired their pistols in the air. One must have known the cattle punching men of roundup skill to fathom their romance for the beauty of a good woman. The name of "Little Peaches" spread to even remote ranches.

We all sat at table with these men, and, firing their pistols and waving their hats as they went, they waved farewell and sped across the plain, beyond the far horizon.

The bugs so plentiful in all pine lumber walked the strands of the baby's hammock and he looked like the capital-studded map of Europe; so he was bidden to the Elysium of the haymow.

I fancy the Count had been refused on the return journey and had threatened suicide. When we reached home, at the earnest entreaty of "Little Peaches," my husband went to Pourtalès' quarters to find his dead body, but the young man was standing with a bottle of Guerlain's perfume in his hand. After a wholesome rebuke, peace and quiet reigned.

Colorado Springs was called a dry town where wild younger sons of titled Englishmen and freedom-seeking youths of every land came. Whiskey was supposed to be sold for illness only by the chemist. The man who bought and sold shotguns and rifles and acted as pawnbroker, sold liquor by the bottle or the keg. After a lark in town many a ranchman reached home sound asleep in the bottom of his wagon.

It is good to have seen the last visit of the Indians descending the Ute Pass. They camped near Colorado Springs on the little stream called "The Fountain." The tepees were pitched and the small fires kindled. A number of young braves, with bows and arrows, mounted on mustangs, followed by cur dogs, slipped from their saddles as we hastened to the camp. A native boy clad in a scanty shirt, dancing an improvised war dance and brandishing a large knife, brought no terror to our hearts. A good pony was held by a squaw in front of the Chief's tepee, from which he slowly emerged, put his foot on the neck of one of his wives, and swung himself upon his steed. One wife was an old and unbedecked woman, and a young one wore beaded leggings and silver bangles. Nothing unpleasant happened, though we had a glimpse of a dying brave sitting upright against the sustaining pole of his tepee, undaunted in the face of death.

To one reared in the confines of a home circle, the discovery of the brotherhood of man was a surprise. Colorado was said to have a population made of those who came for loss of health, wealth or reputation.

One made broths and carried food to those who suffered. My first sight of death was when a horror-stricken wife cried for help as I passed her door, and I went in to see her beloved husband passing away with a hemorrhage before a doctor could arrive.

While at dinner one night I was called by the village physician to come at once to Manitou as the step-daughter of Abby Sage Richardson was dying. The drive in the month of April, over an adobe mud road after a wet snow, was trying. A man came for me from the livery stable. He was just back from the Black Hills. He said nothing was so terrible as the cries of Indians as they came over a hill. "I got two of 'em," said he. "If you come around to the stable tomorrow I'll show you a fine pair of beaded leggings and one not so good."

I arrived to find Mrs. Richardson paralyzed with terror. She who had revealed to me the full beauty of Shelley's "Skylark" as she read and lectured that winter, had no faculty in practical matters. The girl died in my arms at five in the morning.

The servants threatened to leave at once if the body were kept in the hotel. I asked the doctor if he could tell me what I could do, and under his directions I prepared her for her rough coffin which shortly arrived. Driving back in the gray morning, I asked the doctor, "Have you ever seen anyone afraid to die?" "Just once," said he, "and that was a Baptist preacher, literally afraid of 'Damnation and Hell Fire.'"

Mr. Bass did not improve. We resolved to go into camp in the foothills twenty miles north. A dyspeptic north-easterner, with a collie of sorts, begged to come with us. We engaged a teamster from Oldtown, whose barefoot children and wife watched the negotiations.

There was one large tent for sitting and dining, and one for supplies, and the sleeping tents. All slept on the ground on buffalo skins. Dawson, our teamster, hated our boarder and would shout as he shoved in a bowl of rice, "Chinee food for the invaleed!" Going in to look over the supplies, I saw a hundred or two of unfamiliar objects. "What are those things?" I asked Dawson. "Oh, Lord God, Jesus Christ! Jerked buffalo tongues till you can't rest!"

It rained part of each day or night for twenty-seven consecutive days. Mr. Bass grew worse. Our funds were nearly exhausted. Dr. Bell, a close friend of General William J. Palmer, owned in Manitou Park, thirty miles up the Ute Pass, what was called a hotel. I went to Dr. Bell and asked him if he would not open the place. He said, "No, but why don't you take it? Hire a mountain wagon and driver. He can bring guests and mail to and fro and keep you provided with meat and groceries from Colorado Springs, and if you make nothing it will be rent free, but if there is any profit we will divide it at the end of the season." It seemed the one chance to save a man who would only return east to die. Mr. Bass said it could not be. "H. H." said that if I did such a thing I would lose all my friends. I remarked, "Bad luck to bad rubbish," as an Irish nurse of mine used to say. We agreed to Dr. Bell's terms.

The man of the battered face, who had been our camp cook, said he would go to the mountains. A chambermaid of sixty summers was engaged. Off we were for the mountains where the brooks were filled with trout, where the deer met at the Salt Lick in the eerie light of early morning and evening. There were cottages near the hotel of two rooms each, the main house containing a sitting room, dining room, small entrance hall and kitchen.

MANITOU PARK HOTEL

COLORADO SPRINGS IN 1877—TEJON STREET AND CHEYENNE MOUNTAIN

There was living near us, in Colorado Springs, an ultra-civilized Englishman of uncommon culture, born in Genoa, his father an English clergyman, who represented the Church of England in the Italian city. His command of language was pedagogical, hidebound in the heart of the pre-Raphaelite sect in London. His small abode in Colorado Springs was the perfection of East Lake furniture; his walls lined with books. He had imported a quantity of fine Scotch whiskey, but nails having by accident fallen into the barrels, it was of an unusual color. He asked to go to the Park with us where he could sell the beverage by the glass and turn an honest penny, have good food and breathe healing air. He was, in spite of his invalidism, a didactic flirt. With romantic ladies of our circle he read aloud the plays of Augier and Dumas fils, and he lent us Herbert Spencer's "First Principles," and French novels. He was relieved when I laughed aloud at Gallic wit, my associates being too modest to do so. His clothes were made in London. He had white flannel suits with pearl buttons, on which was a blue monogram, and he wore a sort of tasteful blue monkey-cap. There was an amber sky when we reached our journey's end and the Londoner, looking at me, said, "And so you too have seen the light upon the mountains."

All of the ancient families of bed-bugs were in possession of the hotel. I carried at all times a blower of Persian Insect Powder which I squirted in every crevice when I was not scrubbing, washing, or reading Matthew Arnold's verses in the black shadow of a stately pine.

An intelligent policy indicated that good roasts of meat, thick broiled porterhouse steaks, homemade breads and well-cooked vegetables and simple soup were a proper diet for invalids to thrive upon at eight thousand feet altitude. It was soon found that a party who came to spend the night might stay a month. There were sleeping tents to the number of twenty. The meat-safe was a mile up a gorge and was, from time to time, raided by mountain lions.

An intellectual, great, but humorless lady from Fifth Avenue engaged one of the tiny bedrooms as a sitting-room, and she and the esthetic Englishman came to table in full dress at night, she trailing soiled satin finery of a New York season, and together, by an oil lamp, they discoursed on the higher emotions and literature. The mischievous youngsters from the Eastern states who came to shoot, fish and write, went to town and returned with woolen mittens, which they gravely wore at meals.

There were dances at the saw mills. Two fiddlers scraped their bows; standing on a pile of rough boards, the head lumberman called out the dances, while the guests, arriving on horseback, danced on the rough floors, swinging to the strains of the Virginia Reel and quadrille. The head lumberman despised our ignorance as he shouted "balance to partner," "dos à dos," "allez main left," "all promenade."

There were several summer camps along the brook. How they sang "King Charlie's Farewell to Manchester," "My Lodging is on the Cold, Cold Ground," "Three Blind Mice," and "Frère Jacques," as the fierce flames of a pitch-pine bonfire seemed to lick the velvet dome of heaven!

An additional chambermaid from Denver was sent for and arrived, a yellow-haired, blue-eyed girl of twenty, wearing a jaunty sailor hat.

The lady from Fifth Avenue went back to her husband, but behind her, to console her friend, she left a collie. He continued to walk to the hammock where they together had spent their mornings in pursuit of education, carrying between them a school bag of heavy reading and followed by the collie. On a hot morning we heard several sharp shots. The elderly chambermaid and I went *au grand galop,* fearing he had been attacked by a mountain lion. As we passed the barn we called to Dawson to take his gun and follow. "May the beast eat him hair and bones," said our freckled sandy-haired teamster, "I'll not stir." Out of breath we hurried to find our dude gently swinging in his hammock, book in hand, the dog running about chasing chipmunks. "Did the mountain lions attack you?" said we. "Oh, Raffles saw a squirrel in a tree and barked," he replied. "Did you kill the squirrel?" we panted. "Oh, no, I could not hit him," was his answer. On our heels we turned to descend, in full harmony of mind with Dawson.

Once when the lights were out in the tents, there arrived a carefully groomed gentleman and a *comme il faut* youngish woman. Every tent was full, but I persuaded two men who occupied a tent to sleep in the open. With the guests I walked to the open flaps of the tent and said, "Good night." Stuttering and blushing in confusion, the embarrassed man pursued me, exclaiming, "My cousin and I must have two tents." "I will hang some blankets on the ridge pole," said I; "it is the best I can do." The most guileless sometimes must stop to pause and consider. They went at dawn without comment, whether wife, maid or widow.

A Philadelphian of the early school of William Penn always spoke of sin and virtue as though the sin which no form of protest has made unpopular was the only one, and chastity was the solitary virtue.

All communities, however small, have a cosmic resemblance. Did the raucous note of the crested blue jay flitting among the bull pines say, or did I fancy he sang, "Sunshine, a strong wing, and a world to wander. Sin has slyly winked at virtue under the greenwood tree."

Standing on the porch, watching a crimson sky, the sun lost behind the hills, I saw two men drive up with a livery team. One of the men, the head of a religious brotherhood in the Southwest, named De Router, proved to be the cousin of our first German nursery governess when I was a little girl. With him was a blond Austrian architect. The latter was seized that night with a congestive chill. Having an emergency medicine chest and mustard and hot water, the old chambermaid and I nursed him as best we could. In the days that followed I carried his tray to him, adding a bunch of nodding blue-bells that bloomed on the way from my tent. Poor sentimental German, he wept at the sight of flowers.

De Router had engaged rooms for six weeks, but shortly after, one night when the moon was at its full, he said, "We are leaving tomorrow morning,"—a knockdown blow to an amateur hotel hostess. I took the architect by the arm and walked him to the corral. "What has displeased you?" I asked. "Ach, Gott, I love you," said he, and turned back to the house. They started the following morning. That same evening on the far horizon came a gray spent horse and a drunken rider. The architect had fled from the counsel of his religious companion, but returned by the same road within twelve hours.

Going to town on business, I returned to find the personnel in consternation. Dawson and the blonde chambermaid, whose looks indicated lust of the flesh, were leaving for Leadville. I owed him two hundred and fifty dollars. Armed with conscious rectitude, and what seemed to me the oratorical power of virtue, I found Dawson washing his wagon. "What is this, man?" I said, "you leaving your starving children and wife in Oldtown? You can't take this money to spend like that." "Go to Hell," said he. "We go to Leadville!" They departed, she with the blue ribbons of her sailor hat streaming in the breeze, and a keg of whiskey rattling in the empty wagon. Years later I was glad to hear he had ended his life, hanged by a hempen rope, for cattle stealing in Texas.

Life was always full of surprises. As I shook in my bed with malarial chill, the door of my room was violently opened, and a red-headed woman flung herself on her knees by the bed. She was married to a grumpy man who looked like a strangled rat, and she said she should leave him and her four boys to elope with an uninteresting sheep owner with means. I counselled hope deferred and not to act rashly. Years after I met the husband, herself and four boys looking in the shop windows under the arches of the Rue de Rivoli in Paris. Confessions are better given in the confessional box of a church.

The end of days, still light with the sun behind the mountains and before the earth had given out the warmth of the sun, would often find us blazing new trails and riding old ones for long views of the higher ranges. The banker of high finance and a clergyman from St. Louis began to feel the call to return to bank and pulpit. We who lingered to enjoy the warm early autumn loved the ranch house. The cots, tables, curtains made from Turkey red cotton and seats made from barrels half-sawed in the front, and filled with gunny sacking stuffed with hay, invited rest before the wide mouth of the stone fireplace, crowned with antlers, where burned pitch-pine logs that spluttered and blazed. The walls were enlivened with portraits and scenes cut from pictorial magazines; pelts of deer, coyote and buffalo covered the floor, making it a pleasant place to lounge. Palaces and houses of luxury in five continents have left no such human and bright memory as that room in the log cabin beside the flowing stream of Manitou Park, sheltered by rocks and shaded by tall trees.

From the iron-stained whiskey we took no rebate. By the end of the summer during which we had had shelter and good food, we were free of debt and we divided seven hundred and ninety dollars.

The nurse and baby were loaded into the back of the mountain wagon, the surrey was hitched behind, I took the reins and put my foot upon the brake. Mr. Bass cantered on his mustang alongside and the descent of the Ute Pass of thirty-five miles to the plain began, a tax on the muscles of my right leg, which took long to recover from the strain. So we said a tender farewell to Manitou Park.

Again Mr. Bass was for returning home. Stating this situation to Dr. Bell, through General Palmer he offered him the position of General Counsel for the Denver and Rio Grande Railroad and associated Land Companies, with the proviso that I was to go with Mrs. Bell, who was nervously ill, to occupy the great house of General Palmer, Glen Eyrie.

CHAPTER SEVEN

A FRONTIER COLONY

IT used to be said that there was no Sunday west of the Missouri River. Unique Colorado Springs was neither godless nor godly. Once when I said to my brother that I loved Bohemia, he replied, "Oh, it is a dirty place; you would fly from it. What you dream as Bohemia is made of people who know everything, have been everywhere, who, familiar with our conventions, throw them aside." That was, I think, a fair description of Colorado Springs. Into that little town—miscalled, for there wasn't a spring within five miles—swept streams from more than one continent.

Smart people of leisure and fashion touched shoulders with builders of the nation, miners and cowboys, where simplicity prevailed. There were light-hearted dances in the meeting-house, where Sunday, Methodists and Baptists held services; the waxed floor had circles of white for the proper spacing of quadrilles and lancers. The radius occupied by our friends' residences was small. All went on foot even in a heavy snowstorm, to the dances, in high-buttoned galoshes.

A grandson of Lucretia Mott, tall, loose-jointed and as active when he danced as the Wizard of Oz, lived with his sister, who was the wife of Tom Parrish. They sought only the furtherance of the pleasure of their own lives. No mean painter, in his way, was Tom Parrish. Whether Steven or Maxfield Parrish at Cornish, or able financiers in London, New York or Rome, the urge of the artist has been in every person of the name of Parrish whom I have known.

One night at Tom Parrish's there was a ghost story party. We hung on the words of Doctor Solly, the English physician, as in black darkness he told the blood-curdling story of the ghost at Chiselhurst. Suddenly, there emerged from the corner two startling little skeletons. Tom Parrish had drawn them in phosphorus on the bottom of large shoes which he manipulated to our terror. Tom Parrish's wife, Lucretia Mott's granddaughter, lived but a short time. He took to wife later, Anne Parrish, who painted the portrait of my sunny-haired boy seated in a carved oak chair, against a background of books which presaged a literary career which failed to materialize. Tom Parrish read "Uncle Remus" from cover to cover to quiet the restless boy. The daughter of Mrs. Parrish, who painted two portraits of my son, now hanging in the big room of my former home in the Genesee Valley, was the mother of the Anne Parrish who has written "The Perennial Bachelor" and other successful stories.

To those weighing values of long experience, has come the conviction that for joy of living, there was quite as much of a return from those evenings when we furnished our own recreation, as is found where Contract Bridge is played with the sky the limit, or where one goes at midnight to dance at the Ritz, or a great house where the entertainment costs a king's ransom.

One night at the meeting-house, a dance was given in honor of the wedding anniversary of Doctor and Mrs. Bell, English people who lived in a stone house built near the stream at Manitou. There were welcomed with generous hospitality, all traveling nobility and lesser people of worth. Mrs. Bell was a talented musician, who had in her childhood been kissed by Meyerbeer. She was absent-minded, and her friends always asked her an hour in advance of the hour set for dinner. The English women in our community did not dance like sylphs. As morning was breaking, Mrs. Bell and I walked to the dressing-room to put on our wraps. She said she felt uncommonly tired. As she lifted her white satin wedding dress to put on her overshoes, lo, she had never removed them! I ought not to have been astonished, as a few days previous she had come to pay me an early morning call. Putting her baby in the middle of my bed to run on an errand, she had not returned until nightfall, when, remembering the child, she ran lightly up the steps, waving her hands and exclaiming: "Can a mother forget her child!"

Fate forced us into helpful intimacies. There was one who expected to be, and should have been, Marquis of Cholmondeley (pronounced Chumley), but the holder of the title, who faced death, instead produced a son. This raw-boned Irishman, with sandy hair and nose like a hawk, had not met favor in his paternal home because of an infatuation for a Swiss governess. He had a heart of gold. Taking me one day in his shabby buckboard, he was asleep half the time as the horses climbed the Ute Pass. I roused him to look at a sawmill.

"Oh!" cried he, "I worked there a year with never a shoe on my foot. When one gets a good callous on the feet there is no need for shoes."

He and I kept vigil for two days and nights to save the life of a ranchman's wife in a lonely log house forty miles from a doctor. Alert and tender, but for him the exhausted husband would never have had the mother of his new-born baby restored to health.

The striking young woman in the frontier group of Colorado Springs was Queen Palmer, the wife of General W. J. Palmer, who for love of her had built the great house "Glen Eyrie" in a canyon near the Garden of the Gods. Before her marriage a young Indian Chief had seen her. He arrived one morning leading four spirited mustangs; he wore the yellow garter, the badge of courtship. Gravely he offered the ponies to Mrs. Mellon in exchange for her step-daughter. Stoically and sadly, when refused, he went across the yellow plains, followed by his lively steeds.

Finding unknown heights and following streams to their sources, was to make excursions of rare delight. Queen Palmer, climbing stock in hand, rebellious curly hair flying, cheeks aglow, moving as on winged feet, was the spirit incarnate of inaccessible heights. Hats she scorned. She laid claim to beauty as her rightful heritage, whether in a moated English house in Surrey, or in the spacious room in the third story of "Glen Eyrie," where she gathered books, heard musicians and never permitted any but an invited friend to enter.

Warmed by the afterglow of days long past, I wonder now are there still pasture-destroying prairie-dog villages whose dun, rat-like owners seem perpetually scampering to visit one another. It was understood that rattlesnakes made homes with these gentle animals. To me it seemed, for the rattlesnakes, intelligent economics,—no middleman between the consumer and the producer.

A prairie-dog hole was a danger to horse and rider on the plains, and the ominous rattle of the snake among the buffalo grass, halted a horse to shiver and sent a cold chill down the veins of the rider. One watched the flight of hawks, scavengers of the waste. On the highest rock of Austin's Bluff, a pair of eagles built their nest and raised their young. To see them soaring toward the sun was to understand why the eagle was chosen as the symbol of freedom for the United States.

Even a coyote, slinking half-hidden in sagebrush, was an event. On a ride to Austin's Bluff I was ahead of my companions, letting my horse follow his bent. Arriving in a sun-warmed pocket of yellow sandstone, five large gray wolves faced me. Their scent made my horse balk, but neither horse, rider nor wolves were greatly disturbed. Fat flocks of sheep, not far distant, had lined their ribs, and they quietly vanished. I found my friends, who were envious of me as long as my fate had not been that of Red Riding Hood's grandmother.

Around the corner from us was a slab house framed in an apology of a lawn, coaxed and tended as a ewe lamb. There lived dark, handsome, saturnine Arthur Wellesley, near of kin to the Iron Duke. His tall young wife, Katie, with heavily fringed blue eyes, skin of milk and roses, dark hair drawn back from a low brow to coil at the nape of her neck, bore the mark of Erin's daughter, the type of loveliness which foreshadows sorrow. We were vexed, and so were her boy and mine, at the warning of "Keep off the Grass." It was a sickly, tender sward.

Well-born ranchmen, who by day, with quirt in hand, urged their ponies to speed round sharp corners—fit models for Remington cowboys—at night, correctly dressed in evening clothes, handed a fan to shield a woman's face from the blaze of a pitch-pine fire. At Katie Wellesley's perfectly-appointed tea table, English lads gathered and talked of making their pile and going home. There was Claude Stanhope, youngest brother of Lord Chesterfield; he did not always follow the wisdom laid down by his progenitor in Lord Chesterfield's classical letters. Claude Stanhope was a matchless horseman, breaking unruly horses with a light hand, and charming all women with a low voice. No matter how remote the hinterland, one finds the Englishman having his afternoon tea. They carry their habits and impose their customs, and themselves are modified only on the surface of their lives. Colorado Springs had the afternoon tea habit in 1877,—not then the habit of New York and Boston.

I wondered why the men rode heavily armed with pistols and knives and their well-filled cartridge belts, as they ambled over the plains and rode through the mountain passes, while their wives rode and drove without so much as a hat-pin for defense. They needed no protection. However rough of exterior, the man of the West revered and honored women.

Younger sons came from England with Anglo-Saxon land-hunger, equipped with the best of saddles, shotguns and rifles, and coin enough to pay their way. Unfortunately, many had a taste of life en route, and arrived penniless, with their belongings in pawn in Kansas City, or some other hard town, having bucked the tiger in gambling houses. The heart's desire of all was to own a large ranch. Home they sent for funds, and were cheated at every turn. Later, many of them broke stone on the highway. Meantime, they wheeled our perambulators, eager to serve our women.

Mrs. Hamp, mother of six sons, sister of Blackmore, the English novelist, came to Colorado in the desolation of early widowhood. She learned to paint in water colors, and hours each day one found her on a camp-stool before an easel. In my former home in the Genesee Valley today there hangs a water color of perfect Cheyenne Mountain, seen from base to summit from Colorado Springs. We became friends. I think she found peace. We shared a love for dogs, and saying to her one afternoon, "A dog is almost as much comfort as a son," she exclaimed, "Oh, much more!"

If Colorado means "red earth" its name to me brings a sense of sunshine, a good horse, a free rein, where the purple shadows slip eastward from the mountains at close of day, a gamut of delicate tints, unseen and unfelt by those who found no poetry in the American Desert.

Mr. Bass, absorbed in his work for the Denver and Rio Grande Railway, resolved to make his home in the West. It was elation for him to be with those who were state and empire builders.

In 1880, our house "Edgeplain" was in process of building, and we occupied a drab wooden house on Weber Street. A letter came from General Grant saying that he and Mrs. Grant were stopping to see us, breaking their return journey from around the world. We bestirred ourselves to gather as many agreeable people as could be seated about our table, for a dinner in their honor. General Grant was called the "silent man," and was by our friends believed to live up to his reputation. We who had known him in the White House were aware that one antipathetic person in the room would make him speechless. At eight P.M. the leading citizens of the town, with a fair sprinkling of Englishmen, gathered to meet the greatest General since Julius Cæsar. Where was his silence? It was distinctly vocal until the clock struck one A.M.

After half a century, it is not possible to repeat the brilliancy and wisdom of his talk. With those acquainted with the simple, perfect English of Grant's autobiography, his charm and wisdom could be no surprise, but in the days when he was writing his life, he was then the "silent man," not even moaning, but dying with cancer of the throat.

His tour had been an ovation, at every court in Europe, from all the rulers and peoples of Near and Far East. His estimate of the Chinese and Japanese is worth remembering. High class Chinese he believed the ablest of living men of any race, who, given the experience and knowledge of the West, could excel in all competition, which opinion may have been borne out by the supplanting of the Chinese Trading Company in Canton, from which came the fortunes of Boston's valiant adventurers, —Russell, Forbes and Perkins. Having learned the method of the West, the Chinese controlled and absorbed the trade. Perhaps he shared the opinion of Lafcadio Hearn as to the clever faculty of the Japanese educating themselves in Europe and the United States. They used the principle of jiu-jitsu to defeat the West with its own knowledge, by what, in true sport, is called a "foul."

Caps must be doffed to the honor of a high-class Chinese, who would face ruin rather than break his word. Avarice and a desire, against his will, to reform the heathen, has brought old China to a sad confusion. It was a nation which could produce what it could consume, and the pruning of its millions of souls by plague and famine, perhaps was nature's way of taking care of the surplus. The practical rules of daily life of Confucius, and the essence of spiritual Buddhism, with respect for ancestors, served them better than a Christianity that landed in their country with the Bible in one hand and the shotgun in the other,— backed by force and commercial greed.

It has been said that if every man in Jerusalem would keep his house and the street before it clean, it would indeed be the most spotless of cities. So when I look at the faults in our modern city, I wonder why missionaries do not clean up the sin and disorder of their homeland, before being paid to undertake adventurous proselyting in countries where they are as welcome as a sliver in a finger. The squeeze of China is full-brother of the graft of Western lands. Perhaps Korea and Manchuria and the struggles of today with Japan, might bear out the opinion of General Grant, of their racial characteristics.

The dining table where General Grant sat with us is prized by its owner, and has a brass plate saying, "Here sat General Grant." It was sad to have loyal friends turn their faces Eastward. As we waved farewell, we did not know that we should never see their kindly smiles again.

The season of the discovery of gold and silver made the rush for the spot where we spent a night, near the Twin Lakes, on the site of what became the city of Leadville. We had traveled there with a New England ranchman whose nimble, surefooted mules drew the curtained mountain wagon, a place of shelter for my child and me to sleep beneath our blanket roll on a buffalo skin. Gold, silver, zinc and an inferior grade of coal have made great fortunes for many people in Colorado, but for others there came ruin and a permanent investment without dividends. Prospectors tramped the backbone of the continent, and at times they have seemed to me the happiest of our men. Whether they were grub-staked, or finding and working their claims with the bare necessities of life on a burro or on their backs, the expression of their eyes was as different from that of dwellers in towns as are the eyes of the men who open their eyes upon the sea, to follow it until the end of their days. The prospect or Eldorado may be over the next rise of ground, or behind the highest peak. He walked where beauty reigned and the air was pure.

A tall, able Irishman worked for us as carpenter for a short time in Colorado Springs; his name was Walsh. He struck it rich, and was called Bonanza Walsh. I saw him years afterward, when he brought his family to Rome, heralded like a potentate. In ancient palaces ladies of unbelievably long lineage, with a dash of royal blood, entertained them. There were effete sons of old titles, who needed to marry fortunes to replace tiles in the leaky roofs of distant villas and stately palaces. Miss Walsh, his daughter, who afterward married Edward McLean of Washington, editor and owner of the Washington *Post,* refused scions of several great Italian families.

Usually a presentation at Court required weeks in its formalities, but Mr. Walsh commanded, and in two days had invitations to a Court Ball. He was born to command; nature's nobleman, astute and generous.

Among the men of the railway circle was Colonel Lamborne, whose wife was a sister of Bayard Taylor,—a tall, fat, handsome, timorous woman with two daughters who resembled her. She had a congenital terror of Indians, and into the cramped berths of a narrow-gauged sleeper, insisted on crowding the entire family in a single section, that they might, in case of massacre, not be parted. Arriving in the crude little hotel of Colorado Springs, she read in a newspaper that there had been an Indian raid three hundred miles away. She and her daughters, dressed in cloaks, hats and overshoes, sat all night to make their escape in case of an attack. They were lovable people, and my husband asked them to go with us in a special car to New Mexico to the Indian Harvest Festival of Saint Geronimo at the Pueblo of Taos. Now tourists throng to this fête; then, Blackfeet and Apache Indians were the chief guests.

The station agents had been instructed to get means of transportation, to make the drive of twenty-eight miles to Taos from a small town on the line of the railway. We slept in clean beds in small adobe houses, and before dawn we were on our way,— Mr. Bass and Mrs. Lamborne in a comfortable buggy drawn by a mustang, the two fat girls and myself on the back seat of a springless lumber wagon. I thank God I had a strong back. The gallant Colonel sat with the driver.

From dawn until our arrival at ten o'clock at night, we had not heard a word of English. We did not look for comfort; traveling with tinned meats, bread and evaporated cream, we could not starve, if we were unable to masticate *carnecolorale*. It was said that the greasers who lived upon it could be hanged and their bodies preserved as well as though embalmed.

We were quartered in a whitewashed adobe Mexican house. Before daylight we were dressed, arriving at the Indian Plaza to see the tall staff lighted by the first flush of the eastern sky, as the Indians, in procession, followed by a Catholic priest, brought a living sheep, which was hoisted to the top of the pole as a sacrifice, to remain until dark. Two castle-like adobe Pueblos of several stories each, were on either side of the river. Against the blue of a cloudless sky, motionless figures of blanketed Indians in white and scarlet, as stately as Roman senators, watched every move of their tribe, and the sacred ceremonies. Each Pueblo was governed by an alcalde (governor). The Indians who came to dance, emerged nearly nude, save for feathers and paint, from the circular subterranean chamber sacred to government council and religious rites. Guttural cries and chants filled the air as they danced. It was a loss not to be aware of the meaning and significance of their ceremonies, whence French missionary orders of priests have, without offending the Indians, imposed the celebration of mass and the introduction of the cross among these primitive nature- and sun-worshippers. They had never penetrated nor changed the tribal religious customs.

I lunched at the house of the priest. Of the Indians he spoke with admiration. The youths, he said, sang and danced on the banks of the river to greet the sun. The tradition of the white man's coming, in his lust for gold, had meant cruelty to the Indians. No longer they worked their ancient mines in the Ratune Mountains, and their location is a secret held by them, the knowledge of which is passed on to each successor by the head of the tribe on his deathbed. Sometimes the Indians are seen scouting after white prospectors seeking for hidden treasure.

A lamp is supposed always to be lit in one of the circular chambers underground, in memory of Montezuma. No priest has ever been admitted to the mystery of the house of the medicine-man when one of the tribe, facing death, has been closed within its walls.

Twice, since 1878, I have been to Taos. It is now a fête for the world at large. I shall never again see so thrilling a scene as that first sight of motionless Indians at the fête of Saint Geronimo.

For the French missionary order I have profound respect. The priest whom I saw at San Juan Pueblo had not left his post for a quarter of a century.

Taos today is the home of a school of painters, but no white man is permitted in the time of the festival, in the sacred grove beyond the Pueblos. The Pueblo Indians may be descendants of the gentle stock of Toltec or of Aztec stock. They know the rules of irrigation and the gentle arts of weaving and pottery. The greaser is of low type, the descendant of Cortez' army and the cruel Spanish occupancy, and is a demoralizing neighbor for the honest Indians who, during their horse races, can leave their rifles and blankets unprotected without fear of robbery.

If variety be the spice of life, the essence of early village and mountain life in Colorado was highly seasoned. Picturesque and lawless individuals captured my fancy. Two lusty Irishmen, having run through several fortunes, lived just below town. Most women said they were beyond the pale. They were connoisseurs in dogs. Perfect terriers always followed them, as they indifferently walked in town, talking in low-pitched voices the English of scholarly Dublin. My collie "Lady" had an obscure ailment, so I asked one of the fascinating vagabonds to give me advice. He cured the dog, and the day was always gayer when I met him on his route to the pawn broker's. At last we saw the brothers no more, the elder having used his Herculean strength to carry a red hot cooking stove from a low resort below town, setting it in the middle of the narrow road going south. Our roisterers, of the stamp of Lover's eighteenth century heroes, were banished by the sheriff.

Then there was the swarthy Canadian Irmingtinger, whose father was a Governor of the Bank of Montreal and his grandmother the daughter of an Indian chief. He could charm a bird off a bough by singing in a low baritone voice that would have given him high place in a Royal Opera House. His letters to us gave him introduction to what was an exclusive society. He had the Indian's thirst for fire-water, and was distinctly bored by "our best people." I never lent ear to tales of his misdemeanors. He saved my life when a pair of small gray horses got beyond my control and ran like deer. I esteemed his respect and friendship. As one journeys through life the value of Beloved Vagabonds gets recognition.

Then there was an English officer of the Guards, who bought many acres near Cheyenne Mountain, to breed good cattle and sheep. He rode his blooded bull to drive the cows from the plains to the corral, and once sent me, by my husband, a bit of wool from his priceless ram, tied with a true lover's knot of blue ribbon. Being of good family, he was asked to join the drawing class where one found simple jollity and refreshments. One night our subject was "Water." He sent a drawing that could find merit in an art exhibition,—rain falling between high buildings of a narrow street on the umbrellas of a moving crowd. One old maid presented a calla lily with a dewdrop that resembled a chunk of ice, but there was better, if less romantic talent shown.

Our guardsman went for a day off in Denver. Being among the gallery gods at the theater, he insisted on jumping on what he thought was a wooden ledge which proved to be painted paper. He broke enough bones to send him, invalided for life, from the hospital to England.

The dominant instinct in most women is to make men do what sweethearts and wives and reformers believe is right. I was tarred with that brush. A noble young girl from Canada, seeking health, was my friend. She was warmly interested in Jack Wilson, the son of one of the Governors of the Hudson Bay Fur Company. No finer physical man ever danced the polka or rode a bucking bronco. She refused to marry him unless, after a year of probation, he eschewed strong drink.

On coming from the mountains, Mr. Hanson A. Risley, officer of the Denver and Rio Grande, and intimate friend of William T. Seward, whose daughter was adopted by Seward, taking the name Olive Risley Seward, said we could have his small brick house rent-free for the winter, if he might retain his bedroom and live with us. It was a privilege to accept his terms and be in daily contact with an old man whose courtly bearing was founded on the kindness of a warm heart, and the comprehension of human nature and political life. He would bring in a hod of coal from the back-yard to the cook, with the grace of Sir Walter Raleigh laying his cloak before Queen Bess.

We agreed that the Canadian Adonis, who swore fealty to my sick friend and a year of abstinence, should occupy a lean-to shed which opened from the kitchen of the Risley house. He arrived with his belongings filling a lumber wagon, with a large black cat crowning the load. Navajo blankets and pelts made the shed neat and comfortable. He brought his cryptic black pet with yellow eyes, "Pluto" by name, and mighty hunter by profession. "Pluto" had more skill than a group of horsemen with a pack of coursing hounds. It was fine sport for a field of riders to follow towards Austin's Bluffs to corner jack rabbits. The dogs would discover their prey and arrive at the foot of a hill, to see a jack rabbit outlined against the sky, sitting one ear up and the other dropped, sending back a glance to the pack. Breathless, with dripping jowls, the swift greyhounds reached the crest of the bluff to find jack rabbit had twinkled his hind legs, disappearing like a streak of light. So "Pluto," tracking and catching jack rabbits and gay little cottontails, and keeping himself in fresh meat all winter, was an amazement. Music was "Pluto's" passion. At the first note sounded on the piano, he came to listen, and if the instrument was open and the room unoccupied, he walked up and down the keys by the half hour gently pressing the ivory. Was that sleek creature who licked his paws and washed his face by our open fire the king of the nether world?

There was not a cloud the size of a man's hand in the blue heavens. The oldest inhabitant never knew such thirty consecutive days of cold, often ten degrees below zero. The holiday season came. On Christmas eve we asked an empire-builder or two, their wives, and Nicolay, the collaborator with John Hay in writing the "Life of Lincoln." Jack Wilson, with school-boy shining face, molded in Bond Street's best evening attire, repeated over and over again to Queen Palmer, most courteous of women, who sat next to him, an incoherent story about a St. Bernard dog and an express wagon. At that period a drunken man would have had to fall off the floor for me to know his condition. The evening was distressing.

Christmas morning came and I asked Adonis to go to the barn a block away, where our sorrel horse and buggy were kept, saying we would deliver Christmas presents. A plan born of the impulse to get away led him into temptation. He brought me to the house an hour later and returned to the barn to unharness the horse. As he did not return, I went to look for him. I found him in a deplorable condition, reeling. I tried to prevent his return to town. He fell. I buttoned his coat, which had a bottle of whiskey in each pocket, and dragged him over the creaking snow down an alley to our kitchen door. The man of the battered face was courting the nurse and he threw Adonis, limp as a seal, on the cot in the shack to sleep twenty-four hours. He had long deceived me, getting out the sliding sash of his room when the house was asleep to make merry with his boon companions. So "Pluto" and his master found other quarters and a true woman faced lost illusions.

She came to enjoy a Fourth of July a year later with us. Nannie Bristow, the only daughter of the Hon. Benjamin and Mrs. Bristow, was visiting us. She later married Eben Draper, Governor of Massachusetts. All the fireworks were in the stable, and we went across the lawn to take an account of stock. My brave friend was patting the neck of my riding horse. A muffled sound came from her lips. Seeing she was ill, I summoned help. We carried her a few feet, and laid her in the grass. There, by hemorrhage, her life quickly ebbed. At sunset she was carried to our living room and stretched upon the sofa. An hour later her frolicsome young brothers came for the party to be confronted with the figure of her who had been like a devoted mother to them, lying under a white sheet. Perhaps her fate was happier than that of the delicate, plain, intellectual rich girl, near of kin to Washington Irving, who against all protest, married Adonis, to reform him, only to find reformation a dream, and to die broken-hearted in a Swiss valley.

Thoughtless self-destroying sensualists pull down the temple of woman's love in mad thirst for unattainable liberty.

CHAPTER EIGHT

BERTHE POURTALÈS

THE great Chinese Wall may have crumbled before poets cease to love and be inspired by the charm of Helen of Troy, for time has enshrined her fascination.

Five women have shown me that imperishable gift of charm. Four have been artists of the stage. First, Agnes Ethel, of Daly's Company, who, entering my mother's library, was approached by my shy little brother at the age of three, who shunned all strangers, saying, as he put his hand in hers, "May I go home with you?" Her vibrant voice from the past I can still hear. In the rôle of "Frou-Frou," she stood behind the chair of her lover in Venice, looking over his shoulder as he read the Paris paper, she ignorant that within an hour he would find death in a duel at the hands of her deserted husband. She read aloud the notices of the theaters,—"At the Gaiety," she said, "at the Gaiety 'The Last Day of Happiness.'" The entire audience broke into a sob.

Ellen Terry, Duse and Ethel Barrymore,—all my dear friends, all artists,—impersonators of the smiles, romance and tears of living, cling to my memory.

Last, but not least, there came to Colorado Springs she who became the friend of my heart,—beautiful Berthe Pourtalès, a Countess born,—married, when hardly more than a child, to Sebastian Schlesinger, by whom she bore two daughters. She had come from Europe to Cambridge to join her father, Count

BERTHE POURTALES

Pourtalès, scientist and loved associate of Agassiz. In their simple enjoyment of scientific research these two scholars were often seen walking, carrying between them a dripping market basket filled with the organisms they had raised from deep sea soundings.

It was natural that all the undergraduates of Harvard should be hit amidships by love at first sight. Perhaps it was also natural that, fresh from the code of Continental Europe, she, with title and short purse, accepted a marriage arranged with a Jew of wealth, who headed the musical world of Boston and was received in exclusive circles. The magic of her youthful loveliness won, at a glance, the heart of distinguished society everywhere. Her marriage proved a tragedy.

She entered into privileged circles of the Continent and England. Like Joubert, she had the instinct for perfection. In elegant chirography she easily wrote in English, German, Italian and French. When she spoke German, she almost persuaded me that it was not a guttural tongue, unpleasing to one whose ear was attuned to the music, *"lingua Torscana in boca Romana."*

The smart sets of New York and the diplomatic world of Washington, sought her. James G. Blaine said to me, she was the most charming and fascinating woman he had ever known. His long career gives weight to this statement. Sir William Harcourt told me that, seeing her for the first time in London through an open door as the butler announced his visit, he loved her, and should to the end of his life. Arthur Dexter, of faultless profile and culture and grace, of a great Boston family, loved her to the end of his life,—even to the moment when he was found dead in his bed, with his finger marking a passage of beauty which he was reading in the light of a lamp which burned when the light of his life was extinguished.

She was past-mistress of taste and exquisite handiwork, and

unequaled as a housekeeper, in whose house, as in the mansions of Mrs. Wetmore, wife of Senator Wetmore of Rhode Island, one knew that one could walk from attic to cellar in a white satin Worth frock without picking up a touch of dust.

Berthe Pourtalès never suffered the disappointment of Madame Récamier, because the boys of the street ceased to turn an admiring eye as she passed. Man, woman and child paid her tribute as she walked the streets of Colorado Springs, closely veiled, wearing a red cloak tightly buttoned about her throat, with a gray fur collar. She came there broken in health and sad of heart, seeking strength. She had gone first to the Adirondacks with her daughters, where of turkey red calico, she made them dresses—cheap dresses—that were the envy of all campers.

In her luxurious days Worth Père cared as much to design clothes for her as he did to adorn Empress Eugénie and the ladies of the Court of the Third Empire. To his son Jean descended the tradition of serving her,—he who once said to me that taste was a disease from which he who possessed it, suffered. One night the prince of coiffeurs of Paris came to dress my hair for the Opera. Seeing a framed photograph of Countess Pourtalès upon my writing table, he fell into a glow of reminiscence of the woman he had most adored for her grace and beauty.

Thinking of her, I feel the gifts of the godmothers of her christening were high romance and sorrow.

In her simple house in the village street of Colorado Springs, she was the magnet for the homage of international travelers as well as home-abiding citizens. Count James Pourtalès, her cousin, owner of Silesian "Glumbowitz," crossed the ocean in his desire to help her. Like all imaginative men, he was caught in the meshes of mines and processes for their development. Eventually he married Berthe Pourtalès. He was the promoter of the land scheme of the now fashionable settlement known to the world as Broadmoor. A landscape plan of villas and a hotel with imported chef and major-domo, established an elegance of living then foreign to the West. Count Pourtalès said there was but one necessary thing lacking for full success, namely, a few handsome titled European rakes to woo the ladies. Now Colorado Springs and Broadmoor abound in magnificent residences. Charles Baldwin, of Newport, made his home a copy of the Grande Trianon of Versailles, and the mining magnate, Penrose of Philadelphia, has built a princely house.

Knowing Count Pourtalès, one was struck by his simplicity, as one is always when in the presence of really great people. The laughable incongruity of a drive one night with Count and Countess Pourtalès to their Villa at Broadmoor, in a hack drawn by long-tailed black horses,—a negro on the box, who never thought to open the gate,—Count Pourtalès, getting out, said in a low voice, "I always open the gate for a nigger." What a contrast years later going with my boy to Glumbowitz, where, on the night of our arrival, Count Pourtalès walked with us to the Kermess in the village near the Château. Owner of nine villages, he passed among the peasants like a loved father,—old people and children kissing his hands, as with familiar words he greeted them by name, with inquiries as to their well-being. He said, "In all my villages I can find a welcome and a good soup, and when I am forced to take refuge from storm or from a long day's shooting, there is wisdom to be found in the talk of many an old man who can neither read nor write."

Glumbowitz, thirty miles from the Polish border, in Silesia, was built on the foundations of an ancient monastery, where the monks used a series of small lakes for breeding fish. Aged golden carp, of famed longevity, still swim in those calm waters. There were fine roads bordered by anciently planted, now grown gigantic, oaks, giving on stretches of pasture, where herds of shy roebuck grazed. In harvest time peasant girls from Poland, in high-topped boots, wearing native dress, were brought to work in the fields. They were quartered in the villages where no male harvesters were housed. The girls paid the men to come to dance with them in the evening, and bartered for those who were the best dancers.

Knowing how well liked James Pourtalès was in Colorado Springs, where he was considered "a good fellow,"—one took note that he was of feudal stock. His mother, who resided at "Elgute," twelve miles beyond Glumbowitz, was born Princess Putpus, from the Island of Rugen, where her people had, until comparatively late time, exercised the right of life and death over their peasants. After her marriage, she left the distinguished circle of her mother's great house in Berlin to become Countess Pourtalès, and to become a toast at the Court of Empress Eugénie, in Paris, where she was called the "beautiful German blonde," friend of the Princess Metternich. Together they vied in elegance and distinction of attire, dressed by Worth, the creative czar of the world of fashion. He received these great ladies, arrayed in his gorgeous dressing gown, designing with jeweled fingers bewitching costumes for skating or hunting, or Court gowns of rich textiles for balls or races, which he always whispered he had seen in a dream the night before.

It was an age when a lady aspired to make a mode, not to copy one,—not to do as Jean Worth, fils, said Americans did, "copying and following modes like a flock of sheep." Nevertheless, these grandes dames, schooled in coquetry, had an able finger in politics.

In one of my visits to Glumbowitz, the house party included

Baron Wolf, married to the most enchanting Italian singer, renowned as the greatest interpreter of German lieder in Europe,— Felicia Barbais; Count von Farnbühler, Ambassador to Berlin from Württemburg, and Count Moltke, commanding the garrison at Breslau, intimate friend of the Emperor and Empress. He was afterwards disgraced and deprived of rank and estates after the Camera Trials in Berlin, forced by the revelations of Maximilian Harden. Moltke was a natural musician, and while at the piano one evening, a telegram came from the Empress telling him to come for her intimate birthday supper in her small salon.

Count Pourtalès was a strict adherent of Bismarck, intimate friend from boyhood of his sons Herbert and William, and eventually became adviser of Herbert's widow and guardian of her children. A remarkable portrait of the Iron Chancellor, by Lembach, came as a gift from the family Bismarck while my son was at Glumbowitz. Count Pourtalès placed it at the end of the hall, and summoned every man on his estates to come to see it and give it respectful salute. Count Pourtalès had scant liking for the now dethroned Emperor William. He considered him extravagant and vain, and despised the friends who surrounded him, as members of the devil's round table,—an opinion verified by the scandals brought into Court, which touched even members of the Imperial family.

How jolly the lunches in the forest, when the gaily dressed women went to join the guns at midday,—where a hot and beautifully served breakfast was possible only by trained servants, sent on hours ahead! The evenings were filled with music or cards, and long discussions among the men. I pause to glance at the motley medley of memory now, when thrones and kings are going out of fashion. There was talk at Glumbowitz of forms of government, and the edict of the socialistic studies,—a question whether the human race for highest development should not be bred carefully as blooded stock, under government supervision. Now, when Caliban in every country is clamorous to rule, one recalls reading Renan's philosophic dramas, in one of which Caliban usurps the power of Prospero, the Light Bringer. Finding his rule beset with ignorance, responsibility forced him to become conservative, adopting the measures and wisdom of Prospero.

In the time of political discussion, an intensive and pertinent memory of the evening when James G. Blaine came to dine in the country near Washington, links Washington to Silesia. He had desired to meet the eloquent, colorful, charming orator, Bourke Cochran, but recently elected Tammany Member of Congress. Blaine sat reflecting the mellow radiance of wisdom in age, informed and tactful as Richelieu or Mazarin, his face softened by abundant white hair. Bromidically I stated that it were better to have for President one term of office of six years duration. He gently turned to me, answering: "Oh, no. Four years is quite sufficient, for a President of the United States wields more power than any other living ruler." That was more than thirty years ago. Today, when federal bureaucracy is omnipotent and state rights almost ignored, I wonder if one term for a President, without power to play for a second nomination, were not wisest, and that we should demand that all Presidents should have historic wisdom, be politically minded and a judge of men, and not an autocrat.

One night at dinner, when the guests had had the excitement of a successful *chasse,* the winding of the gamekeeper's horn called us to the terrace overlooking the lake. Every man arose, clicking his heels and kissing the hands of fair women, as he wished them good digestion. On the terrace were arranged all

THE TERRACE, GLUMBOWITZ

GLUMBOWITZ

the game killed, an assistant gamekeeper guarding that of the individual he had served. Each man standing straight, with a flaming torch, the light of which streamed across the water, made an old-time scene not familiar to republican eyes.

Sometimes we drove to "Trachenburg" over the fine roads bordered with fruit trees and owned and policed by the state. Fürst Hatzfeldt, who could either sit or stand or wear his hat or be uncovered in the presence of His Imperial Majesty,—I cannot recall which—was the owner of Trachenburg, built for defense in the seventh century. The land consisted of eighty thousand acres. Even during my visit there, there was grave shaking of heads as to whether the Polish border, about thirty miles away, might not be crossed by Cossack invaders. It was an ungentle background for Russian-born, sympathetic Princess Hatzfeldt. Here the Emperor bestowed the expensive honor of coming with his large suite, to shoot in the height of the season.

At Glumbowitz, where James Pourtalès planted an acre of lilies of the valley in honor of his bride, the garden was in the shelter of walls thirty feet high, erected in earlier days for defense. The walls of the wine cellars at Glumbowitz, where never a woman was permitted to enter, were of such massive thickness that there was no change of temperature the year through. They were filled with the finest wines, regularly added to every year, from every famous vintage.

At noon, when we breakfasted, our chatelaine presided over a perfectly appointed table, near her hand a gold-mounted book, in which she noted every fault in food or service. I sometimes long for another taste of a saddle of larded roebuck, with sour cream sauce. My Scotch maid, reared under the care of the Duchess of Argyll, was thunderstruck at being called to sausage and beer at ten A.M. The Germans eat early and often. Coffee and dried goose at the first meal; at midday, so-called breakfast, of many courses; on our return from an early drive, coffee, tea, cakes galore, and potted meats were served.

Whether in Colorado Springs or Germany, James Pourtalès was full of merriment and glee, as on the day when the Archbishop and attendant clergy, in long soutanes, were walking in procession from the newly consecrated village Catholic chapel at the Château. Black swans sprang from the lake to the path to chase the priests. As they fled with lifted soutanes, James Pourtalès drove back the swans, saying to the Bishop: "That was a moment for you to pray, not to run."

At the command of the Emperor, all the landowners grew potatoes and built distilleries for the making of alcohol, which the Emperor believed would become the fuel for locomotives and all mechanical driving power of the future.

There were vast cow stables where the animals were born and bred their young, and were killed in old age, having been fed on the refuse of the distilleries. Sometimes their hoofs grew inches long, as they never left the roof which sheltered them.

Count Pourtalès inherited his income from the scientifically grown and tended pine forests, planted by his grandfather. As he had no children, his estates passed to Count Jacques Pourtalès, his French cousin, and Glumbowitz was confiscated by the German Government during the late war because of its French inheritor.

After the marriage of James and Berthe Pourtalès in a church on Fourth Avenue, where Mrs. William Churchman of Philadelphia and I were attendants, we saw them on board the steamer bound for home. They returned now and again for call of business.

Coming to lunch with me at Edgeplain one day, the Count

was wearing a new London suit. His wife exclaimed, "Why, what is the matter?"—and glancing down, he saw his trousers covered with bright yellow spots. "Oh, chemicals," said he, as he drew a corkless bottle from his pocket. He was a student of chemistry, and lost, as many others, a fortune in an effort to discover a new process for the treatment of ores. Builders of railways say that between the Mississippi and Rio Grande Rivers, there are enough scrapped and abandoned smelters, the iron of which might have furnished rails for commerce from the Atlantic to the Pacific.

Berthe Pourtalès died in California under the surgeon's knife, refusing the relief of anesthetics. Of a hot afternoon I met Count Pourtalès at the station, and we followed her body to Hoboken to be placed in the cabin of an ocean steamer. The morning he sailed he brought me the cornflower brooch of sapphires and diamonds given by him to her as a gauge of faith on the day of their betrothal.

In the family chapel beneath the ancient trees of Glumbowitz, James and Berthe Pourtalès lie near the tombs of his father and mother.

CHAPTER NINE

"H. H." AND OTHERS

THE Antlers Hotel, Colorado Springs, on Pike's Peak Avenue, was the center for the floating population and citizens as well. I wonder if a grandmother living in Buffalo, wife of a leader of the Democratic Party and owner of an influential newspaper in Buffalo, recalls an incident of her girlhood, when she was seventeen. The morning after her arrival at the hotel, she had seated herself coquettishly to rock to and fro on the porch, wearing bright red stockings and slippers of the same hue. She watched a freckled faced, red haired boy, whose trousers were held by only one suspender. He raised the dust as his copper-toed shoes shuffled. Clapping his hands, he sang:

> "I danced all night in my summer pants,
> My night tonight."

Two tight-fisted New Englanders answered the glance of his entreating eyes by tossing him a quarter. In that time, the smallest coin in circulation was a silver dime, whose purchasing quality equaled one cent at the Massachusetts seaboard. A group of laughing youths, far from home, loafed by on horseback. Spying the pretty, plump girl, they needed no court chamberlain to present them. After consulting in unfettered mirth, they rushed to the village house painter and returned with the hoofs and legs of their mustangs painted bright scarlet. Taking a tight knee-grip, and putting their ponies to spur and whip, they forced them to mount the stone steps, scattering in dismay the guests upon the porch. Drawing rein, they flung their sombreros at the dainty feet of the startled girl, crying: "Oh, naughty, naughty, Totty Cough Drop!" Later, they were her gallant escorts to distant picnics.

There was a happy contagion in the free, generous spirit of the sparsely settled town, that lulled apprehension and strengthened the hope to live. Snobbery and ultra-sophistication do not thrive in the vigor of high altitudes. Far from kith and kin, utter strangers served one another as brothers. There was, I think, a recognition of real worth.

No doubt today influential grandfathers are settled in England who will recall with gratitude Mr. and Mrs. Green. By speech and bearing, he betrayed education in an English University. They lived in a small brick house, where the best of young Englishmen lodged when they came for a lark from lonely ranches. Rotund, bright-cheeked Mrs. Green was said to have been an English barmaid. She looked the part, but she mothered those homesick fellows, put them to bed, helped them to return to the Plains. In their absence she brushed, cleaned and pressed their evening suits and best clothes, caring for them until they came again for "a hot time in the old town." Into her ears these repentant boys poured their woes and shortcomings, seeking the comfort and censure of a really good woman. It may be that the sailor keeping watch beneath the stars on trackless waters, and the adventurer in distant lands, dreams most often of his mother. The very world seemed young in Colorado. Pranks and mischief are part of youth. But on the whole, society was clean, with decent ideals.

When we moved from the double house, where Helen Hunt's

affectionate thoughtfulness made privations for me easily enjoyed, she went to her new house, which was so built that her windows got every ray of sunshine. Though two years older than my mother, she was a boon companion, and together we laughed over trifles. Gleeful, when being told that I had been instructed that to save the juice of beef it must be seared in a hot oven, I had followed instructions, and upon opening the door of the littlest of stoves, was frightened by the fierce flame that swept over the kitchen. She had shared the Thanksgiving dinner where I had bought a turkey so large that when its head was in the oven its tail was out, enveloping it in linen and bacon, I sat on the floor basting it all the afternoon. The bird was delicious, and one did not have Agassiz' friend from Cambridge, gentle Count Pourtalès, every day to dine. No one minded that there were no two water glasses the same size, nor two plates the same color, on the table.

Of Helen Hunt it is difficult to write. Swift of thought, the gray-green eyes of genius lighted a face responsive to all moods. From the intellectual association of Thomas Wentworth Higginson, Emily Dickinson, and the society of a university town like Amherst, of which her father had been President, she had gone to Newport, marrying an Artillery officer, who later, in the examination of a cannon, was smothered. She faced the loss of two sons, and brought a wounded heart to Colorado, to lift up her eyes to the "everlasting hills." She met William Jackson, a prosperous banker of Colorado Springs, from Chester, Pennsylvania, and she loved him. To me that union was as unnatural as the wedding of a skylark to a turtle. The Brahminical élite of art and literature in Boston and New York, were her friends.

She was early to rise and early to bed, and worked at her writing table in her bay-window from nine A.M. until noon. Then came long drives in the afternoon, to find the first wild flowers of spring, or a sheaf of autumn-touched leaves and purple asters to brighten her living-rooms. A stream of notable people lunched and dined with her, in which feasts she included Mr. Bass and me.

The thought came to my mind that if one would sit still in Colorado Springs, or at the corner of Twenty-third Street and Broadway, the entire world would pass and be within call.

She loved Cheyenne Mountain. Twenty-seven Sundays of one year we picnicked there, generally on the spot where she afterwards asked should be her grave. Whenever she left the town she gave me her manuscripts for safe keeping. Later, I read with her the proofs of "Ramona."

The author of the Saxe Holm stories was a mystery; so, piecing two and two together, and a chance remark at a picnic luncheon, I said, "Why, you are Saxe Holm." She turned white, then scarlet, and I hung my head after having discovered and loudly voiced the truth.

She was buried on Cheyenne Mountain. Her grave became a shrine of pilgrimage, and every traveler added a stone to what became a huge cairn. There was too much expenditure and difficulty for William Jackson to secure in perpetuity the rights of that sterile mountainside to hold for her and the world who loved her. She and I had seen together long stretches of mountain range and endless plains. Her heart was in those heights, and healing came to her from them. One of the disagreeable shocks of my experience came when, driving up the rocky road to lay another stone on that love-built cairn, I met Mr. Jackson and a driver with her coffin in an express wagon, taking it to the village cemetery in the shadow of Pike's Peak.

The world is never the same after the loss of such a noble friend as Helen Hunt. Entering a room she vitalized it. Mrs.

Daniel Goddard, wife of the editor of the Boston *Advertiser*, said: "Helen Hunt laughs too much to be happy." She echoed my thought, for I knew she wore a crown of sorrows. I met Mrs. Goddard through Helen Hunt,—a high soul who was childless, and should have been the mother of great lawgivers and jurists. Older by many years than her husband, they walked together happily. In their house gathered young writers, finding in her a kind friend and discerning critic, a helpful Egeria.

Mr. Goddard's death ended her life soon after she came to our cottage at Cohasset, where Minot's Ledge Light stared in at the windows. She was grave and annoyed at the kindly people who came to offer their help to buy her mourning. She dressed as usual, and said to me, "My husband, wherever he is, is as unhappy without me as I am without him." Helen Jackson and Martha Goddard were loyal friends of one another and to me.

The cottage at Cohasset was owned by Edward Cunningham, one of the Boston group of China traders. He owned, and occupied with his large family, Brush Island, just off the shore. They led an amphibious existence, and I watched, with interest, father, mother and several children walking from their cottage door to a long springboard reaching over the harbor on the rocks, gracefully diving into deep water as easily as seals. The youngest girl, Hilda, aged seven, taught my son to swim, an ordeal for a mother to watch, whose brother had drowned because he could not swim.

The most marked event of our stay in New England was our first visit to Mr. and Mrs. Jack Gardiner's, at Brookline. Mrs. Gardiner was not born of the inner caste of Boston. Her striking individuality, whether as patron of arts or as a siren, enlivened the talk of every dinner table. Knowing she had no beauty of face, I expected to see a dark woman of the George Sand type.

She met us, as we entered the front door, with outstretched hands, —a small, perfect figure, a genial, ugly face framed with a mat of yellow-drab hair. She wore a simple surplice-like white crepe frock,—her necklace, belt, bracelets, brooch, earrings and rings of superb cabochon turquoise.

Adulation was the incense of her days, but she gave flattery with both hands to those whom she would honor. She saluted me as "one whom she had long wished to meet,—the cleverest woman in the West," saying, "My night blooming Cereus will open for you." She really knew no more of me than a hole in the wall. At the end of the hall were masses of purple Darwin tulips, then unknown to American gardens. Trees eight or ten feet high, all pyramidal pink azaleas, lighted from the floor with pink shades, made a picture of ravishing beauty. Before nightfall, she showed us her conservatories, one filled with a new variety of pink begonia.

Her salient attributes were worship of beauty and exercise of power. She had a gift for gardens. Her Italian garden's walls, inset with fragments of Roman and Greek sculpture and inscriptions, wore the seeming patine of antiquity. It was the only Italian garden in the United States that seemed a part of Italy.

At dinner she wore her celebrated pearls and a giant ruby. I agreed with the verdict of one of her admirers, that the fairness of her skin put pearls to shame.

We met at long intervals for many years, every meeting a remembered pleasure. She came to luncheon once with me in Washington, where she met her friend, Marion Crawford. It was the first time since he wrote "To Leeward," of which the reading public said she was the heroine.

Whether in the Curtis Palace, on the Grand Canal in Venice or at the Shrine of Nikko in Japan, her stay and passing left a luminous trail. She traveled with a spring bed, which fairly broke the backs of the coolies who carried it from Yokohama to Nikko, where it rests in peace.

About three months before her death, as I was in Boston en route from the wedding of a daughter of beautiful Mrs. Bayard Thayer of Hawthorne Hill, a note came from Mrs. Gardiner asking me to come to see her. When I arrived, she was lying on a couch in a lower room of the palace-like museum in whose third story she lived. Sargent had but recently made a sketch of her in a wheeled chair, enveloped in white mosquito netting, placed among the flowers of her dream court. My back was to the picture. She was impatient for me to turn and give my opinion of the portrait. I could honestly say it looked like a sybil who, knowing the past, foretold the future. In my estimation, Sargent's portrait of her, which had the fascination of the Empress Theodora, was a fuller expression of her power.

She was swathed in cashmere shawls, about her wrists strings of perfect pearls, on her head a Mandarin-like cap of corn-colored grenadine, with satin bound petals, in front sticking straight out, the longest tail-feather ever grown on pheasant or any other bird. Did she wear it to excite curiosity? I do not know, but one could not give sign of thought of eccentricity. Her mind, clear as youth itself, was interested in the recently acquired painting of one she considered a rare artist.

In any assemblage she stood out, small as she was, as an individual and a personage. Not all women liked her,—some feared her. Duse told me she would not accept Mrs. Gardiner's invitation, for she had tried to vulgarize Venice.

Yet she was one of the women of whom America should be most proud.

Once, when the husband of another woman had paid court

to Mrs. Gardiner, for which he had been seriously criticized, Mrs. Gardiner said to me, "Why do they not keep their little husbands? I keep Jack."

She never missed a Boston Symphony concert. She was in sympathy with the genius and intelligence of Henry Higginson. In speaking of her to me, he told of the financial sacrifice she made, and the things she relinquished, to give to Boston that unique and most personal temple of art ever given to a city. When she died, I felt Boston had nothing left to talk about, and she was a greater loss than that of Bunker Hill Monument could have been.

Laying of the corner stone of our new home, Edgeplain, was by my boy, aged three years, now a grandfather. In kilt and tam o'shanter, yellow curls blowing in the wind, he used the trowel and set the stone with hammer's blow. There was a large gathering. Champagne was not a sin; he broke a bottle on the stone and we served it with a bountiful repast, in a tent near the foundations. Through my husband's success and my father's generosity, we had John La Farge's jeweled glass in the transoms of our connecting rooms and lighting the staircase hall. From the western bay-window we learned to be weather prophets. Pike's Peak dominated the range. Whether it was cloudless, or wore a nightcap, or was hidden in mist, we took counsel, as did the Israelites from the Pillar of Cloud.

Perhaps those days in Colorado may have been a narrow life, walled by the complementary lines of mountain range and fenceless plain. A Shakespeare evening, a play read and discussed, and in the intermission, our throats cleared by angel cake and hot spiced claret, gave more of pleasure than we now find in the purchase of a ticket for twelve dollars to see the Follies.

Beautiful rugs covered the floors, and our servants enjoyed the laying of the table with Venetian glass and Dresden china, and preparing the best of food.

To us came the wisest man of his time, Charles Perkins, who for twenty-four years was President of the Chicago, Burlington and Quincy Railroad. His children played house in a piano-box in our back yard with my son, while their elders sat at meat. These delightful little girls grew to superb womanhood, worthy of their powerful father, who thought no man was to be praised for doing his duty, but only commended when he exceeded it. Their mother was born Edith Forbes, niece of Mr. John Forbes, Daniel Webster's financial backer, who had at his own expense sped a heavily-laden ship of food to Ireland during the great famine. Mrs. Perkins felt she would perish if she did not see, for a part of the year, the sea from the shore of Massachusetts. Half the year she lived in Burlington, Iowa.

We visited Mr. and Mrs. Perkins in the environs of Boston, and enjoyed the untrammeled activities of those dark-eyed girls and boys. When visiting Mrs. Perkins I always asked that Uncle John Forbes might come to supper, and I sat spell-bound listening to tales of great achievement of one born to be a practical realizer of dreams.

Mrs. William Hooper, the eldest of the daughters, today lives, dispensing generous hospitality at "Elsanes," at Manchester-by-the-Sea. Mrs. Edward Cunningham built a Spanish house, set in a peerless garden, at Montecito, on the hillside where her Uncle John Forbes a half century before planted a bare mountainside with a wilderness of eucalyptus trees. She has written and published chronicles of her distinguished father and mother. A sparkling face, and always in suitable attire, she is one of the influential citizens of California. Her sister, brilliant Peggy, now

Mrs. Herrick, heads with energy all great causes for the advancement of philanthropy in Boston.

As for fascinating Mary Perkins, fond of books and travel, she shares a ranch with her brother Charles, on a great well-watered plateau, where, in their haciendas, they have a life enabling them to raise blooded horses, and to ride to their hearts' content.

Cameron Forbes, former Governor of the Philippines and now Ambassador to Japan, is of the same virile stock, and he, like his forbears, has left the mark of high achievement in his private and public career. What does not the game of polo owe to him, both in his maintenance of it in the Philippine Islands and for the playing of the officers in the United States Army? In his unique country home at Dedham, built of rare woods from the virgin forests of the Philippine Islands, one looks across a well-kept polo ground, which he generously maintains for his Boston friends.

The piano which came in that box in which the children played, was one of the early miracles of Steinway, for it is used with pleasure after half a century. On it played the poet of the piano, Josefy, whose touch was as clear and rhythmic as the falling of a summer shower. Through the appreciation of beauty come blessings. Josefy was my guest. Coming back from his concert, I asked a question as to one of the posthumous Mazurkas of Chopin. He seated himself at the piano and played that Mazurka, and until morning I had a feast of Mazurkas, Preludes, Polonaises and Nocturnes, and sat under the spell of Chopin.

There, too, came Remenyi, the Hungarian wizard of the violin, who, on our return from his concert, walked and played with passion, as he improvised variations on "Way Down South in Dixie." He considered that tune original, and America's best contribution to music. Liszt was his dear friend. He told of Liszt's coming to pay him a visit, and when he raised his eyes from his violin, as Liszt sat at the piano, his mother was standing in the doorway keeping time with a soup spoon, too entranced to think of the dinner cooking in the kitchen.

Poor Remenyi in his later life, forced to fiddle in small towns, to ignorant audiences, died, I fear, with the iron of defeat in his soul. He sent me from Old Mexico lovely Mexican rubies, with fire in their hearts.

Our last meeting was one night on Broadway, and he said: "Quick, there is a lovely new ballet by Delibes being played in a theater on the next block." I now hear it often, always with the memory of my gifted Hungarian friend.

The square, large porch at Edgeplain, when completed, was a loafing place for the young and idle.

Many a week-end John G. Milburn spent with us, reading and watching the cloud shapes on Cheyenne Mountain, receiving the tribute of all the young and pretty women in the town. His one request was that I give him the promise he would be asked to go nowhere.

To have beautiful menu cards and flowers on a prettily laid table, to write appropriate quotations or original verse for honored guests, and to superintend their arrangement, was the privilege of the hostess.

It was an education to listen to friends of Mr. Bass,—the D'Acosta brothers, Samuel Dickson of Philadelphia, and others who were neither Bulls nor Bears, but constructive Americans.

There were musicians and charming singers who came west for healing sunshine, and in our living-room germinated the society which grew into the foundation of the greatest musical society west of the Mississippi.

Seeking health came the young Yale Class Poet, Louis J. Swinburne, of Albany. He mounted on his chestnut horse, Rex, together we explored untrodden gulches of the foothills. For me his acquaintance was an epoch-making experience. He brought me John Morley's "Life of Voltaire," "Diderot" and "Rousseau," and his "Eighteenth Century Essays," which revolutionized my attitude toward Marie Antoinette and Robespierre.

Years afterwards, John Morley took me in to a small, brilliant dinner at the Asquiths', at 21 Cavendish Square. He was greatly pleased at my enthusiasm over his "Lives of the Encyclopædists," and became my cordial friend.

It was real life to spend forty-eight hours in the saddle, come back to a bath, tea-gown and tea, where young men and women, under the spur of my flail, studied Browning, and spent six months trying to know about the Jesuits and the Jews.

Mrs. Garston, an antiquated English lady whose father wrote "The Life of Defoe,"—he who was of the circle of Coleridge—knew profoundly English literature. She read with me twice a week, and tempered Milton's "Areopagitica" and "Samson Agonistes" with Byron's passion and spur to wander in the wake of "Childe Harold's Journeys."

In these days when I am in haste going nowhere, I ask myself if a picnic were not a greater pleasure in North Cheyenne Canyon, where the blue columbines nodded by a running stream. There for all winter I had cooked each day our dinner, in the warmth of the sun, sheltered by high rocks. In the early morning the sorrel mare was hitched to the buggy and my boy was strapped to the seat. We took home-made sauce for spaghetti, made in the remembrance of the flavor of an Italian journey. When we reached the Canyon, the hammock was swung between spruce trees for my baby's nap, and a bonfire built on which to heat a flat rock. No chef could prepare more toothsome dish than thick Porterhouse steaks, lamb chops or chicken done to a turn on a hot rock. Many guests entreated to come to share our meals in Cheyenne Canyon.

Within us all there is a response to turbulent nature. Today I am roused by the thought of an electrical storm in South Cheyenne Canyon, fiercer than Henry Irving ever depicted, of Walpurgis night. Hastily the pony was tied behind the buggy, Mr. Bass and the baby getting all the protection possible under the cover. It was black night. Forked lightning rent the sky, and was my only light as I led the sorrel mare down the slippery rocks beside the stream. Wet to the skin, there was still an exaltation and gladness at the clean fight with nature, though the lights of Edgeplain welcomed us home.

Dearer than the remembrance of court balls is that of the hazardous ride with General Palmer, when the thermometer fell forty degrees in as many minutes, announcing a dust storm, and an icy gale rushed from the north. We take the elements in their friendly moods as a matter of course—air, water, fire, earth—never reckoning with their destructive forces. At the end of that mountain ride, coming down the foothills, spiral columns of dust rising from the plains, and black clouds of the sky to envelop us, we could not see each other. General Palmer's calm voice said, "We must trust to the wisdom of the horses to find their way." Our eyes blinded, clothes and faces caked with dust, and half frozen, we at last reached the road. At our journey's end we found an affrighted household,—but a bright fire, clean clothes and a good dinner.

Strange that there comes a clarion note of triumph from having faced fear and conquered,—a finer recollection than hours of gaiety where danger did not threaten, and better than that of the following flawless morning, when we could not find a cloud the size of a man's hand in the azure sky.

CHAPTER TEN

POLITICS AND MORMONS

EVERY other year the Colorado Legislature convened in Denver. Mr. Bass and I spent the full session at the Windsor Hotel, where the Railway Lobby had headquarters.

The thread-like narrow-gauge railway from Denver running south, needed to grow to broad-gauge, and make trans-continental connections to the Pacific Coast. The question of right of way, whether by state condemnation, barter or purchase, was vital. I doubt if the legislators, or those who acted as middlemen in influence, had ever heard the name of Horace Walpole. They held his faith that every man has his price. I have seen a bright-eyed, clever little Jew, Otto Meyers, a genius of adventure and railway building, as his autobiography proves, with his hands full of greenbacks and additional ones peeping from his pockets, leave the Committee room in the purchase of human beings. A man bought rarely stays bought; he's apt to pocket his gains and sell himself again to a higher bidder. At the time I felt, and still do, that the Jesuitical code of "the end justifies the means," was essential, and the only workable scheme.

The Denver and Rio Grande Western must reach Salt Lake City. However, the morals of Colorado were rather higher than those in the time of the Rotten Boroughs in England.

Diaz was dictator in Old Mexico. In General Palmer's mind was conceived and matured the glorious project of the Mexican

National Railway. To that end he set out to enter Mexico from the north by private stage-coach. Mrs. Palmer and Rose Kingsley, the daughter of the distinguished writer, the Reverend Charles Kingsley, and Governor Hunt, the former Territorial Governor of Colorado, shared the adventure. Banditry was rife on the stage route. The gentle robbers, with discrimination, killing only the men, stripped the women, leaving them only stockings and garters. General Palmer's party was fully armed. As they were nearing the outskirts of a large town, a band of highwaymen attacked them. General Palmer and Governor Hunt acted on the Persian code—to "shoot straight and tell the truth." I asked Governor Hunt if he killed anyone. "I cannot say," replied he; "there were seven dead Mexicans on the road and a fleeing band." The following morning the authorities of the town threw the party into jail for assaulting and killing peaceable citizens. General Palmer entered into negotiations with Diaz. Contracts were signed and work begun, all to be nullified when Diaz' rule ended.

When George R. Coppell became President of the Denver and Rio Grande, the rights of way were no doubt secure, but from then on the policy of the Company attempted no further expenditure to influence the flexible minds of local politicians.

In the expansion of the West, the men who had engineered and laid down railways had been chased and wounded by enraged Indians. They, however, acquired a Machiavellian knowledge of the minds of the men with whom they had to deal. To negotiate with Brigham Young and the Latter Day Saints called for tact and enlightened selfishness. Several times the officers of the railway went to hold sessions in an uncomfortable hostelry in Salt Lake City. On these journeys I accompanied them.

Once I had a return of malarial fever. Crawling from my bed

POLITICS AND MORMONS

one evening, I knocked on the door of Kate Field's bedroom across the hall. She had tiny feet, shod in coquettish bronze slippers, which rested on a side-saddle as a stool. She was engaged in a powerful penetration of all the stupid and sacred Mormon literature and tenets. She came to Utah under contract with an Eastern publisher. As I entered, she raised her eyes, and wearily said, "I am sick of Jesus Christ."

The following day, kindly wishing to lift up my spirit, she asked me to walk with her to the house of Mrs. Orin Pratt, whose story she intended to hear. As we went, we passed many one-story houses, with four front doors facing the street. They were the residences of Mormon husbands, whose four wives were expected to enjoy the marital justice of spending one week every month with their husband. Kate Field seized my arm, exclaiming, "Don't look at those houses as if you were seeing a ghost." Imagination might easily supply the vision of the hand of a disillusioned wife, whose soul died under hard work and slaughtered womanhood, raising the latch of the door which opened on the street.

The walk was not long to the unpretentious house of Mrs. Pratt. As we entered, she met us in a wheeled chair, crippled by deformity of rheumatism. Her head was intellectual, like a New England woman of the highest type. Kate Field's entreaty brought forth a tragic story in as simple language as that of Aeschylus or Sophocles.

At seventeen years of age she was a convert at Norvu under the fiery eloquence of the accomplished classical scholar, Orin Pratt. They loved one another, and she bore him four sons. Their domestic life was ideal, marred only by the missionary journeys to Scandinavia and England for converts to Mormonism. Pratt taught his boys in the evenings, Latin and Greek. Joe Smith had not then announced the doctrine of polygamy as obligatory. Later, with a heavy, sinking heart, Pratt told his wife of Smith's revelation, and was resolved not to accept it. Later, he announced to her that, rebellious as he was, he must take a second wife or his power would be broken. He annexed their servant girl. The barbed arrow struck the heart of his noble wife. She submitted, and with their family they made the terrible journey from Norvu to Salt Lake City. She fathomed the avarice and lust of power of the Mormon Elders, the size of whose collars was rarely less than seventeen inches, a measurement that a witty man once said "needed the charity of their fellows."

In Salt Lake City, in terror of her life, she dared not flee. She put her boys to bed, her lips close to their ears in the dark, in the arraignment of Mormonism. Those sons, who later were important citizens of Salt Lake City, were Gentiles.

The visits of Pratt became fewer as he added to his quota of wives, and when he died the wife of Heber Kimball, one of the most powerful of Mormon Elders, rushed to see his widow. Mrs. Kimball had been lecturing that afternoon to young women on the virtue of being a plural wife, who would take a high place in heaven instead of that of a servant. While Mrs. Kimball was seeking to console Mrs. Pratt on the death of her husband, Mrs. Pratt looked her between the eyes and said, "My husband died years ago. Mr. Pratt's death is a matter of no regret or importance to me."

I listened to the heartbreaking record of that woman and burst into tears. She said, "Don't cry, my child, it all happened long ago."

The blow fell. The law of the United States suppressed polygamy. What a trial for those men who had to take as mate the elderly first wife, and like Lot's wife, wished to look back over their shoulders at forbidden joy—the society of their young and pretty ones.

In the Temple I heard Cannon, who represented Utah in the United States Senate, say, "I tell the mothers of my children they must be industrious and support their offspring."

Brigham Young, acting on that theory, gave his youngest wife, number twenty-eight, a sewing machine, which she promptly threw downstairs. It was she to whom in a moment of weakness, he gave a jeweled breastpin. The early wives set up a hue and cry of protest, forcing him into the extravagance of buying twenty-seven duplicates.

There was exchange of railway courtesies among the connecting and contesting lines,—courtesy of passes, special cars, and at times, special trains for railway officials. In the splendor of privilege, I often felt a self-satisfied condescension as I looked out the car window to other less fortunate passengers. Pride came before the fall. I, who as a matter of course expected passes, express and telegraph franks, was advised that it was better to write a letter than to go to the expense of a telegram.

In a special car we went to the end of the lines under construction, to a town built in ten days. We were accompanied by Governor Hunt, who, having been Territorial Governor, was double-dyed in knowledge and experience of the Western man and the aboriginal Indian. It was a revelation,—the movement in the dusty streets, the rough boarded one-story houses, where, in the parlance of the people, everything was "wide open,"—faro-banks at every turn; gaily painted women flaunting their gaudy frocks. One young ranchman we saw gallop up to a gambling hall, hitch his pony and stake his earnings of six months. Having in a brief time lost his pile, he came out, flung himself into his saddle and galloped toward his ranch, saying, "Easy come and easy go."

Many interesting excursions we made. My husband commandeered a sleeping coach, on the platform of which was put an ice-chest filled with roasts of beef, mutton and chicken for our guests, who demanded no great luxury. Just before meal time there was silence or petulance, but as soon as food and drink were served, laughter, merriment and good fellowship were established.

Doctor Swinburne, the eminent surgeon of Albany, was with us. He had worked in France during the Franco-Prussian War, and had introduced antiseptic surgery into the United States. He was a cynic, highly critical of spinsters, of whom he said, "Nearly all become cranks."

Mr. Sherman S. Rogers and his family, of Buffalo, were of the party. He fell into a rage with me when he found I had ridden on a cow-catcher with Colonel Lamborne, seated beneath the headlight, having faced the danger of a vagrant hog, which would have cost us our lives if he had not lifted his hind leg from the track at an opportune moment.

Our guests were eager to kill a bear and shoot wild turkey, having chained dogs in the baggage car. Starting a flock of wild turkeys on the mountainside, those handsome bronze birds seemed to go slowly, but they left the hunters far behind, spent with breathless following. Nor did they kill a bear, but they shared the revelation of grandeur of the remote visions of the glorious Rocky Mountains.

I recall shivering with exhaustion as we drew into Pueblo, when handsome Dick Haines, man of fashion of New York, concocted an ambrosial remedy called whiskey sour, more potent than that quaffed by the gods on Olympus.

Now people dash in high powered motor cars or express trains, from place to place. They are like swords dipped in oil and drawn through the sea, taking nothing therefrom and leaving nothing behind. Though I was reared in luxury, the joy of a life as near freedom as human nature permits, paints the palette of memory in brilliant hues.

The business of the Rio Grande gave me the privilege of crossing the Sierras, and to strike down among the orange groves to California. We arrived at the charmingly set, modern hotel at Monterey. Under a full moon the gardens were as magical as Klingsor's. Hedges of white calla lilies, banksia and Maréchal Niel roses climbing to the roof, the air heavy with standard growing heliotrope and white jasmine, made the passion of a summer night. The luxuriant bushes filled with large tea roses were a disappointment. They lacked the fragrance of the roses of the East,—even of the June grown cabbage roses in an Eastern kitchen garden.

General Palmer preferred the saddle to a carriage, and with him I explored the tangle of wooded hillsides' unbroken trails. At last he relaxed his courtesy of dismounting to help me mount or dismount, and treated me like a boy and a good companion.

Despite General Palmer's grasp on all things practical, he was at heart romantic. In the laying out of the railway from Denver to Colorado Springs, he explored the foothills on horseback. Finding a fantastic gorge and flowing stream near the Garden of the Gods, he said, "Here I will build my home when I marry." He named the spot Glen Eyrie. Doctor Bell, who rode with him, chose a site near Manitou, where he would build his home. For both men the dream was made manifest. There they built their homes, took their wives and fathered their children.

In the study of his home General Palmer surrounded himself

with the portraits of his friends, painted by a celebrated artist, and the one of Mr. Bass came to my son at General Palmer's death.

The cedars of Lebanon on the cold heights between Damascus and Balbec have no greater beauty than their brothers at Monterey, against the red glow of sunset. We used to ride slowly as we followed the shore; the plaintive cry of the unmolested sea lions emphasized the desolation of the loneliest of all oceans—the Pacific, and silenced our talk by the sadness of its unutterable beauty. At that time, going to and from the Far East, one could be at least a month without sight of sail or steamship.

We made excursions to crumbling and as yet unrestored Spanish Missions, or stood in wonder, looking through the green heights of the red-barked giant sequoias. I can read without emotion that thousands have been swallowed in a Chinese flood, but the felling of one of those great trees, whose rings register centuries of summers and winters, fills me with hot indignation. The lumbermen who then laid axe at the root of those giants, were men of little imagination, and full of greed for the lumber to build houses for small men. We turned our backs upon California with regret.

The social affiliations of Colorado Springs were with Boston, Philadelphia and New York. The Middle West said little to us.

Young Herbert Timmins flashed into Colorado Springs. He was a nephew of Mr. and Mrs. Martin Brimmer, of Boston. He bought and financed a pack of English hounds, huntsmen and stud grooms, and was followed by a field of those who wore Busvine habits, English boots, Tautz English breeches, and who scorned aught but the best made of English saddles. So the unaristocratic coyote was hunted in the aristocratic garb of England.

Timmins's mother was an Italian Countess and his father one

of those cultivated sons of New England who went to Europe in the spirit of Heine's verses—"The pine who sighed for the palm."

As Master of Hounds, Herbert Timmins looked as Italian as Rome. He no doubt quickly emptied his purse, and our following the hounds ended, but it was fun as long as it lasted. He liked a good dinner and fine wine and a woman. He was a born lover; courting was the chief of his diet.

He married the daughter of the historian Prescott, whose "Conquest of Mexico" fired our imagination. She was a handsome girl. Her sister Edith, wife of Roger Wolcott, former Governor of Massachusetts, today stands as she did then, as the standard of great ladyhood. Mrs. Wolcott said of Mrs. Timmins, that she could do without the necessities of life, if she could be surrounded with its elegancies,—an opinion which was borne out when the bride arrived with gorgeous presents of art and silver. With her own hands she kept shining, in the little cottage on the edge of the town, enough plate to furnish Westminster Palace.

The visit to her of Herbert Timmins's sister, Minna, began for me a glorious friendship. She once said that those of mixed race needed much charity. As I reached the Timmins cottage I saw a long necklace of clouded amber beads hanging on a cottonwood tree, where, she remarked, they were "taking a sun bath."

Some friendships are like conversion—instantaneous. Such was ours. Tall, dark, with the face of a benign lion or sybil, her every movement free and untrammeled,—she was a true child of the South. She and her sister, Gemma, and two brothers, had been brought to Beacon Street and Pride's Crossing on the death of their mother, to make their home with Mr. and Mrs. Brimmer.

Of Mr. Brimmer remains the tradition of one of Massachusetts' greatest and most luminous citizens,—a cosmopolitan, a traveler and a patron of the arts.

The two girls were eager for learning and were loved in their new home and developed fine intellects. They were welcome guests in New York and Philadelphia.

Quaritch sent out his catalogue of fine books, in which was listed a costly, rare copy of "Calderon." After much consideration, they ordered it by letter as a birthday gift for Mr. Brimmer. Going to pass the night with Mrs. Jack Gardiner, they found the book in their room, under the light of a reading lamp. Mrs. Gardiner had purchased it by cable.

In our visits to Boston we found at delightful dinners, Judge Holmes, until recently Justice of the Supreme Court, gifted Percival Lowell, and Mrs. Whitman, whose portrait of Mr. Brimmer is prized by the Boston Museum. Lowell's fascinating book inspired Lafcadio Hearn to go to Japan.

On the walls of the Brimmer house were fine paintings. "The Turkey Tenders," by Jean François Millet, was valued at twenty-five thousand dollars. It was purchased by Martin Brimmer when, as a young man, he and William Hunt, the painter, were in Barbizon. Being told by Hunt that Jean François Millet was in destitution and on the border of starvation, Martin Brimmer sent him two hundred and fifty dollars, and received "The Turkey Tenders." The painter was so overjoyed with more money than he had ever possessed before that he burst into tears.

In that inner circle of Boston, Cabot Lodge was always a political suspect. They thought they believed in statesmen, not politicians, and were hypercritical, not realizing that a successful politician after death becomes, in the public eye, a statesman.

The business circles of London and the Continent as well as

the United States of America, financed the mining and survey growth of the West. We spent months of each winter in New York, where the best legal talent was retained, in the interest of the Denver and Rio Grande Railroad.

Many a dinner was enlivened by the two great wits of the American Bar—Joseph Choate and Charles Beaman. Charles Beaman, who became a familiar friend, had as wife the daughter of Senator Evarts.

One spring, when Mr. Bass was tired, and the work of the winter, in which he was assisted by Edward O. Wolcott, the Assistant Counsel of the Railway, made them both long for sunshine, it was decided to go to Havana. Today, when the luxurious see the gayety of Cuba, the picture of our hasty trip is an anti-climax.

We went aboard a steamer that rounded, without killing me, the home of the four winds of Heaven, Cape Hatteras, but that stormy point past, we realized there were tranquil southern waters, and flying-fish that soared over the ship's rail to die on the deck.

The evening before we were to land at Havana, the sea was oily and smooth as glass. All passengers were at table except a seasick man on deck, and my belated self, who was combing my hair in a stateroom which opened on the dining-cabin. As I stood near to the port-hole something shot past, and a shriek sent me to the dining-room crying "Man overboard!" Captain and everyone were quickly on deck. The seasick passenger was throwing deck-chairs over the rail. Under a blood-red sky the steamer turned about. A Quartermaster who had been an Able Seaman for twenty-one years, had fallen as he worked at adjusting the gangway stairs for the landing the next morning. He wore heavy boots and had never learned to swim. Until darkness fell, the ship slowly moved over the face of the waters, and then, to the waiting crowd, an officer said, "A shark got him."

I, who hate the sea and am almost seasick at the sight of water in a hand-basin, had the conviction that if, on that evening, a man could not be saved, I would as well say with Swinburne, "The salt entombing sea," for a stout swimmer had poor chance for his life in that sea. It was a horror-struck beginning for a jolly vacation.

There is nothing more picturesque than the entrance to Havana Harbor with Moro Castle darkly outlined at dawn or in the warm color of a sunset sky.

After the Spanish War, General Wood set order and cleanliness in that sink of Cuban dirt, where the streets were filled with all sorts of débris and refuse.

Nasty little boys were making indecent gestures as they played, trying to attract our attention. On our visit to the tobacco manufacturers to order large special cigars, wearing gold bands with the owners' monograms, these urchins, back of the manager we followed, made filthy, suggestive signs. I have spent a year in the Far East without ever meeting with lascivious behavior. Perhaps the mixture of negro, Spanish and indigenous Cuban is a poisonous amalgamate.

At the hotel, in prostrating heat, our nights were passed on canvas cot-beds, with a sheet to cover our sweat-drenched bodies.

The magnificent Government buildings and the residences of the wealthy planters and tobacco manufacturers were the setting for an elegant Europeanized gay society. The pure-blooded Spaniard was the cream of society and outranked the Cuban. We were invited to luncheon in a magnificent private residence.

After a delicious repast we adjourned to a marble room with a plashing fountain in the center. Along the length of the room were ranged two rows, facing each other, of bent-wood rocking- and straight-backed chairs, between which were ranged in rectitude, china cuspidors. One was expected to smoke and converse. Conversation in broken English is as pleasant to me as eating from broken china, and I was relieved to get back to the novel sights which one saw from beneath the arcades of the hotel.

An alarm of fire sounded, and the hose brigade, as they pulled their cart, lighted cigarettes as they ran. With the regal carriage which carrying burdens on the head can give, a gigantic, white-clad negress strolled, as the Empress of the world's black empires should walk, her bandana handkerchief-covered head bearing a colorful basket of fruit. She puffed an enormous black cigar and hastened to the conflagration.

We drank glasses of the most delectable of beverages made of the juice of ripe pineapples, and ate with relish the tiny yellow bananas which melted in our mouths.

We decided to make a journey to the Valley of the Eumerie, renowned for beauty, where miles of famous caves bristled with stalagmites and stalactites.

At the station we entered a *volante,* a huge vehicle like a *calêche,* moving on two gigantic wheels, the horses guided by mounted postilions. There are still extant pictures of fine ladies wearing Spanish veils and carrying fans in these elegant chariots which negotiated the rough highways. As I bowed to the populace, I felt nothing less than a descendant of Ferdinand and Isabella, and saluted with reverence one of the earth's beauty spots.

At the entrance to the caves, Mr. Bass said, "Fanny, is not a cave a hole in the ground?"

I said, "Yes."

"Well, that's what I have been fighting against for years. I will stay above ground."

It takes courage to joke grimly under the sword of Damocles.

A tall, fat woman from Brooklyn, clinging to the protecting arm of a thin wishbone of a husband, was ahead of us. In the steaming hot gloom of that subterranean chamber she suddenly exclaimed, "Oh, my! if I had only known what this was, I would have worn my dressing-sack instead of ruining my new dress."

Mr. Wolcott was of boundless energy and always got what he wanted when he wanted it, and being told that every cabin was engaged on the return steamer from Havana to Key West, he succeeded in commandeering the cabins of three officers. I heard our fat lady from Brooklyn say to her little husband, "How I hate that man! You might know he would own the whole steamer."

The Caribbean was calm and, though ungodly, we uttered the prayer that the flat-bottomed steamer might not be overturned by storm, or wrecked on one of the myriads of coral reefs. Sitting on deck in the bright light of a waning moon, we watched the jaunty Captain as he promenaded the deck with the well-rounded wife of an absent Connecticut Member of Congress on his arm. She was of the age which the French call critical and dangerous. In the caressing voice of a Southern man, he said, "That was the winter I was waiting on Miss Blake of Mobile." Suddenly a smutty-faced coal-heaver stuck his head out of the hatch and said, "Captain, the Engineer wants to know who the Hell is steering this boat, and where." The budding romance got a foul blow below the belt, and we safely came, in the beauty of the lifting of the pearly mists of dawn, to the quays of Key West, and all fears of shipwreck vanished, but we noted a mass of sunken craft and stacks of steamers pricking the surface of the Bay, where ill-fated ships had been wrecked.

Key West was largely populated by the makers of Havana cigars. I think I smuggled in a few boxes of delicious guava paste.

Off we went to Charleston for a drive along the sea and under the sad waving moss on the live-oaks.

A brief stop in Washington enabled us to pay our respects to Mr. and Mrs. James G. Blaine, the meeting with whom was always a stimulating pleasure. But in recalling the charm of the plumed knight one must never forget his devoted wife, an original, notable individual, broad of sympathy, with no belief in consistency; for with all her humor, she was never able to appreciate fully the remark Winthrop Chanler made to me when I repeated it to her. "She is a great woman who could have been in a Turkish harem for thirty years without changing a hair."

CHAPTER ELEVEN

NEW YORK IN THE 'EIGHTIES

FOR a quarter of a century, Colorado Springs was my home. The harmonious colors of the record of experience were woven woof and web, as by a swiftly flying shuttle. North, south, east and west, risking the torment of sailing many seas, enjoying enlightening contacts in cities ancient and modern, we always returned joyfully to our Colorado home.

It is a revelation to those who pass beyond the rim of static and conventionally ordered Eastern towns, to face the simplicity of life in the early days of the West.

Many stricken people made death familiar; but death has less horror without expenditure of wealth and the successful rapacity of undertakers. There was a natural acceptance of the inevitable, without discussion, feeling that king, beggar or dog, with life extinct, were one and the same, and should without delay seek quick combustion in the earth.

One year I spent twenty-eight nights between East and West on Pullman sleepers. We went back gladly to the romance and ease of Colorado, where the dome of heaven seemed higher and the stars brighter.

The months in New York were stimulating. What lovely young women made me welcome! Florence Lockwood, now Mrs. Grant La Farge, had just returned from London, where she had been the intimate friend of the much talked of "Circle of Souls." In her children are united the artistic strain of John La

Farge with her own omnivorous mind. Christopher La Farge, the anthropologist, who wrote "Laughing Boy" and "Sparks Fly Upward," is her son, and his twin brother is the beloved architect, artist and actor who vivifies the Comedy Club.

Through Florence Lockwood I was invited to lunch with Helen Benedict, the wittiest of bright-haired girls, who was then as plump as a partridge. It was before Poiret, the French dressmaker, resolved to dress the *petit baton*. The crusade had not begun that made it a crime for a woman to have rounded curves or well-padded bodies. The heroines of the novels of that time glided into the room, not striding like a prize fighter exercising on the track.

Every new book was sent to Helen Benedict by the publishers. She was a musician of head and hand, the sympathetic friend of artists and writers, a perfect horsewoman, whether in the saddle or driving a four-in-hand down the Champs Elysées or through Central Park. She was socially at ease abroad and at home. John Alexander's painting of her is his best portrait. She carried a kindling torch wherever she moved, with her inexhaustible, inherited brilliancy. She bred the tiniest of Pekinese dogs, and owned perfectly trained hunters. She was the delight of her father, Commodore Benedict, the explorer of the Amazon. He was the friend of President Cleveland, and the host of the leading men of his time. It is a loss to the historical records of our time that his memoirs of early Connecticut, and the excitement of Black Friday, are not in their annals. In speech his English was perfect, and in his tribute to Stanford White, who never failed in kindly words and acts, he said, "He was a first nighter, an every nighter, and an all nighter."

The loyal friendship of Helen Benedict, later the wife of Thomas Hastings, has been one of my life's richest assets.

The fermenting group I came to know included beloved and able Charles F. McKim; Stanford White; Mead, whose dream, now realized, was the American Academy crowning one of the Seven Hills of Rome; St. Gaudens; Richard Gilder; John La Farge, painter, with a mind as iridescent as the gleams on the throat of a mandarin duck; and Whitney Warren, a duality of Bohemian and aristocrat, who stood out in charm in any gathering, dressed to suit his emotions and his personal taste.

Now, with the roar of streets, one rarely stops to pay tribute to St. Gaudens as we pass Farragut's statue, or the most perfect building in the city, the private library of the late Pierpont Morgan, built by McKim in the manner of the ancients, without mortar, and of faultless proportion; but the memory of McKim and Stanford White is dear to those who knew them. No more do we see the uplifting in beauty of the tower of Madison Square Garden, the inspiration from the Giralda Tower in Seville, designed by Stanford White, where the graceful gold statue by St. Gaudens carried our eyes to the heavens, which we so rarely see from the streets of New York.

Later, I went one day in Paris, to the Salon with St. Gaudens to see the plaster model of his statue of Sherman. I asked him if the model was not placed too low. "Not for me," said the sculptor. "All my life has been spent in looking at the bellies of equestrian statues. I would like the face of the statue to be seen."

My friendship with St. Gaudens gave me the privilege of long talks with him in his studio, where more than one horse died of boredom as he modeled the statue of Sherman, led by Victory, in the Square of the Plaza.

His statue, made in honor of the wife of Henry Adams, gave him renown and created much discussion. I think Mr. Adams asked him to express Nirvana, and St. Gaudens asked me to give my conception of that future state. As the doctrine of Buddha and a future life has always seemed to me the only one that did justice to mankind and gave every man his chance, I had quite a distinct idea of Nirvana.

Whether or no sinning and repenting and struggling onward, one surmounted the spirals of many planets until one was purged of all dross; the belief that at the end one could be absorbed into the harmony of all comprehension seemed to me a far greater end to aspire to than a heaven where one retained personal individuality. St. Gaudens contended that my idea was all too Western, but the Far East and the Near East have taught me it was not half enough Eastern.

The night after the unveiling of St. Gaudens' statue of Farragut, the base of which was designed by Stanford White, I went to that charming house of the Richard Gilders', in Fifteenth Street, in a reconstructed stable, to the party given in honor of the occasion. Helen Hunt and John La Farge were guests. There was also Maria Potter, who later became the wife of Kennedy Tod (all the young men of New York seemed chained to her chariot wheels—and I did not wonder); she looked as though she had stepped from a painting by Gainsborough, a picture hat on her soft hair, a lace fichu held by a rose at her breast, and wearing long suede gloves. She attracted by her wit as by her beauty.

My friendship with John La Farge began that night, and afterwards I ordered glass which should be a heritage to my descendants. Whether I talked with him by a cast-iron overheated stove in the bare studio, or in the comfort of a luxurious boudoir, I felt I had spent an hour with a master. When I returned from the studio, a friend said on meeting me, that my hat was askew and there was a new glint in my eye;—such is inspiration.

In the reading class which met at Etta Dunham's, was Elizabeth Chanler, who, after the death of John Jay Chapman's first wife, Minna Timmins, married him. Rearing his children, she was both artist and saint. Her portrait by John Sargent has eyes which haunt one's memory. James Dunham's large household was presided over by his daughter Etta, who was a distinguished hostess, and acted as mother to her sisters. In her library Royce of Cambridge came to enlighten us as to Kant's philosophy. Of his revelations I understood little at the time, and remember little now, save that I hung on his words of wisdom.

One evening stands out, when Etta Dunham asked a French explorer and his wife to dine and give a conference. They were fresh from work in the jungles of Yucatan, uncovering Mayan temples. For the occasion he had borrowed from the Ambassador to the United States from Brazil, a replica in color of one of the seven extant books of Mayan ritual, the paintings undestroyed by the ferocious bigotry of Spanish priests. He showed us a pamphlet of cryptic hieroglyphics by Maspero, giving the three sets of characters used in Egypt by the royal, priestly and warrior class and the lower classes. He believed that the mysterious shepherd kings who created the Egyptian hieroglyphics, and who ruled Egypt, were the race which developed the high civilization and built the temples in Central America. From the Mayan record he fluently translated by use of the Egyptian characters, the loss of the romantic continent of Atlantis.

Years after, when Cardinal Merry del Val introduced me to the German head of the Vatican Library, I saw and held in my hand, the original small volume of the Mayan Book of Ritual. A reproduction of it is under glass in one of the ante-rooms.

The covers of the book are of olive wood, mounted in silver, and embellished with uncut semi-precious stones. It was kept in a safe —never shown even to great personages or ambassadorial representatives. The learned German curator of the Vatican Library totally repudiated the theories of the French explorer, but I have heard of late that the Frenchman's theories have again been considered.

One amusing recollection of that period was dining at the table of one of New York's leading lawyers, of old time New York tradition. At the board sat plutocratic, rooted social conservatism. William H. Vanderbilt had recently moved from his house on the corner of Fortieth Street and Fifth Avenue, to occupy the house built for him of brown stone in a box-like style, designed for him by the Herter brothers. Now, when the name of Vanderbilt in the eyes of Europe spells rank almost royal, the conversation of these dyed-in-the-wool Presbyterians, whether they should or should not call on Mrs. William H. Vanderbilt, is laughable. One woman remarked: "Mrs. Vanderbilt is a fine woman, and she tries to bring up her sons well." The atmosphere betrayed that curiosity and respect for wealth would make for visitors to the new mansion on Fifth Avenue.

All questions of social privilege broke when Mrs. Cornelius Vanderbilt issued invitations for an entertainment in her new Henry IV palace on the corner of Fifty-eighth Street. The greatest artists of the Metropolitan Opera House were to sing. The critical snobs fell over one another to secure a card of invitation, but Mrs. Vanderbilt asked no one not already of her own friendly circle.

The Vanderbilts must have had prepotent forefathers. Among Commodore Vanderbilt's descendants there have been men of ability, character, and originality. We sometimes forget that the same soil can produce the pure annunciation lily and the deadly nightshade and riotous weeds as well. There has never been any mystery about the Vanderbilt men. Some were bold and some were shy, but the press and the chatter of society have put them in the glare of publicity. Of George Vanderbilt, no American artist of his time but found in him a patron and an aid in climbing to achievement. Of the women, New York recognizes no better strain. I believe they all play untouchable bridge, which means clear thinking. The energy and talent of Gertrude Vanderbilt Whitney, her generosity to every struggling artist, and her gifts to New York and to Europe, would alone make her a monument, but she has, as well, put her dreams of beauty into marble. Miss Ruth Twombly was, for years, the financial brain of the Colony Club, and could command the high salary of a professional in any important banking house. Gracious Mrs. Jay Burden is now President of the Colony Club, beloved and admired, and rejoices in talented children. The energy of the Vanderbilts has made women of boundless philanthropy, filled, as they have been, with the desire to make their city and the world better than they have found it.

The winter that John Sargent painted Mrs. Twombly and Edwin Booth, he asked me to his studio to see the paintings. As I looked at Booth's portrait, which now hangs in The Players Club, I said, "Why! You painted all his past dissipation in that face." He replied, "I didn't know he was ever dissipated. I only painted what I saw."

There were a few elegant cosmopolites moving easily in New York society. Egerton Winthrop, of the direct line of the first Royal Governor of Massachusetts, maintained a dignity and elegance of surroundings which made him a social leader. Far in advance of his time, he brought to his house in Thirty-third Street tapestries, rare furniture of the eighteenth century, and *objets d'art*. The painting of him by Sargent reveals the man who paid tribute to the conventions of a well-ordered world. His son Bronson, today one of the ablest of our lawyers, carries on the tradition of his race. His only daughter died while I was in London, leaving her newborn daughter, who is now Mrs. Robert L. Fowler, Jr. Her father, Harry Cram, had been a friendly intimate at Edgeplain in Colorado.

Frank Gray Griswold is still living, the last, I think, of that American strain,—cosmopolite, great gentleman and man of fashion. As I first recall him, tall, lean as a coursing hound, at home in London, Paris, Rome or Vienna, squire of dames, master of hounds, sportsman, yachtsman, man of letters, he made me say that a débutante or a woman of three score years stored a happy memory when she sat next him at dinner. An English belle of the diplomatic corps attracted his attention, and one of her friends remarked to her at the races, "You had better tie a knot in your handkerchief to recall that you have a husband in London." His reputation was that he could turn a sweetheart into a lifelong friend.

In this hasty moment when one can raise an umbrella and stop a taxi, 15c—5c, and is welcome at a church wedding in sports shoes and a tweed suit, the rule of hurry and utility is with us. A horse and milk wagon or rubbish cart may clatter to the door, and those poor red-faced coachmen who stand outside the door of the Plaza Hotel seem poor understudies for the time when a thoroughbred hackney sped around the Park; and now, driving in a broken-down victoria as it toils around Central Park, one vainly strives to summon the romance of a vanished past.

There never has been a great house in New York such as those of the political hostesses in England and of the titled literary salons of Paris. The national capital has furnished only sporadically diplomats and officials of the national government to New York society. We used to wish that Florence Lockwood might marry a multi-millionaire and establish what would be a great house.

Mrs. Astor's balls included pedigree and fashion, but were cramped in scope. Easy and friendly relations of small coteries are, at present, almost impossible.

Perhaps no one, at that time, had a larger influence than Charles A. Dana. He had produced the best newspaper ever edited in America. He and Mrs. Dana had been members of Brook Farm. It may be that deep-dyed cynicism is born of the lost illusions of an idealist. I have always believed that Charles Dana was an idealist. A high-spirited, cultivated, unusual man, he spoke, read and wrote twelve languages, and he acquired Russian after he was seventy years of age. To hear him read verse or prose was an unqualified delight.

He bought the island Dosoris, off Manhattan. No tree or plant so rare, which could survive our latitude, but grew on that estate. He was as great an authority on coniferæ as was Professor Sargent, of Boston, of Arboretum fame. He was one of the first collectors of Chinese porcelain. His Sunday mornings were spent in dusting and arranging his treasures, and his grandchildren called them "grandfather's playthings." I was fortunate enough to have him more than once show me his rare possessions. On the bare walls of a neutral-tinted room hung the painting of Courbet's "Wave," and the vitrines were tastefully arranged with porcelains. He once took out an apple-green vase, around which was a stout scarlet silken cord, and he said to me, "This was once owned by a powerful Mandarin. The Emperor coveted it and he sent to the possessor the stout scarlet cord, which was a polite command that the owner hang himself, which he did at once, and so His Imperial Majesty received the apple-green vase and the scarlet cord with the assurance of the owner's death." But no man has been able sanely to endure or survive absolute power. Perhaps that Emperor went mad.

Of Charles A. Dana, a brilliant writer has said, "He was the fiercest journalist of all time, and he could go nowhere without meeting people he had scalded." He had bitter enemies everywhere, dating back to the War, when Stanton sent him to investigate the conduct of commanding officers and report on them. He was the kindest of husbands and fathers and a loyal friend, but I imagine he shunned people rather than being shunned by them.

Among his descendants are those of creative artistic ability. His youngest daughter Eunice, with a trenchant wit, has the spirit of a reformer, and in her fight for Women's Suffrage, through storm or shine, would face prison and speak eloquently from soap-boxes, but she has never converted me to the belief that I should be happy in a hag-ridden world.

His daughter Ruth, who married Dr. William Draper, our family physician, produced among her large family of children, three of artistic drive. Ruth Draper, the most original diseuse or monologist of her time, creating the characters which she represents, occupies an unique position in the professional world. The late Paul Draper, lovable of nature, and a singer, opened many portals of beauty to me, and the world was a colder place when he died. Dr. George Draper is well-known for his scientific investigation and original methods of approaching nervous diseases.

Mrs. Schuyler Van Rensselaer was New York's leading intellectual hostess. Interested in young writers, she was the friend of all eminent people. She often said to me that Arthur Brisbane had a quicker and more interesting mind than that of any young man she had known. In 1888 he was London correspondent for the New York *Sun*. He returned to the United States, and, if I remember correctly, was not yet twenty-one years of age. His family was prominent in Western New York and Buffalo. His father, Albert Brisbane, left his homestead in Batavia as a young man. He commanded the flawless admiration of his son, Arthur Brisbane. Standing on the bridge over the tiny stream which ran near his house carried his thought to the sea, toward which the water rushed. He pondered on the contradictions of belief and civilization. He felt he could get more information about God and the status of woman in the world if he went to the Far East. He packed his bag and departed at once to board an outward bound steamer for Europe. A man of great learning, he became a leading Fourierite. He was an intimate friend of Humboldt's, and the door of every great and important house in all countries was open to him.

The Arthur Brisbane of today is strongly influenced by his adventurous father. I have always thought that a monument should be erected to Albert Brisbane for his notable success in domestic science. At one period of his life, he had four living wives who loved him, though divorced, and neither to him nor one another, indulged in rancor or recrimination. Cordial relations were enjoyed by all.

His cousin in Buffalo once asked him why he ceased to love his first wife, a beautiful Italian. "Oh, she loved me too much. She was a Catholic and would fret at a civil marriage only, and I thought she was better in her own land enjoying the pleasant offices of her religion and the inheritance of her large fortune."

Is it because memory gilds facts that the 'seventies and 'eighties in New York seemed to have more social brilliance and friendliness than today?

The Sherwood Studios were a bee-hive of artists, a real fraternity, painting hard and spending little. Mr. Bass's portrait by William Rice was notable. The one of me, to my eyes, had a face suggestive of a Semitic mule. I felt he must be a great artist as he sometimes forgot to put on his shoes, and at times wore a slipper or a slipper and a shoe. I was restive and bored at having to be painted, and not even his flattery that I had beautiful arms could reconcile me. Many were green with envy who were not included among the privileged few in the party at which Stanford White introduced Carmencita, at Carroll Beckwith's studio. After the theater, an exclusive crowd was seated on the floor in tense expectancy. At last the tardy dancer, who had lingered after the theater to put on glad attire, stood in the doorway, framed like an orange flame, while artists, more skillful with modeling clay or use of paint brush, strummed bravely the dances of Spain on manifold guitars. As she entered the room, so Sargent painted her in the portrait bought by the Luxembourg.

As for the Horse Show, nothing but being laid low with smallpox could have kept a woman home during that jolly week. It was a woman show as well as a horse show. Stanford White had made a fitting background for the amusement of crowds.

When Seidl raised his baton at the Metropolitan, he accompanied great singers. Who will ever forget Calvé dancing in the court of the smugglers? She made the world long for youth and sin. The De Reszkes, Plançon, Melba, Lilli Lehmann, Ternina, Schumann-Heink, were interpreters of Wagner and Verdi to lift one's soul on waves of song.

After a perfect performance of "Faust," as the curtain fell, Mrs. Calvin Bryce turned enthusiastically to me, saying, "There may be better music in heaven but I doubt it."

And what of, at an early date, the color of Rubinstein, though at times he hit a wrong note? Paderewski, on his first visit, his golden aureole of hair making him a reincarnation of the Hindu Sun-god? Women who did not know even the difference between a major and a minor scale, crowded to the front of the stage at the end of a concert to worship him. Mrs. Draper, née Ruth Dana, gave him loyal support and artistic appreciation, and his friendship for her children lasts until this day. He was nearly killed with kindness and hospitality.

Neither Mrs. John G. Milburn nor I was really musical, but through curiosity and an impulse to honor the greatest of musical interpreters and to find in him a creative composer, we girded up our loins and left Buffalo for New York. We had taken seats on the left hand side of the front row of the orchestra circle for the first production of Paderewski's opera, "Manru." We commanded a view of two-thirds of the boxes in the Diamond Horseshoe. Until the curtain was raised on the Second Act, all first tier boxes were empty save the one in which Paderewski sat with his friends, and that occupied by Mrs. Taylor, née Josephine Johnson.

One cannot, with impunity, get between a dog and his bone, or disturb the feeding-time of those who, at that period, found music an aid to conversation. Sympathy alone tells me that the dregs of humiliation and bitterness were that night in the heart of a brilliant and pampered artist. The orchestra and galleries were filled with an expectant and respectful crowd. Of the opera I recall nothing, though I believe that an audience under like conditions in any Italian opera house would have hissed the late-comers, and as for Germany, it would have been worth a man's life not to have given the opera silent attention and respect. One of the boxholders of the Metropolitan once said to me, with self-satisfaction, "I have never heard the overture of any opera, nor seen the first act of 'La Boheme.'"

The prestige of the First Night of the Metropolitan season of those days is only a tradition. Perhaps the tiaras and diamond necklaces may be in safe deposits. The long locks of old women and young are shorn. No longer a hairdresser creates individual coiffures that could hold the glitter of a diamond round crown which, by right, was worn by royalty, and as a Bond Street jeweler said to me, "I only make them now on order for American ladies."

Down the years, in imagination, comes the echo of voices of all the greatest singers of the nineteenth century, and the auditorium where we heard them, in the march of democracy, may go to the Radio Center.

The vanishing dream of fair women holds the vision of Mrs. Jack Astor, born lovely Ava Willing, who held the palm for distinction and compelling charm, and she seems to wave a graceful adieu.

I still smile when I recall Schumann-Heink's saying to me that she had sung at the Metropolitan in the rôle of "Brunhilde" the night before the birth of one of her sons. As I raised my eyebrows she said, "Oh! but I carried a shield," but I could not picture her scudding through a stormy sky with her sisters, giving the cry of a Valkyr, as she bore a hero to Valhalla.

In those days, it was whispered, there were a few women who enameled their faces and dared not laugh for fear of cracking their beauty. Millions now are spent yearly on cosmetics, and uplift is not a matter of morals but of the muscles of middle-aged women's sagging faces.

The anciently recognized sign of the harlot did not then flame on the mouths of virginal débutantes. I have some sympathy with the dying roisterer and philanderer who, a few years back, said to his neglected wife a few hours before his death, "There is one comfort. I shall never again have to taste lip-stick."

Lily Langtry was much in evidence at race meetings, arriving in the smartest of broughams, drawn by the finest bred horses. The red heels of her patent leather shoes accentuated the simplicity of her perfect attire and a face free from paint.

A matriarchal head of a powerful clan, in a stately house on the Hudson, smoked a large black cigar in the mode of ill-fated Empress Elizabeth of Austria. Then one often saw Baroness Rothschild in Paris, walking in her riding-habit after a canter in the Bois, crop in hand and a large cigar in her mouth. Why carp? Did not our admired scholar and poet, Amy Lowell, puff the largest of fragrant Havanas after dinner, as she edified her guests with original talk?

Few ladies then smoked cigarettes. The world moves fast. I hope nursing babies may not be weaned on Lucky Strikes and Old Gold cigarettes in the near future, as their young mothers puff in unison. I hold the faith that no charming hostess should encourage smoking cigarettes between courses at dinner. It is no compliment to the flavor and perfection of her cuisine.

Most of loose living comes after midnight. Possibly the days of our delightful girls and boys might be more efficient had they not the urge for the wee small hours in Night Clubs, where picturesque vice rubs shoulders with virtue.

I am no reformer and do not cry, like Billy Sunday, who dramatized his hatred of sin by throwing himself on his abdomen and spitting into Hell. New York is not, and never was Hell. It revels in being the great modern world. The elegance of Canfield's exclusive gambling house, his courtly manner, and his collection of art, strike a different note from the adventurous dens that were frequented by Rothstein and his gang.

New York is noisy and full of poisonous gas from automobiles, and it's "catch as catch can" to cross the streets, but we can pause and remember, were we standing in a ten-acre field twenty miles from a railway, the short and long waves of the radio would still be passing through our bodies and carrying a lilt of Jazz and the wisdom and folly of the spoken word of man.

Our conventions have changed. The Diamond Horseshoe does not follow the standard of those *qui se tiennent sur leurs derrières*. European royal circles, where the family escutcheons of the women held many quarterings, filled them with a desire to be seen as well as to see, holding themselves as great ladies.

It is not so very long ago since an old leader of inner circles invited the wife of one of our Presidents to a Gala at the Metropolitan. Afterwards she said to me, "Why, my dear, she doesn't know how to sit in a box! She lolls on her spine." But for some of us, New York is a chronic cheerful disease. Criticize it we may. Love it we must.

A sad-to-see change has today paled Newport. It remains solid, beautiful, in setting and climate, occupied by people of elegance; but modern youth has found other shores on which to sport. For years Newport was the aristocratic playground of America,—the high note of social aspiration. Someone has said it was a town of palaces and paddocks. While the leisure class of New York predominated, Newport's inner circle was recruited from Boston, Philadelphia, Baltimore and Rhode Island.

The diplomatic world sought to establish there the summer Legations and Embassies, to escape the torrid heat of Washington. The children of the ultra-rich of the Far West turned their faces eastward towards Newport as the followers of Mahomet turn theirs eastward towards Mecca.

There was a good residential society of retired Army and Navy Officers. It was the "happy hunting ground" for foreigners in quest of young and pretty heiresses,—a paraphrasing of the cry in the tale of Aladdin's lamp, "old titles for new gold." A friend once said to me, "The girls at Narragansett are as pretty and well-turned-out as ours at Newport, but there is a difference in the men." Possibly she had in mind the appearance, beauty of grace and wide-world polish of Winthrop Rutherford; but his standard is never produced by the dozen.

In that period, though men and women were possibly no more moral than they are at present, they wore more clothes both in the water and when visiting on the beach.

Astors, Belmonts, Wetmores, Vanderbilts, who lived in palaces called cottages, spared neither ingenuity nor money to give superb entertainments. The gardens at Newport are still peerless, and at this moment, there is a strong movement to make the social pursuits more interesting. Theatrical performances and the entertainment of the gifted people of the stage are included in their pleasures, but the nouveau riche and would-be snob without Newport's gates no longer fiercely struggle to break into the charmed circle.

With the death of Freddie Gebhard and the departure of Berry Wall from New York and Newport, disappeared the last dandies of the turf.

Going back to Edgeplain, from where we could see the College buildings, due in large part to the generosity of General W. J. Palmer, who had given beautiful parks and money, time and thought for the advancement of learning, we realized that General Palmer purchased the bare plain where Colorado Springs stands, laid out the town, the irrigation system and planted trees everywhere.

He rode every day one of the two spirited horses used by him in the last year of the Civil War. They were old in point of years and fairly unmanageable in spirit. General Palmer was thrown as his horse stepped into a prairie dog hole, breaking his leg. The horse was put out of his misery by a shot, but General Palmer was never again able to move. He who had spent his life in acquiring rights of way for railways, inveighed against the unlicensed freedom of motors which could go where they would without let or hindrance. But in those terrible years when he faced pain and inaction, his only excitement was to lie prone in a motor driven at breakneck speed.

He was a friend whose loyalty knew no turning, and in the debacle following the death of Mr. Bass, he took charge of my boy's education and the sale of Edgeplain.

Later it was bought by Alan Arthur, son of President Arthur. There I, who had figuratively been born in Buffalo on a paving stone, had planted a garden, hedges of mock orange trees and box elders and the cottonwoods whose reputation was that the earliest spring could never fool them.

CHAPTER TWELVE

CAIRO

IT was hoped that a winter in Egypt might benefit Mr. Bass, and with meticulous care the details of the journey were arranged with Thomas Cook's New York office. After Christmas in 1888, Mr. Bass, my mother, my son eleven years old, who at that time answered to the name of Metcalfe Bass, and a remarkable Scotch woman, Maggie Grant, who had been in my service many years, and accompanied us as maid, embarked in January for England. We then shared the persistent prejudice against the French Line, and debarked at Liverpool in vile weather. We were billed on the quickest transit possible between Havre and Brindisi by the Indian Mail. The crossing on the Channel Steamer left me limp. The luxury of the Pullman sleeper so vaunted in Cook's Travel Bureau was laughable. We had the drawing-room and two sections in the ramshackle earliest brand of Pullman car. The train was packed to discomfort. Then came the plea from the conductor, that the wife of a high officer in the Indian Army, who had been suddenly called to a sick husband, should sleep on the sofa in the drawing-room with Mr. Bass and me. Distasteful as it was, we were human and acceded to the request.

Oh! that awful Italian roadbed! I hung on, tooth and nail, from my upper berth, to save myself from being dashed out to the floor as we swung around curves. Meantime, the English lady tried to beguile us at night with tales of hunting at Melton-Mow-

CAIRO

bray. At that time, sulphonal, a coal-tar product, was used as a sedative to produce sleep. I took it and stumbled exhausted onto the P. and O. steamer at Brindisi, to fall into a berth, in which with difficulty I awakened on arrival at Alexandria.

We set out for Cairo. Before leaving America, Count Pourtalès suggested we would be wise to go to the Hotel de Nil in the heart of old Cairo, adjoining the main artery of native commerce, the Mouski.

The hotel was built about a palm-shaded court with second-story galleries. We were early to bed, but sleep was banished by heart-breaking continuous cries of mournful women's voices, who watched with the dead. They were paid and accomplished mourners, and their cries did not cease until the corpse was borne, at break of day, on the shoulders of men, to the cemetery the following morning. Awakened at sunrise, the sound of the notes of a reed pipe called us from our bed to the balcony, where our eyes were arrested by the motions of a squatting snake-charmer. Having taken two cobras from a stout bag which he turned over to a young assistant, he placed his child of not more than two years of age before him, making the child grasp the snakes behind their heads, and spit into their open mouths. The horror of the exhibition was not lessened when at table that evening, a young English Army Officer, returning from Southern India, told us that for years he had known and seen about Calcutta, a skillful snake-charmer. The poison glands of a cobra are removed, but start almost instantly to grow again. From the bite of a cobra the heart is paralyzed and death is almost instantaneous, but the wretched snake-charmer of Calcutta, of whom he spoke, believing the cobra safe, died in forty-five minutes from the strike of the reptile.

The Government of India at that time had offered ten thousand pounds for a cure for snake-bite, as eighty thousand inhabitants in India died yearly from the bite of poisonous reptiles, as the bulk of the Indians walk bare-footed.

Since the winter of 1888, I have spent months at Shepheard's famous hotel, now not patronized so greatly since all official England made it its headquarters. The tourist now prefers the winter palaces open for a few months near the banks of the Nile.

I recall a Cairo that was a less clean but more Eastern town, camels, beasts of burden at every turn, an occasional Bedouin Shiek, whose clean-cut features bespoke an Arab of long lineage, as did the steed he rode. Hawari horsemen or the turbaned Bedouin were picturesque. Always the smell of roasting coffee and the fumes of the burning camel dung,—the fuel of the desert,—assailed our nostrils. In the dark bazaars the squatting merchants sold cigarettes perfumed with ambergris, vials of attar of roses, and favorite perfumes beloved of women of the harem.

The fez came to Egypt with the Turk, and we paused to watch the beating of the wool to required form, and the dyeing and modeling of that ugly modern head covering. The turban, such as Abraham may have worn, lends dignity.

If one is wise, one is reverent toward all religions, and a traveler can comprehend a little beneath the surface of that compelling faith of El Islam. The pundits in the courts of the vast university at Cairo teach that the world is flat, and it is of record that many students, unable to read or write, have learned to repeat by heart the whole of the Koran, which would take twenty-four hours. The daily prayer of the smallest boy is that the infidels may be cut down with the sword, and their women delivered to the conqueror. But one salutes the monotheistic faith of Mahomet who, like all founders of the ruling religions, launched a simple faith, to be encrusted and corroded with the superstitions of their followers.

The conscientious Mussulman is abstemious, clean of body, serving God with prayer, generous to the poor, diligent, unfailing in answering the call of the muezzin who summons the faithful to prayer, facing Mecca and Medina with fixed rules of prostration in the worship of one God whose Prophet is Mahomet. How welcoming the cleanliness and beauty of the mosques were when we were tired of noise and dirt!

It has occurred to me that in the Koran there must be voiced a terrible punishment for all time for him who takes his own life. Were it not so, I should think all male Mussulmen, by whatever path, would pass the gate of death.

On reaching the gates of Paradise, the stature of the faithful changes to the height of a palm tree sixty feet. He is met by seventy beautiful houris of suitable stature to mate his own. Black and sparkling eyes with long lashes are the seal of their beauty. He is to sit under a tent woven of sapphires, rubies, emeralds, pearls and all precious metals. Three hundred delicious viands are served on three hundred gold dishes by three hundred servitors. It must be Elysium for both gourmand and gourmet, as the last crumb of food is of perfect flavor and satiety is unknown. As the wine of Paradise does not inebriate, the faithful may drink to their hearts' desire, and beget children without limit. If they wish, they can be joined by their wives, but whether the girls they leave behind them, if solicited, grow large enough to gambol on flowering fields with the houris of Paradise, is not stated. Those whose piety is flawless, can at morning, noon and eve, spiritually look on the face of God.

The narrow streets of Cairo were filled with blackly clad fellaheen women who bared their breasts and covered their faces with a strip of black cloth held at the nose by a gold clasp. Women of higher class rode upon donkeys and were guarded by eunuchs and old women. Donkeys were everywhere. Sometimes a mother and child, winding their way through the narrow streets on an ass, recalled the flight into Egypt.

The ewe lamb, eventually to be sacrificed, went to mill and to meeting with the lower class, gayly beribboned and led by children; now and again we saw an English woman seated behind her easel in a colorful slipper bazaar, where her maid tried to repel the curious, and later on, after her return to the hotel, cleanse as best she could her garments from fleas and vermin collected in the dust.

A strict Mussulman turns his eyes from the Christian, but long bartering with Israelitish merchants is enticing, one being served Turkish coffee as one accepts the comfort of squatting on soft cushions in small booths. Forty years ago, in the dim bazaar, one might come across a Persian illuminated manuscript or a superb copy of the Koran. One needs a "poker face" to earn the respect of the Eastern merchant. He may be convinced that the word of a Frank is as good as his bond, but in his heart he despises a purchaser from the West who pays him his price, and he loves the wiles of bargaining and pitting the subtlety of the Eastern mind against the crudity of the West.

One afternoon I went to the Mouski to shop. As we stopped, a handsome white-haired Greek merchant, carrying a heavy gold-headed cane, wearing a carefully-brushed beaver hat and long, shiny broadcloth greatcoat, was jostled accidentally by a heavily over-burdened native. White with wrath, the Greek merchant began beating with his cane the offending carrier. In my indignation, I jumped from the low carriage, and beat the Greek over the head with my umbrella. Before he could conquer his astonishment, Mahomet seized me by the arm and thrust me into the

CAIRO

Victoria, telling the driver to whip up his horses. I only hope that Greek had a black eye and many bruises; but thanks to the discretion of the dragoman, I had no disagreeable settlement to make.

The judgment of the traveler coincides with the wisdom of those who have traded in the Near and Far East and had cause to weigh the characters of Israelite, Greek and Armenian. The opinion is condensed in the saying, "No Israelite can survive where there is a Greek. No Greek can survive where there is an Armenian." The Armenian is detested by every race save his own. I do not wish to smirch all individuals of any race, and certainly, in spite of the brutality of the Greek in Cairo, many a successful merchant has given to his native land noble buildings and museums, but, as far as I have traveled, the underdog never wags his tail for joy.

In 1888 it was not difficult to unearth the rarest of Persian carpets, cabochon rubies, and Damascus weapons. The dignified merchant, in garb of long rich broadcloth and well-placed turban, embroidered waistcoat in delicate colors, or broad sash which the man of the East wears day and night to prevent chill on the liver, makes odious the ugly suit of civilized men. In the native town, we constantly met these finely dressed tradesmen, walking in friendly relation, hand in hand, as children do,—and we were captivated by the washable textiles that made their under-robes.

To the artistic and unprejudiced mind, Cairo spread a rich feast, and though one shrank from the sight of children whose eyes were covered with poisoning flies, street scenes were absorbing. We went thirsty rather than drink water from the well-filled skins of goats, or lemonade from purveyors with brass vessels of graceful form so coveted now by the collectors.

We wondered why all the processions, whether for betrothal,

circumcision, feast, or funeral, were led by six or eight blind men.

The sound of the hautboy, drum and pipe, as well as the chanting of texts from the Koran by boys and women, was a call to interest.

President Cleveland had asked not only diplomatic representatives, but consuls to show us every courtesy. The United States, in Egypt, was represented by a man and his wife from Texas. In that state I think he must have been an able politician. Their name I do not recall. They were not people of the great world, but kind and generous, and had a little daughter who chattered Arabic. They asked us to dinner, and we met there a powerful German banker, financial adviser of the Egyptian government, and other officials from Austria and England. The mind of the Texas lady was surprised by the sight of a lady smoking, as well as by the knowledge of polygamy. Later we were asked to dine with Austrian diplomats of title, to which dinner were also bidden the Consul and his wife. After dinner, the men came to the salon with the ladies and cigarettes were passed to the hostess first. She lighted hers and my mother followed suit, as did I, to the amazement of the virtuous woman of the Southwest. It was a surprise to find that men liked women and enjoyed talking to them. American men may love one woman or more, but they do not like women when they have the superior pleasure of talking to their own sex.

At our Austrian friends', we saw tables and seats made from the stout saddles that Napoleon I furnished to his soldiers so that two could cross the desert on one camel. They were of stout hardwood staves, prettily ornamented with engraved steel and brass. The dragoman of our Austrian friends was instructed to search the stables in Cairo for some of these saddles, which were made into unusual seats and tables, now in the possession of my son.

There we also obtained a *mushabiyeh* screen from the court of a native house. The name comes from the unglazed water bottle which is placed in a niche through which the wind can pass, cooling the water by evaporation. The old beautifully-turned open-work screen enabled the ladies of the harems to watch the life in the courtyard and enjoy the suggestive dances of the Orient, in which their lords and masters reveled, as they smoked their long water pipes, hoping to incite their ladies to warmer love.

Mr. Bass and my son went to see the Khedive, and I and the ladies of our party were bidden to the wedding of an Egyptian Princess. One had to have a larger knowledge than I at that time possessed, not to shrink from the sight of richly attired resplendent dwarfs giving the *danse du ventre,* but they seemed to give joy to the bride and her attendants. The monotonous beat of the drum, played by deft fingers on a parchment drumhead, was as resonant as though beaten by drum-stick. The reiterations of flute-like pipes were to arouse love.

We were shown places as for prominent guests of honor, while the bride, by her bondswomen, was dressed and undressed to exhibit her trousseau. We were served coffee and heavy syrups and delicious Turkish Delight, but the heat and monotony exhausted us, and we were glad to reach the open air.

Sir William Grenfell was Sirdar of Egypt and had a fine old English garden set behind high walls. We were welcomed at dinner and receptions there. His socially gifted wife, a skilled hostess, sister of General Wood, was generally liked. I shall always believe that she died all too soon by making for herself the smallest waist ever possessed by a grown woman.

Sir William Grenfell's graciousness made Cairo a delightful place socially for us, and we enjoyed his friendship for many years.

Cairo was rife with strange true stories to which we listened breathlessly. Back of Shepheard's Hotel a palace surrounded by walls thirty feet high was occupied by a Princess of evil repute. She was believed to have the hunger of a vampire, and many handsome young English soldiers were kidnapped by her people and never seen again.

We saw walking about, and later met, a splendid looking blond doctor by the name of Grant. He had been summoned to that palace as a physician. At times an English doctor, in a case of life and death, went to a pasha's home. Dr. Grant was sent for and left his house in a brougham with two eunuchs on the box and two footmen. He was blindfolded as he entered the brougham. Arriving at the place of his destination, he was hurriedly shown along many passages to the door of the Princess' apartment. He was shrewd enough to have counted his steps and noted the direction of every turn. After being detained three days and nights, he was told he could leave. He was a powerful athlete, and counting his paces as he neared what he thought the exit, he struck his attendants felling blows behind the ears and made his escape.

Another current tale, believed by English officers and residents, was that an Egyptian Prince who had married a Turkish Princess, found himself occupying a position in rank greatly inferior to her own. The rule and etiquette of the East is that no man may court the slave of his mother or his wife. Being asked to eat, one evening, in the apartment of his Turkish wife, a large covered silver dish was passed by a slave of his wife as they squatted on the floor around an octagonal inlaid table. He spoke in admiration of the beauty of the arms of the serving woman, and removing a bracelet from his wife's wrist, he clasped it on the arm of her slave. His wife made a noisy protest, but he felt that all was peaceful when he left. A night or two later, going for a like repast, when another serving woman brought the large silver dish, the cover being raised, there lay the severed arm of the admired attendant of two nights before, wearing the bracelet with which he had encircled it. He told an English General that, because of his wife's position—for the Turk was in power in Cairo—all he could do in punishment was to lock her in the watercloset for two days. Possibly, as Orientals thrive on jealousy and passion, he was flattered by the action of his wife.

I wish my recollection of Sir Wilfrid and Lady Blunt were clearer. Reading his letters recently, I know how great is my loss. The talk one night at dinner at the Sirdar's was of the miraculous permission the Blunts received to penetrate Arabia in the interest of breeding pure-bred Arabian horses. One must belong in the East to realize fully how carefully treasured and guarded is the purity of strain of the Arabian horse. Perhaps we recall that the Sultan of Turkey presented to General Grant a white stallion of royal lineage, called "Leopard." That stallion later I often saw in the stud of August Belmont's daughter, Mrs. Sam Howland, in the Genesee Valley.

How could I have been so stupid in meeting Sir Wilfrid Blunt not to have recalled that my heart had throbbed with romantic emotion in reading his little volume, "The Love Letters of Proteus." Now it seems almost a tragedy that we were not able to accept the invitation of the Blunts for a cruise on their yacht. The one thing on earth I hate is a yacht.

It was possible then for any traveler to go to the services of whirling, howling dervishes. It was before the English closed all dervish activities. After the organized army of the Mad Mullah, all indulgence in religious hysteria was a threat, and these sects had secret cults akin to Masonic mysteries.

On a Friday we went to the cemetery, where the women gathered to make the feast of their dead. The repast is left on the graves for the nourishment of the dead. I suspect the jackals devour it after nightfall.

Our dragoman arranged that we should be asked to the country estate of a plutocratic Arab merchant. In a small kiosk, surrounded by palms, he received us, as all visitors are received, in the *samlik*, removed some distance from the house occupied by the women of the family. As usual, slaves passed coffee and the sickening sweet syrups from which cloying drinks we shrank. After long pauses in difficult conversation, we were taken to the main house where he respectfully introduced us to his old wife, number one. My boy, being young, was permitted to accompany us. There was a statuesque young negress wife, standing with a baby son on her arm; a coffee-colored charming Arab of the same age, with a little child of lighter hue. The younger women seemed deferential to the eldest wife and courteous with one another.

If one has to be shut in a harem, a plurality of wives must militate against stagnation. A spice of love and jealousy might not be unwelcome. Eunuchs are the only purveyors of news from outside the walls. There is always a sprinkling of concubines, and should one of them bear a son, she may be promoted to the honor of wifehood.

Through the influence of the Texan Consul, we were received in a house occupied by the direct descendant of Mahomet, where he is maintained with large revenues in an immense house built seven hundred years ago, lined with Persian tiles of unbelievable beauty. As we entered the great hall, the master knelt on his praying-carpet, prostrate for his noonday worship. Devotions past, he greeted us cordially and put us in the custody of a tall, very black young eunuch, who raised the canvas curtain, covered with brilliant patchwork of texts from the Koran, which marks in Cairo the entrance to the apartments of women.

We found the ladies of the harem of various tints of skin ranging from the glossy fine texture of black negresses to a pale Circassian from the region of the Garden of Eden. They were all shod with light tints of satin slippers, but clad in slovenly calico robes. The Consul's daughter, a clever child, glibly translated in Arabic to the wives and from Arabic into English for us. There seemed a superabundance of babies in the arms of slave nurses.

We were served coffee in large gold cups encrusted with diamonds, rubies and emeralds, and golden sweet dishes richly enameled and decorated with sapphires and pearls. I tried to talk with the Circassian wife, and on saying, "You must some time come to America," she bitterly replied, "How could I, who cannot go to shop in the Mouski without a guard and a eunuch, ever see anything?" All the women joked with the tall black eunuch, slapping him on the back like children at play. They were curious about my attire, lifting my petticoats, examining my underwear, and, feeling my stiff corsets, they inquired what evil I had done that my husband so locked me up. Fountains plashed and the women lolled on luxurious couches, pillows thrown on superb tile floors, to rest on rich rugs, but it was a prison as guarded as Sing Sing.

Beset by beggars and donkey-boys, we had our first view of the Sphinx and Pyramids. I fully intended, in my youth, to climb to the top of the Great Pyramid, as I knew Mrs. Dexter, of Boston, had at the age of seventy-six, but starting to make the ascent of the high steps, being dragged by my hands and boosted from behind by voluble Arabs so disgusted me that I turned back to have my fortune told by a lying Arab in the sand, in which it was prophesied I had better beware of the treachery of a dark woman.

The head of the foreign missionary body, Mr. Lansing, was a personage in Cairo, and came to see us. He had been for thirty years in Cairo, establishing schools and trying to make converts. The natives were avid in desire to learn English and secure a degree from the American head school which would enable them to establish private schools with the encouragement of Missionary Boards, and under the law, to have illumined before their door that they were graduates of the American school.

Being full of legitimate curiosity, I asked Mr. Lansing how many converts to Christianity he had gained in his long service. "One," said he. The history of that proselyte is worthy of record.

Two Moslem boys were able scholars. The elder of the two, proud of his acquirements, had established a private school under the ægis of the American Mission. The younger one remained. He approached Mr. Lansing with the statement that he was determined to join and be baptized into the faith of Christ. The boy, from his earliest childhood, had lived at the Mission. The elder brother, being informed of the facts, came repeatedly with arguments and tears to alter the lad's determination to abandon the Moslem faith. As his endeavors failed, he said he would kill the lad. The Mission had two houses with an alleyway between, but a bridge connecting the two houses on the roofs. Mr. Lansing detected the elder brother skulking about with a rifle, trying to take aim at his brother.

At dusk one night, the boy was seized as he tried to cross the small path between the two houses. Mr. Lansing notified the police at once, but no trace of the boy could be found. A few weeks later, Mr. Lansing was aroused at midnight by a veiled woman demanding audience. She was the mother of the two youths and said that the boy had been imprisoned in his father's house. The chief men of the University had labored day and night to change the boy's mind. Having failed, the decision was reached that he should be killed, but his father said he would not stain his own residence with his son's blood, and he hired a house in which the murder was to be perpetrated. The mother fled secretly to tell the missionary of her son's place of hiding. All the ingenuity and power of resident diplomats and missions was called into action. There was danger in arousing the religious frenzy and antagonism of the Arab population. However, the boy was found and rushed under cover of darkness to a man-of-war. A Scotch Duke, returning on a Nile steamer from upper Egypt, heard the story. He assumed responsibility for the maintenance and education of the Arab lad, giving him a home and admittance to a Scotch University. When the Arab boy received his degree of Doctor of Medicine, his generous patron arranged to have him sent as a full-fledged surgeon and physician to a Mission in India.

It would have been death to put his foot on the soil of Egypt or to try to see his family. The hatred of the infidel is acute in the mind of the Islamic world.

There had been a fanatical massacre of Christians at Tanta fifteen years before, where thirty thousand Copts,—the world's oldest sect of Christians,—had been put to the sword, and the native women marched in parade with cries of triumph, the entrails of the infidels wound around their necks.

CHAPTER THIRTEEN

THE NILE —AND TANTA

THE day set for embarkation on the Nile steamer came. We were to see many temples before reaching the Falls of Assouan. One really finds few truly interesting people in an excursion anywhere on earth,—rarely on an ocean leviathan. On board our steamer was an energetic editor of a newspaper in Troy, New York. He had the adjoining cabin to mine, where his abusive language to his wife destroyed my sleep. The great-nephew of Fanny Burney, an English clergyman, in correct attire of well-fitting gaiters, was accompanied by a purse-mouthed wife; they asked why such persons as the editor from Troy ever traveled. With us she would be quite content to have a fortnight's holiday at Margate, said she. No one could have hated the editor from Troy more than I, but American loyalty answered, "I suppose an American of any class has more intelligent curiosity than an Englishman." That onslaught made them very friendly to me.

Now all sorts and conditions of people make the Nile journey, but then it was a surprise to find, among the more privileged class, some illy-fed man, in a linen duster, possibly even without a collar. He usually had full knowledge of the Bible, and was spending his last cent to see Pharaoh, who forced the Egyptians to make bricks without straw, exposed in a glass case in a museum, and to stand by the monolith at Heliopolis where Moses was steeped in the wisdom of Egypt. Maggie Grant, our beloved Scotch maid, kept us *au courant* with Biblical facts.

Mahomet, Cook's Chief Dragoman, was of those who inherited the right to wear the green turban of a descendant of the Prophet. He ruled passengers and donkey-drivers with a rod of iron.

Each night the steamer was tied at the bank. At dawn we went ashore. Fat and lean, old and young, mounted donkeys, all heads protected by pith helmets, and scurried on, a crowd in stifling dust for a day's excursion.

I may be unperceptive, but in my comprehension, the architecture, the life, religion and mysteries of ancient Egypt, even to the adventurous modern scholar and excavator, must be an exotic mystery.

We arrived at Assiout to visit the town, it being "market day." There we saw many mummies of cats, which were held sacred in the worship of the Sun God, and I, having recently read Eber's "Princess," thought with sympathy of the poor Greek arriving with two pet cats, to live at a tower in the village. He had to shut himself in, and as he dared not destroy an animal, in the end he had to be either massacred by the fury of the religious believer, or eaten alive by the cats he had bred.

In the marketplace, for the delight of the crowd, both men and women, very frank and indecent dances were enjoyed.

On reaching the landing to go into the Temple of Abydos twelve miles away, we were off before false dawn, old and young with outstretched hands, demanding bakshish money; sturdy boys we passed killing birds with a sling such as young David used to slay the giant Goliath. Mahomet mounted me on a fresh young gray jackass whose gait suited me until the return trip to the steamer. The joy of distant courtship and a measure of corn called my mount. He laid back his long ears, no bit could hold him, and he ran like a streak of light. It was more merriment for the onlooker than for the spent rider. I wondered why one of those able boys would not aim a stone behind his ear and give me safety, but at last he slackened his pace. It is much more of a tragedy than a comedy to be run away with by a gay young jackass on the Plain of Abydos. Such exercise and fatigue made the eating of the meat of the usual frolicsome kid at a none too good dinner not unwelcome.

At Denderah we visited the Temple,—the least ruthlessly destroyed,—and one took leave of it with regret.

The repetition of stately processions, ritual, and offerings of fruit and flowers, one could follow. They were all attributes of the earth's vital and creative force, which penetrated, more or less, our understanding. Osiris, Isis and Horas, the trinity of the worship of the fecundity of the Nile's flood and recession, is as remote from the imagination of the globe-trotting American, as would be the feast of the Greek gods on Olympus. At last we reached the holy of holies where the roof still remains, of cerulean blue studded with golden stars. Here, shorn of their splendor, the ruling monarchs of Upper and Lower Egypt alone must face with humility their God. A touch of awe seemed reflected back and made us silent, for each and every one of us must alone face the profundity of life and death.

As we steamed up the Nile, I never tired watching the rhythmic motions of naked natives toiling the day through, raising water from the river by the rude shadoof. The unfamiliar sails of small river craft, the flight of egrets, or now and again the crimson flash of a flamingo, strings of camels outlined against the sky, made one reluctant to leave the deck.

Reaching Thebes for the first time is a striking experience.

In 1888, to visit the ruins of Karnak was as fatiguing as it was impressive, and the moon being well-grown, my boy was heartbroken when I refused to let him accompany some venturesome Englishmen at night to kill jackals. I hope he has now no bitterness in his heart, for they returned empty-handed. The table of our steamer was the better for my son's shooting of the dark-meated Egyptian quail which yearly migrate across the Mediterranean to Capri and Southern Italy. He kept the larder well supplied.

Every native was a searcher for scarabeus Egyptian beads and the blue faience effigies of the dead who strove to be remembered as long as one's effigy existed. I suppose it was dishonest to buy from a dragoman the winged scarabeus which had been rifled from the breast of the mummy of the High Priest of Pharaoh, but I still possess it. Then it was not difficult to buy a scarabeus with well-executed cartouche of rulers and priests. One symbol tickled my mirth; that the scarab or beetle,—with whose energy in America I was familiar, as he pushed his ball of manure down the lane to the cow pasture or in the dirt of the highway,—should in Egypt be worn on the crown of kings and used as a symbol of eternity everywhere. As children we called them "tumble-bugs." The Egyptian believed that they were bisexual, having within themselves power to recreate forever.

In my fumbling ignorance, I tried to plumb some of the symbolic meaning of the decoration of tombs. In one slanting shaft to a royal tomb, there were unmutilated frescoes indicating the struggle of the spirit to reach perfection, and to that end they were represented as passing through the bodies of serpents to attain eternity,—an ancient purgatorial idea.

Minna and Gemma Timmins were keen to rise before daybreak on the various excursions to temples, tombs of kings and queens, and the vocal Memnons which rise on the Plain of Thebes. Mahomet, looking at Minna Timmins, said, "You belong to us. You have the eyes and straight brows of the Arab." Seeing her with saffron scarf about her throat at dawn, I felt he was right. She inherited the understanding of all time. Indeed, she and Mr. Brimmer were interested in writing the essays in a charming book called "Egypt" on their return to America.

It is said that the tiny, dusky maidens who transport water from the Nile in lovely black pottery vessels to assuage the thirst of the excursionist, are a vicious lot. Life is none too easy for them. I am glad if they can find joy in either good or evil.

We were informed that the English Consul would entertain us and we should see the famous dancing girls of the Nile. When we arrived, seated on the floor were men beating with their fingers on a parchment-headed drum, strumming the strings of a rude guitar-like instrument made of cocoanut shells strung with catgut, and one blew a rude flute, with which our ears were familiar in every village procession.

The understanding was that this entertainment was for us alone. At that time, none of our party had ever seen the *danse du ventre,* and we were shocked. Every World's Fair, every vaudeville show, whether with white, mulatto or black performers, has hardened the youngest child and the oldest inhabitant in America to-day, into familiarity with the Eastern dances. The crowning moment was when the women went through their muscular contortions carrying a flaming candle on the head. The exhibition was repellent and my mother would have gladly fled. Suddenly the door was flung open, and two exhilarated Englishmen came in. No amount of protest on the part of the Consul could drive them away, and so we gladly retired to the hotel. One bore a proud title, and at four in the morning, in his drunken cups, he hammered on my door in the vain attempt to gain entrance. He was the scourge of the small water-carriers of the plain.

At that time, I believe J. P. Morgan was financing American excavations, the result of which has made the Metropolitan Museum one of the most informing and intelligent means for the study of Egyptian lore. One prized composite photograph of Cleopatra, taken from the reliefs of Ptolemaic monuments, was filched from me. Among what is termed honest people must be born intelligent kleptomaniacs who have robbed me of many literary treasures.

At last we reached Assouan, where the Sheik flag of seven black hawks on a white ground floated at the prow of Mr. Wilbur's luxurious dahabiyeh named the "Seven Hathors." His handsome daughter was the wife of Edwin Blashfield, the painter. Not only his open-handed hospitality warmed the cockles of our hearts, but his archeological excavation and interest enriched our days and gave him a proud place on the Nile.

What cheerful dinners on the deck of the dahabiyeh, and strangely enough the persistence of individuality brought Lady Duff Gordon often into the conversation. She had been dead eleven years, and yet there was no native between Assouan and Cairo who did not think of her as a Princess, a mother, a sister. She had the nature of a world mother, and a mind too broad to be sectarian. One of the most intellectual and beautiful women of her time, the friend of every great writer and diplomat of her day, fearless of mind, a distinguished authoress, she was courageous of speech in defending the weak and suffering of whatever race.

She had come to Assouan in the hope that the sun and the sustaining nourishment of warm camel's milk might restore her to health. It was a time of hard traveling, poor accommodation, and few individual comforts. She did not meddle with what she could not influence. The fact that an unfaithful wife was thrown into the Nile, or that the wife and her paramour were lashed and thrown into the flood together, she accepted as a judgment she could not change; but she fought the wrongs of the cudgeled fellaheen farmer, whose feet were often tortured with the bastinado until he fled for refuge from the inexorable tax-gatherer in the dusty desert. Her mercy would relieve the unjust taxation of the dancing girl who had been rifled of her wage by the stony heart and sticky fingers of the tax-collector from time immemorial. The attitude of the Arab toward the dancing girl is that she belongs to another race akin to the wandering gypsy, and is set apart for the vicious indulgence of mankind.

Lady Duff Gordon and Mrs. Robert Browning were the two best known of the women writers of that day. Lady Duff Gordon's chief desire seemed to be to face death bravely without giving pain to those she loved. In this hasty moment of a busy world, there is no better reading for a quiet hour than the vivacious "Letters of Lady Duff Gordon."

We resumed excursions. One day, having heard much of the riding of camels and leaving our party at luncheon, I went near the landing to where Mahomet's son had tethered a camel. I said to him, "I wish to mount and make an excursion along the bank. How much?" He named an exorbitant price, which I cut in half.

The beast knelt; I adjusted myself in the rough saddle between his hump, and suddenly felt that I was being thrown to the height of a mountain. The boy guided the camel who was shaking his long neck and making hideous noises. I became aware that that portion of my anatomy which the ancients say is the seat of the emotions, was disturbed, and that that beast could be fittingly described as the "ship of the desert." As the camel continued to emit alarming sounds, I exclaimed, "What *is* the matter?" "Oh, camel very hungry; camel very angry," said the boy. "Stop," said I, "I wish to walk." The signal given and acted upon, the sensation came of my being sent toward the bottomless pit. Through sand above my ankles under the rays of the noonday sun, I regained the steamer a sadder, wiser and subdued woman.

The stranger in Egypt is struck by the mysterious rapidity of the promulgation of news, as well as the persistence of memory of the Arab of the stranger who has once lingered within his gates. The donkeys' pace is a slow one and they seem impervious to moral suasion or the whip.

I was in sympathy with the boy who asked his father for the gift of a pony, and being refused, he was offered a donkey. He said, "Oh, father! Please give me a pony, for some time I might be in a hurry."

On starting on an excursion, the greatest compliment a donkey-boy could offer an American was to call his beast "Yankee Doodle," but they were vicious youngsters. Having irritated an open sore on a hidden portion of the donkey's body, they spurred him on with a long steel instrument like a skewer. I have dismissed more than one youngster from my service because of such cruelty. When I mounted "Yankee Doodle," accompanied by my son on "Hoopla," under the red-hot sun, perhaps our beasts seemed like lazy palfreys.

We went to the Falls to see the shooting of the rapids by the natives. To a lover of bronzes, nothing could be more satisfying than the torsos of those black men, but from the European point of view, the legs lack beauty; the heel bone being longer, the calf and thigh lack the Greek line of symmetry which the torso would suggest.

These swimmers had a cast of feature which I think was Abyssinian, and their vociferous shouting for the coins, which seemed to me inadequate to repay their skill and bravery, were both harsh and joyful.

From this section of the world, lower Egypt was furnished with eunuchs, and the mothers in this region were well paid for the mutilation of their infant sons. The little fellows, after castration, were buried in sand to the height of their navels, that the warm sand might disinfect and heal their wounds. I was told that death among them was not frequent, and there was let loose on the Islamic world the sensual dreamer and rapaciously mercenary abnormality who guarded the harems of Egypt.

To those who had the privilege, before the building of the great dam, of seeing the Temple of Philæ, most delicately refined of the Egyptian temples, its poetic proportions made a strong appeal. The mysterious shrine was erected to a god whose name was so sacred that it was not uttered.

My memories of Philæ are a record of the Temple as I first saw it, and later, as its roof and columns raise above the clear waters of the Assouan Dam, and its beauty was veiled and mysterious beneath clear waters as a boatman gently rowed to give us full vision of its hidden beauty. It reminds one of Debussy's "Cathédrale Engloutie," and one fancies that the sound of the High Priest's horn may at nightfall come over the placid water.

Speaking of the persistent memory of the Nile inhabitants, my own experience has been interesting. My mother spent many winters in Cairo or on the Nile, an honored friend of the Americans who were uncovering the hidden tombs of Upper and Lower Egypt. Mr. Bass had the desire to educate, at his own expense,

Mahomet's son in a good school in the United States, but Mahomet courteously refused the proffer. I asked him why he would not allow his son to have the advantage of an American education and he replied, "Because he might become a Christian." "And what would you do if he did?" asked I. "Kill him," he said quietly. But our friendship for Mahomet was born of respect for his virtues, and one amusing experience with him brings a smile, even at this late day.

During the World's Fair in Chicago, Mahomet was sent to Chicago in charge of the Arabs in the Egyptian section. My mother asked him to pay her a visit in Buffalo en route for his return to Egypt. He accepted, and when he arrived in magnificent embroidered raiment, with carefully adjusted turban, and a myriad of mysterious bundles, the curiosity of the North Street neighborhood in Buffalo was at white heat. The family were in consternation upon learning that we should be obliged to send an express wagon to the stockyards to bring back a foolish American sheep to be drained of his blood, by the code of Islam, in the carriage house. Children seemed to spring from the earth like a swarm of flies, and every groom in the neighborhood crowded into the driveway. None of the family assisted at the butchery. Mahomet was a welcome visitor, but ideas and vocabulary for exchange of thought were too restricted not to make conversation soon wearisome. He made us twice glad,—his coming and his departure. A great sigh of relief came as he saluted respectfully from the end of the train. It may be glorious, but very inconvenient, to entertain one who has the right to wear the green turban of a descendant of the Prophet.

But honors were easy when my brother, Dr. Metcalfe, years later reached Luxor. Mahomet killed another foolish sheep who had nibbled and fattened on the bank of the Nile, and it was roasted on a spit as a gesture of hospitality in honor of my mother's son.

When my granddaughter, Susan Bass, and I arrived at Luxor in 1920, we were taken in charge by the son Mahomet had refused to have educated by Mr. Bass, and there was not a donkey-boy or an inhabitant of Luxor that did not recognize me and spread the tidings that Mr. Bass's granddaughter was in Egypt.

The weight of years had crippled our stalwart Mahomet, but he arrayed himself with his ancient elegance and came to pay us tribute of respect, and made us laugh describing his return from the World's Fair to Luxor where, on being met by the leading men of the district, they sat about him on the ground to listen to his stories. Filled with undisguised curiosity, they touched their brows as though he had gone mad or had become God's worst liar.

Our return journey was delayed by now and again running on a sand-bank. On our last night on the Nile, there was a crescent moon, as there was on the night when Mahomet began his Hegira. That crescent is the sign on the banners of Islam for war or peace.

Mr. Bass had won Mahomet's heart. He longed to convert us to his own faith. Standing by the rail of the steamer watching the river, he asked me to raise my right hand and say after him in Arabic, "There is no god but God, and Mahomet is His prophet." Truthfully I repeated the words. They were a fitting finis to a journey which had aroused interest in the hidden mysteries of the universe.

The Nile falls rapidly in the spring, and when we reached Assiout in March, it was a red-hot day. The news of the great New York blizzard reached us by telegram, and the fact that Roscoe Conkling had died from the effect of his being caught in the storm was a shock. A great political figure as well as a powerful lawyer, not often kind, often supercilious and contemptuous, a brilliant, bitter adversary without magnanimity or the power to forgive one who had wounded his vanity,—the bed of his stately loving wife and charming daughter was not a bed of roses. His beautiful descendant, Mrs. Oakman, recently died in England at the age of seventy-five, so the saying is made good, that "Great men have no continuance."

It was the moment when the prostrating wind from the desert, the *hamsun,* might blow for three days on end. The feast of fifty days of Ramadan was near. From sunrise to sunset the faithful believer must let neither food nor water pass his lips. But human nature is resourceful. If they fasted all day, they feasted all night. The sanitary rule of Mahomet, like the Lenten fast of the Christian, makes for good health and self-control.

On reaching Shepheard's Hotel, Minna and Gemma Timmins were delighted to be welcomed by Captain Silsbee of Salem, Massachusetts. He belonged to those aristocratic East India adventurers who founded many of the great fortunes of the Massachusetts coast. He had traveled greatly and was an enthusiastic student and appreciator of Shelley. He read in the Brimmers' drawing room an interesting article he had written on Shelley. In his passionate love for the poet, he had shrewdly spent a winter in a pension in Florence where Jane Clairmont lived. She possessed many of Shelley's letters and Captain Silsbee coveted them, and by hook or by crook he resolved to get them.

Gray, wiry, hirsute, with a scrubby beard and mottled complexion, he bore no imprint of a gay Lothario. However, he said that he had been pursued to quiet churchyards and Campo Santo by the ardent chase of English spinsters and unattached widows, their blood warmed by Italian skies.

Jane Clairmont, the most predatory of women, must have been taking a half-holiday in her home-wrecking poet-chasing career for Captain Silsbee secured Shelley's letters.

He was vastly intelligent and of unvarying kindness, and finding that I had not observed that one of the Pyramids still retained part of the highly finished ancient facing, he asked me to drive with him to see it. When we reached our destination near the close of the day, and we started to wade across the sands, the excursion promised over-fatigue. Being surrounded by a howling crowd of Bedouins, four were engaged to carry me. Two Arabs clasped the wrists of each other, the other two following as a relay. The natives, probably demanding bakshish, made the quiet sands pandemonium. Captain Silsbee, swearing oaths he must have used to control a mutiny on the high seas, jumped up and down in a cloud of dust of his own making. At my entreaties he became quiet, and I motioned to the clamorous men, pointing to the rising of a full moon in the East, and the color of the setting sun in the West, staining the golden sands as with crimson blood. I put my finger to my lips, a silent spell upon us, and the barefooted, white-garbed Bedouins walked silently in the glory of color which Egypt alone reveals. The black shadows of the rifled tombs of kings dead centuries gone by, laid the spell of silence upon us all.

The road back to Cairo was white with moonlight, the sun-heated sand still reflecting warmth, though one must always provide against the sudden penetrating chill, which makes fur coats a comfort.

The gem-like beauty of the windows lighting the Mouski, inspired Minna Timmins to copy them in the blocks made of plaster, set in frames in which the inserted glass is in the seven prismatic colors of the rainbow. It was no easy task to get the blocks of plaster, which I fancy were made of marble dust, and a trying experience to cut out the design in which the glass was fitted. The success of her endeavor later embellished the residence of her husband, John Jay Chapman.

Through Mr. Brimmer, we met Maspero, and how I longed to become the proud possessor of one of the remarkable bronze cats which graced his collection. I remember the cats, but have forgotten Maspero's face.

Schliemann was in Cairo and we met him frequently. It was said that he had taken an oath to marry no woman who could not repeat the Iliad by heart in Greek. I believe his beautiful wife answered the requirement. He told me she wore the bracelets of Helen of Troy found, I believe, at Tiryns. He remarked he intended to seek for the tomb of Cleopatra near Alexandria. I exclaimed, "Do leave us something to dream about, and not put Cleopatra, spiced like Pharaoh, in the glass case of a museum!"

His table manners were unpleasant, as he sucked up his soup and carelessly let the long sleeves of his tweed coat dip into his soup plate.

We took farewell regretfully of the Sirdar and Lady Grenfell, and boarded the train for Alexandria, watching a string of camels loaded with fine cotton to enrich a British company. Wherever a son of England treads, there may be a spur to personal gain rather than philanthropy. The building of dams and the engineering feats of the sons of Great Britain have increased the yield of lands enriched by the floods of the Nile to the production of many crops per acre in a year, and the value of land in Egypt makes it worth per square foot, about as much as a corner of ground at Wall Street and Broadway.

The Nile trip being ended, Mahomet came into Mr. Bass's service as his personal dragoman. He had acted in that capacity for the Duc de Chartres and many other men of prominence.

I consulted him as to the feasibility of making the excursion to Tanta. He suggested that for safety, he would like to engage two other well-known dragomen, as he had heard that after sunset, license and debauchery were rife. No European woman had ever ventured to that fanatical feast. Mr. Bass would have found it too exhausting, but Minna and Gemma Timmins were aglow with excitement at the thought of the trip.

The proprietor of Shepheard's Hotel was an Austrian. He prevented the trip for the two girls by telling Mr. Brimmer that it would be an outrage to allow them to go to Tanta where he himself had never been, and that the reports were such that no decent European woman would dream of undertaking the risk involved in going to such scenes of uncontrolled moral license. Of course we were aware of the murder of thirty thousand Christians fifteen years earlier, but my fastidious mother, who shrank from danger as a sheltered woman should, agreed to go. She and I with three richly clad dragomen, reached the railway station to find Mahomet delirious with joy at the sight of Sir Ernest Budge. His renown was known the length of Egypt, being, as he was, the head of the Department of Egyptology in the British Museum. A travel-stained, powerful-looking man, one would have known he was somebody. He shared our compartment. He had that moment, we learned from his tale, returned from the desert on his journey back from Bagdad.

Mamma said to him she rather feared we were going to be shocked by rude scenes at Tanta. Impatiently he answered, "What has been the life of the people for four thousand years should not shock. Should it do so, it will be for your good to be shocked."

In the midst of the desert for a brief quarter of an hour, his life had hung in the balance. A group of war-like Bedouins rushed towards him with murderous haste. He gave a courteous salutation in the mode of Islam and addressed them in their own vernacular. Their mood changed and he became to them their son and brother, and they begged that he would sleep beneath their tents and share the honorable feast of a roast sheep bled and killed according to the Koran.

After a night about their campfire, at dawn they set him on his way and escorted him for miles, he relieved to see them gallop away.

Bagdad was then a true city of the Arabian Nights. I yearned to cross the sands to Bagdad, but the very sight of the motion of a camel turned me ghastly sick.

What Sir Ernest Budge said of Egypt was enlightening. My mother, who had the grace of a woman accustomed to entertain as well as be entertained, had spent many winters in Egypt, so she gave him a Roland for his Oliver by speaking of the opening of the Suez Canal. She prized the memory of meeting de Lesseps and showed, with pleasure, the small photograph of his wife taken with a string of nineteen children, which I think was the number of his offspring by one lady. With color and vivacity she spoke of the performance of "Aïda" in the opera-house built in eighty days for the production of Verdi's opera, given in honor of Emperor Napoleon III and Eugénie. Doubtless there was no more slave-driving when the Pyramid of Cheops was built than during the construction of the largest operatic stage in the world, in intensive work, day and night, for less than three months. The stage crowd and supernumeraries were composed of native Egyptians, but the best of operatic actors and singers were imported from Europe.

As we arrived at Tanta, the dragomen, in their resplendent elegance, told the noisy crowd that we were in rank nothing short of royalty. Most of that day I was in pain and my mother, in distress lest I fall ill, burned brandy and sugar at intervals to calm my vitals.

The great mosque is on the site of the ancient ruined Temple of Bubastis. The chief men of the mosque received us as personages, surprised at the sight of two foreign women.

Reaching the shrine of the tomb which was without the mosque and protected by a grill of rare ironwork, crowded about were women pushing and striving to touch it, uttering a queer high shrilling birdlike note. Their aspiration was to produce sons, and the touching of the sacred shrine and ancient things was supposed to promote fertility. During the week of the fête, as many of the faithful as could be accommodated were sheltered within the mosque where they unrolled their beds on the radiantly colored floors, and free of charge were fed with durra, a preparation of crushed corn made into thin cakes. We entered the vast open court with a sherif and his escort, who guided us through the curious crowd to an improvised bench on which to stand to watch the self-hypnotized worshipers. In the face of that fanatical crowd we were given durra to eat. I said to my mother, "I cannot eat it. The smell is like that of mummies, and it looks like their skin." "Swallow it," said she, and I did. Thousands of eyes were pinned upon us. Standing about were those who, I suppose, were saints or holy men, some with eyes fixed on the relentless sun from its rising to its setting. There were those who uttered harsh cries of the name of Allah until, frothing at the mouth, they fell writhing in a fit. Such can the incessant reiteration of a holy name bring to those half mad.

It was a relief to have the high men of the mosque blaze a

way for our exit. Mamma said to Mahomet, "If we fall on rude scenes, protect us." I felt I should like to see the very heart of this fanatical town, cost what it may.

We hurried to the camel and horse market where five thousand camels and dromedaries could be bought and sold. Some of the purchasers, as they led what seemed to them a young camel to their homes, found he was an aged beast of skin and bones, that had been blown to youthful lines by inserting a quill under his skin. Gradually he would return to old age.

The exhibition of horsemanship of the Hawari, with their floating cloaks and rich silk turbans and cords of gold, raised us to a high pitch of excitement. One who has never seen a fantasia given by the horsemen of the desert, has missed one of the thrilling panoramas of the East. There was jousting with spear and lance, and races where the chiefs on their fast steeds rushed, with weapons high in the air and black cloaks floating out behind, like great birds of prey, uttering harsh cries to speed their horses. On the side-lines one saw an occasional camel with the palanquin of veiled women who, to urge on the victors, uttered that queer clarion-like thrilling note, which seems as little of earth as the beautiful note of a hidden lark.

We were fended from the obscene frankness of men and women dancing, watched with eagerness and delight by surrounding natives. We came upon a slender young woman,—an improvisatore. After a few words with Mahomet, we who knew not a word of Arabic, sensed the beauty of rhythm and accent as the girl, in verse, told of our crossing the seas to bless with our largess, the poor and needy. We "greased her palm" with coins.

Snake-charmers there were, eaters of glass, burning cotton and scorpions, but those exhibitions had more call for the Arab than for us.

The lack of sanitation and the filth of places of retirement were revolting. We finally wandered to the outskirts where was a tribesman who, in dignity and apparel, suggested the prophets. Back of his large white tent, his henchmen guarded flocks and herds while he, on cushions with the Koran on a pillow before him, expounded the moral law. The protecting grill of rope lattices of the tent reflected the veiled shadows of the traveling harem. My mother waxed fatigued and grew timorous as the day wore on and increasing numbers of worshipers reiterated the name of their god until they dropped in epileptic seizures.

We had been told that when dark fell, there would be scenes of revelry and unbridled lust as fierce as in the days when Herodotus wrote of Bubastis. Whenever I have defied Thomas Cook and the advice of my friends, I have been rewarded with unusual experience. I left Tanta in the mood of the boy who, asking to swim on Sunday, was told by his mother that boys who disobeyed their mothers were usually drowned on Sunday; but he said, "May I not go to see the bad boys drown?" 1888 is a long time ago, but not one day since we turned our backs on Tanta but I have regretted that I never saw the phallic revelry on the lighted barges moored on the branch of the Nile, to the music of strings, drums and flutes, and I felt, with Sir Ernest Budge, that I would have been the better for being shocked. We crowed with delight over the rarest unknown experience, which could have harmed no one who carried decency beneath his hat. It would not have stained us to have had a glimpse of what the Western cowboy calls "hell let loose." It is one of the few times in life when my sin was one of omission. Our trip made the thrifty firm of Thomas Cook and Son advertise to take venturesome spinsters from England to succeeding fêtes.

CHAPTER FOURTEEN

ASIA MINOR AND CONSTANTINOPLE

IN 1888, those who went "down to the sea in ships" knew no luxury. The best transportation was by small Austrian Lloyd vessels. The united forces of the Brimmer party and ours had secured the best passage months before, on the ships going from Alexandria to Constantinople.

My cabin commanded a view of the forward deck, where pilgrims, bound for Jerusalem, Mecca and Medina, huddled to eat, drink and be sick, in a stench that was overpowering, including the scourge of all shipping in those days, bilge.

By train to Alexandria, we reached the steamer to mount the gangway of our ship. Finding Professor Schliemann leaning over the rail, each and every one in the party secretly resolved, as we were bound for Tiryns and the Gate of the Lions, to do a little independent brain-picking from his store of knowledge. Professor Schliemann gave no outward sign of the scholar or romantic adventurer in search of hidden treasure.

Our first stop was Port Said, the sewer of poisonous humanity from every quarter of the globe. The jostling crowd was picturesque and colorful, and they found a call to easy sinning in every shop window, but what a kaleidoscope of nations it was, of races who had not been converted to the wearing of coats and pants! All our passengers rushed to buy cigarettes of pure Turkish tobacco, drink Turkish coffee, finding their cabins to deposit parcels of Oriental trumpery.

As we left Port Said, wind, a cloudy sky, and a slate-colored sea foretold tempest, but we hoped to land at Joppa. The courier of the Brimmers was stylish, wearing a beaver hat, a black frock coat, rings galore, and a heavy gold chain. A storm on the open roadstead at Joppa is no joke. We arrived in the teeth of a tempest. The steamer was tossed like a cockle-shell in the churning waves, but the anchor held, and we were quickly surrounded by a howling mob of native boatmen. The pilgrims were thrown over the side into the clutches of these seeming pirates who, getting a full craft, started for the breakers. Reaching the edge of the full fury of waters, the boatmen demanded money far in excess of the dues agreed upon. Between being robbed and terror of a watery grave, the miserable creatures who had been cast like bales of cargo over the side of the steamer, had to submit.

The Brimmers' elegant courier had to go ashore. The tails of his frock coat standing taut in the wind, he stood brandishing a brace of pistols to subdue the Levantine thieves. We left him to his fate, to meet him later on in Beirut, and we turned our faces toward Beirut with relief. Night put a calming hand on the high waves, and we arrived at Beirut on a sunny morning.

We reached the quays in the midst of a clamoring crowd and were almost cross-eyed watching our luggage at the Customs. The trunks were opened, contents dumped and stirred as with a pudding-stick. Suddenly a shadow fell, and the tall clerical figure of the Reverend Mr. Bliss, head of Roberts College, was rebuking the noisy thieves. He helped us re-pack and asked us to luncheon at his house. A little home food did not seem amiss.

Edward O. Wolcott had asked us to look up the grave of his father's first wife in a cemetery at Beirut. His father, one of the earliest of the Near East missionaries, the Reverend Samuel Wolcott, was an orator, an adventurer by nature, a scholar and a clergyman by profession. He had always believed that, descending into a well, he had found the subterranean entrance to Solomon's Temple, and I daresay he had. His young wife and child died in Beirut. We scrambled through an unkempt cemetery after luncheon, hot and discouraged, and found nothing. At last, going into the walled cemetery reserved for the families of missionaries, under the shade of tall cypress trees where birds were mating and singing, we found a well-kept tomb of the young wife who died at twenty. Samuel Wolcott returned to America, married Miss Pope, and in 1886 was the father of eleven grown men and women. I suppose when his first wife died, he thought he would never recover from his grief, but he was evidently mistaken.

My intelligence has never been able to cope satisfactorily with the subject of foreign missions, and Heaven knows, I have sailed many seas with American missionaries and their families. They are the only body of people I have known that are paid for having children, and with a rising ratio of support for the youngsters as they mount to the dignity of pinafores, short pants and roundabouts. I have no sympathy with proselyting what the righteous call the "heathen." If we must promote commerce and scientifically protect ourselves from the thousands of poisonous germs which breed in the East and follow the lines of travel, medical missionaries have their place. Like Colonel Bob Ingersoll, I feel that an honest God is the noblest work of man. All races create their gods to suit their imaginations and their particular needs. Why should we curse our souls with sins of omissions towards the unregenerate of our own land?

The first impulse on touching land is to shop, and we bought two fine silver daggers in Beirut, one in scimitar form with which a powerful bandit with skillful hand could rip a man from down up. Both weapons had traces of human blood near the hilt. We still treasure with pride that blood. It gives added glamor to our pride of imagination, and we still wonder who was disemboweled.

Another purchase was a beautiful silver marriage horn, two feet high, which a bride of the Druses fastened with silver chains to her virginal head.

We were in haste to push on. Mr. Bliss helped us to set off in our victorias for our long drive to Damascus. We were told that the fierce and predatory Druses were for the moment behaving themselves, and that we should be able to pass through their wooded hills unmolested.

We had not counted on a heavy snowstorm, but it fell. The weather was no colder than my fear for the attack of winter upon Mr. Bass. Shivering, we reached the hotel kept by the most ill-tempered German of the Near East. In America, we had paid Thomas Cook and Son for the best accommodations. When that ill-tempered Teuton tried to force an invalid to climb two long flights of stairs, I talked pure unadulterated American. He said I ought to thank God that I could find a roof over my head where thirty thousand Mussulmen were thirsting for my blood. There had been, not long before, a massacre of Christians in Damascus. At last we were given a fair-sized room, up one flight of stairs.

We circled around a shining polished large brass brazier, which ate up all the oxygen in the air. We laughed and tried to joke about the delights of travel. What we had, had as much relation to the cheer and comfort of home, as gathering around a hot-air furnace radiator in a north hall bedroom in a hotel in the Indian Territory.

Warm sun changed gloom to joy, as we set blithely forth for

the Street called Straight. The thrill of the unexpected spicy mixture of the conversion of St. Paul, the romance of Scheherezade in the Arabian Nights, and the mystery of the desert which hemmed us in, banished fear. We understood the swelling heart of that donkey-boy Mahomet, poor and ambitious, who looked down from the tawny dust of barren sand to the rose gardens and merry plashing waters and fountains of the world's most ancient city. It is not unlikely that he had a coin and bought a sweet in the world's oldest candy store where, for all time, it has served a shifting populace of the crowded bazaar of the Street called Straight.

I wonder did Mahomet, at that early moment, plan to launch the most compelling and powerful religion of the Orient.

There were superb palaces in the year 1888, large marble courts rich with Persian tiles, which I fear, since the fighting of the Great War, have been leveled by shot and shell.

We bought abayas of hand-made silk, inwrought with gold, a garment the shape of which, for centuries, had gracefully draped fat women and revealed the lithe contours of slender youth.

It was suggested that the women of our party should see a Haman or Turkish bath. No one but myself cared to venture. The dragoman and I wound our way through narrow lanes to something with low domes that suggested a lime kiln. Arriving, a repellent-looking black woman opened the door and helped me to remove such of my garments as I was willing to remove, to have them held by our guide. She ushered me into a series of seemingly dimly lighted rooms where groups of naked women were washing their bodies and swishing in the water heads of lettuce, but their eyes shot ill-natured glances and their tongues chattered hate. One feels antagonism though unaware of the words in which it is expressed, and I reached the open air relieved that the uttered wish for my death had not been granted.

After months of hearing many tongues and understanding not a word save "attack," I dreamed it might be a pleasure to be told to "go to the devil" in English.

I was sorry not to see an incoming camel train which, for three months in the olden days, was wont to wend its way from the Far East, bearing to the bazaars of Damascus the wealth of the Indies. The Suez Canal has destroyed the commerce and color of Damascus.

The journey back to Beirut was free from incident, and traveling on schedule, we embarked on the ship which, through the wonders of the Grecian Archipelago, would lead us to Ephesus. The landing was a little disappointing. The Oracle is mute, and the Temple, at a distance from the city, is ruined.

Mr. and Mrs. Brimmer and their nieces were in quest of the Consul, who was reputed to have the largest and finest collection of Tanagra figurines. Mr. Brimmer had generously presented to the Museum in Berlin a large number of Tanagra figurines, many of which the German experts considered spurious, which sorely wounded him.

Mrs. Brimmer had an ardent wish to possess a specimen of unique beauty and value, as well as a string of the largest beads of clouded amber ever born in the spume of the sea. Mrs. Jack Gardiner, alert of mind and quick of decision, had such treasures carelessly displayed under the soft light of a lamp in her boudoir. It took many years for me to comprehend thoroughly both the taste and ability of Mrs. Gardiner to find and get what she wanted, no matter who competed with her. Mrs. Brimmer returned to the vessel without the figurine, as the man would sell only the unbroken collection, but she had the amber in her portmanteau.

Central Europe has produced supermen, who might have been those spoken of in the Bible as the sons of God who descended to mate with the daughters of men. Nicola Tesla belonged to the races of Central Europe. His clerical father was an inventor, and his mother, born somewhere where the Garden of Eden should have been, was also an inventor. I should think the invention of twelve males was sufficient contribution to electricity without working in a laboratory.

I believe that Tesla, now no longer young, is an American citizen, still working on inventions for the perfection and efficient growth of the telegraphic and telephonic service. He had a wiry figure, lean and energetic, and seemed to me one of the tallest of men, though, if I remember, he told me he was the shortest of twelve brothers. Years ago, he was more or less sought out by New York intelligent society, to which he was an enlivening addition. His brilliant eyes were unreadable and Oriental. He asked a party with whom we had been dining, to accompany him to his laboratory to see his invention of powerful electric volts transmitted without wires, to a great distance. A piffling previous engagement lost me a great opportunity.

Standing by the crumbling Temple of Ephesus I was reminded that Tesla told me he believed the Priests of the Temple of Ephesus had full knowledge of the power of electricity as modern scientists now reveal it, and that the scoffing unbelievers beyond the circle of worshipers had been struck down by such volts as he now produced.

It is years since I last saw Tesla in the Palm Room of the Waldorf. For a time he sent me books on Oriental religion, as he seemed mistakenly to think that my chief object in life was the study of comparative religions. As far as I know, I have never been profoundly interested in knowledge of any sort. I rejoice that there are able men who can put a hand in the breast of a well-made coat, and who guide the finance of the world, advancing their own fortunes,—I wish they could mine,—but wearing the air of unconscious arrogance of conscious wealth. In contribution of charm, one could endure their going on the steamship *Leviathan* to the Port of Missing Men rather than to lose the spell-binding quality of Tesla, or a glorious hour with the illumined soul of Professor Pupin.

During that Asia Minor journey, there was the more or less historic appeal of Tyre and Sidon, and we climbed the great bluff where the priests of Baal made sacrifice in their temple of black bullocks and little children, to call rain from Heaven. If the priests of Baal were destroyed by the lightnings of Heaven, the prayers of the Chosen People were answered.

The cries for rain from above give birth to kindred rites in many lands,—for the routing of famine and the yields of the earth's increase, and for sons from the fertile wombs of women.

The same spirit which inspired the prayer of the American aborigine in the snake dance of the Hopi Indians on the steep rocky crags in New Mexico, was born of the world's needs. Their prayers I saw answered, after their solemn service with their necks wreathed with snakes,—the knowledge of their medicine men made them immune to the poison of a rattlesnake,—one man's throat I saw thrice struck, and yet he lived. The ceremonies being over, the reptiles sprinkled with sacred cornmeal, they were released to carry their message to the springs beneath the ground. A sudden blackness of night covered the heavens, which were rocked with forked lightning. Beating rain and hail poured in floods from the clouds, while the Navajos and Hopis made a joyous cry behind their teeth. Suddenly the storm ceased, and springing from horizon to horizon, two rainbows bridge the plain. At that moment I, like the Israelites or the Indians, could but acknowledge the efficacy of prayer.

I have no desire to be a scoffer when I say I do not hold with the modern civilized dream of a perfect democracy, the utility of pants, and the adoption of health-attacking unventilated shoes. The ankle is a pivot, on the line of which should rise the torso of a man. If you box it, all symmetry ends. The perfect arch, as given to the men who wear the pointed sandals held with thongs of leather, enables the handsome giants of Central Europe to cross mountain and plain without fatigue.

A medium-size Captain of the Indian Army, one of the clan Campbell, who serve their Sovereign wherever the British flag floats, showed me a pair of shoes, saying, "I have walked in them fifteen thousand miles on my good flat feet, in Turkestan,— Russian and Chinese." I said laughingly, "You might continue and finish the tour around the world without wearing a hole in them." His experience bespeaks the integrity and the skill of the London bootmaker, but perhaps had he never worn a shoe, he might have had a strong arch instead of his "good flat feet." With Bernard Shaw, I agree that unventilated shoes contribute to human disease.

Those who, a hundred times a day, put the shoes from off their feet in reverence for their shrines and the cleanliness of their homes, are erect of bearing; and the practice builds for health of body.

Again on board steamer, we sailed the sapphire waters, which no one who has not coasted off Northern Africa, or sailed the land-locked waters of the Grecian Archipelago and Ægean Sea, can realize. One almost longs to spend a third of a lifetime under a lateen sail such as the Phœnicians used in the small craft touching the Biblical Ophir in the island the moderns call Ceylon, and as far west as the Gates of Hercules. If one had enough Latin, Greek and Arabic to be fluent of speech, and were not seasick, there is no port of the Grecian islands that would not yield him joy. One should have as companion, the most charming story ever penned for man, "The Wanderings of Ulysses," literally translated by Butcher and Lang, Kinglake's "Eothen," the most glamorous book of travel, and journey with Sir Richard Burton as he, disguised, faced death hourly in his pilgrimage to Mecca and Medina.

Our curious eyes were lifted as we passed, but didn't land upon the Plain of Troy. How thrilling to be able to stand at the gateway where the greatest compliment ever paid to woman was voiced by her father-in-law, Priam, the blood of whose eighty sons had stained the Trojan Plain. Sitting with Antenor at the gate as Helen passed, he understood, without bitterness, that for her beauty men must fight and die, but did he know that when those dead were forgotten, poets would be still singing of her charm?

We passed Naxos and I could almost hear the sighs of Ariadne mourning when deserted by young Bacchus. Tintoretto's painting in the Ducal Palace at Venice has fixed the type of the vine-crowned Bacchus and the sorrow of Ariadne in our minds.

There were days of idle coasting. Mrs. Brimmer and I were fortified against ennui, for in our coat pockets we carried belated numbers of Littell's "Living Age," and we blessed those maiden ladies of Philadelphia who furnished our refreshment. Golden and tempting medlars in a measure quenched our thirst, but they were made chiefly of huge brown seeds. Huntley and Palmer's biscuit and a tea-basket abated our hunger. Minna Timmins and I, one night beneath a waning moon as we traversed the waves that poets once said brought the last cry of that Pagan god Pan, strove to hear his farewell, and we were sad and our eyes were wet with tears. *"A dire adieu est mourir un peu."*

The journey from Ephesus found us impatient to cross the water where Leander nightly swam the Hellespont to visit Hero, and reach the land of waters of the Golden Horn.

Forty years ago the port of Constantinople was where the East and West met, and turbans were as numerous as fezes. Dragomen in bright hues, in uniforms rich with braid and embroidery, Greeks in European attire, dusky faces from the Far East, with their flowing garments, gave infinite variety. It took a little experience not to mistake the Semitic Syrian for the Jew, but the Christian Marianites and Copts had the outline of the Semite. Jewish merchants stated frankly, "I am an Israelite." The ramshackle houses of wood of modern construction are built on the vast foundations of ancient palaces of splendor.

The hotel to which we were accredited had been the home of Lew Wallace when he was diplomatic representative of the United States; and it was there he wrote "Ben Hur," the graphic picture of the Holy Land which he had never visited. It seemed hardly a dignified residence for a Minister of the United States. Neither he nor his successor, Sunset Cox, were men of fortune, but both were scholars and writers. Sunset Cox, an able Member of Congress, found his book, "In Search of Windsor Sunshine," widely read.

When we reached Turkey, Oscar S. Straus had arrived shortly before we did, and he had bought a large house where he might fittingly represent his country and stabilize his own position. The Sultan had treated our former Ministers in a cavalier fashion, and it was difficult for them to make appointments and transact their business with him.

Sunset Cox was a small, dark man with a rich, sonorous voice. All the people we met talked and laughed at the tale of his going to the Seraglio where, if he were denied or kept waiting, he would pace the passages and into chambers, swearing until the air was blue. The Sultan, being made aware of the row, would at last receive him. Sunset Cox never took "no" for an answer, and generally accomplished the object which he sought to attain.

Mr. and Mrs. Straus at once issued invitations for a large diplomatic dinner in our honor, followed by a ball. No stone was left unturned to get interesting privileges for us, and to proclaim that we were people of importance.

The Sultan was always in danger of assassination, and protected himself against an uprising in the palace. He never slept two consecutive nights in the same room. When he grew tired, he slept where he found himself. There is more than a grain of good sense in the standard of no fixed hours in the Orient, save for prayer. To clap one's hands when the pangs of hunger prompt, sit cross-legged on the floor, at a richly ornamented octagonal table, to be served by slaves or concubines, suits the needs of Oriental rulers.

Abdul-Hamid II was one of the ablest of royal politicians, balancing his policy of power between Asia and Europe. Forty thousand soldiers were reviewed on Friday to guard him and to impress Europeans and his own subjects as he went to and from the Mosque to pray. Naturally we were eager to reach the Samlik, —agog to see the show. At the end of the morning, moving troops swept the regiments of fierce Bashi Bazooks, Turkey's mercenary troops. Their unkempt hair was like that of horses' tails. Their shouts turned my blood cold. They were supposed to be the fiercest fighters in the Turkish Empire.

Diplomats and distinguished visitors were received with ceremony. Refreshments, sherbets and coffee, cigarettes bearing the Sultan's monogram, and small gifts were passed by attendants.

As the closed carriage of the Sultan, surrounded by troops, swiftly passed, we could see him but dimly. His devotions finished, the doors of the Mosque were opened, he stepped into the doorway, surrounded by his Ministers, descended the steps, entering the large open phaeton, took the whip to drive himself; while he lashed the horses, his pashas and viziers, in heavy uniforms, puffed up the hill, unable to do more than pantingly follow the equipage, their gait impeded by clanking swords. The guard fell in behind and the Sultan retired to the privacy of his vast palace on the hill.

After the Great War, my granddaughter, Susan Bass, went to the Samlik and saw the last sad Sultan go to pray, followed by but few servitors, and the fashionable function at the Samlik was shorn of much of its glory.

The jewels of the Sultan are supposed to make pale the treasure of Ali Baba. Under the eye of Ministers of State, we were shown enough fine and sick jewels to load a ship. The extent and volume of the hoarded treasure of the Sultan were only to have been determined by the conquerors after the Great War.

Years dim one's memory, but the sarcophagus of Alexander the Great, as well as the Oracle, the Temple of Ephesus and the Hippodrome in the Square at Constantinople are still impressive.

Harsh winds tearing down the Black Sea tempered joy in drives to the sweet waters where kohl-outlined eyes of harem beauties peeked over the yashmak which veiled their brows and chins. English soldiers sought romance at times in flirtation with these charming ladies, and some of them found sudden death. At that time, an over-venturesome European could disappear and no sign of him be found, nor redress possible. Cut-throats and robbers found security in the ancient runways of the old city.

We made excursions to the deserted summer palaces of former Sultans on the Bosphorus. He who arrives to rule in the Orient has no desire to conserve the buildings of his predecessors, but rather to set forth his personal glory in newly built palaces.

We were told that the slave market was still operative. Circassian girls were brought, given Turkish baths, fed upon sweets, and, when their skins were free from blemish, were sold. The Oriental man likes them fat. In one of the summer palaces the attendant showed us an immense marble room with vast circular pool and fountains. "Here," he said, "the Sultan bathes with his ladies." An adjoining large marble chamber and a black ill-smelling hole in the corner used as a *cabinet d'aisance*. The East has never known sanitary cleanliness. The women's quarters hung over the deep, rushing Bosphorus. An unfaithful wife would be flung out, speedily meeting death. Women of the harems are reckless in intrigue and love, and in spite of eunuchs, they seek escape, and are not always fastidious as to the color of their lovers' skins.

In a lonely garden overlooking the water, an aged tiger paced his cage. He had few teeth and was powerless for battle,—a sad emblem of a departed ruler.

Among the faithful there was a tradition that the Turk would be driven from Europe, and they sought to be buried in the soil of Asia. We crossed to see the cemeteries. The headstones on the graves showed by the form of the turban by which they were capped, the rank of the man beneath the sod. As we were going to the Asiatic side, we were given a letter to be presented at the gate of one who was supposed to be one of the most interesting pashas in power. Our coachman and guide pounded and knocked on the gate of the high-walled park. Finally a eunuch opened the gate a few inches, took the letter, disappeared and never came back again. Such was the opinion of the pasha of the traveling American.

The Turk is respected both as a man and an adversary, and is considered a gentleman by those who have been in touch with him diplomatically. The present black-eyed Greek has no such meed of admiration; though he still carries on under the name of the blue-eyed Greek who made the glory of Greece, he is not of the stock which gave the world rich heritage from the age of Pericles. He is of a more shifty and untruthful quality.

Of course we wandered about Sancta Sophia, remodeled from a Christian basilica, to have its simple stone of worship facing the east where Mecca and Medina called them to pilgrimage. One feels the dignity and rightness of a faith that banished statue of man or beast to be used as a symbol in the house of God.

Whether from a tiny mosque in the desert, or from the tall minarets of Islam's finest places of worship, the call of the muezzin has always stirred in me an emotion. I have been told that those who summon the faithful, five times in twenty-four hours to pray, are generally blind.

All travelers spend many hours in the crowded, shadowy bazaars. It is like seeking for hidden treasure, only one spends instead of finding gold. There are no shrewder traders than those of the East. As an English traveling gentleman remarked to me when I asked for the address of a shop, "No matter where you go, you will be done in the eye." Still to-day I rejoice to own one of the largest undamaged Rhodian embroideries and a curtain that the experts in New York say is a museum piece, whose date and handicraft they cannot yet name. We bought a scimitar-shaped Damascus dagger, than which, in the Wallace collection, there is nothing finer. At that time, someone who had thousands to spend, might have bought a hanging enameled Arabian glass lamp. I bartered with a Persian for the possession of a Persian begging bowl,—a mass of turquoise whose color would never change. One curses one's stars at what one left unpurchased, rarely for what a keen eye brings away.

We were excited by the invitation to go on Easter Sunday, which, in the Greek calendar, is thirteen days after that in the Roman calendar, to the palace of the Patriarch, to a notable midday function. There we met dignitaries, Mohammedan as well as Christian, and one, the Patriarch himself, who looked like the High Priest Aaron in his tall cap and rich flowing vestments. At that time his power reached to the farthest boundary of Russia. The Papacy has always been sleepless in its effort to absorb and unite the Eastern rites to the Romish church. The Patriarch shared power with Islam. The vestments of the prelates of Rome no doubt are of tradition coming from the High Priests of Israel, but the dress of the clergy of the Orthodox church deepened my feeling of an unbroken line of Eastern priests. All the diplomatic circle, England leading the list, were present. Sir William and Lady White represented England. The British Foreign Office recognizes the truth,—that the Orient respects large embassies and evidences of wealth, and the belief which England has impressed upon the East, that the word of a Frank is as good as his bond, has force.

Sir William and Lady White showed us every courtesy at dinners and balls given in our honor. There was a fly in my ointment: the Sultan did not seem cognizant of the prestige of the American wife and mother, and I was not included in the audience granted to Mr. Bass with the Sultan.

What a blessing for the world it would have been, and how much less battle of Cross and Crescent, if the Empress Helena had never discovered a piece of the True Cross, which became the bone of contention foreshadowing war, like the contended-for apple which Paris threw in the contest for beauty.

The witchery of dome and minaret from the cold brilliancy of the Black Sea called us, as did the beauty of Seraglio Point, but the day to set sail for Greece came all too soon.

CHAPTER FIFTEEN

GREECE

TO a group consisting of Greenough, the sculptor, Martin and Mary Ann Brimmer, his wife, he a patron of art, she a stately woman loving laces and all fine textiles—the fruits of all skilled handicrafts—, Mr. Bass, student of philosophy and law, my mother, a lover of beauty and a real traveler, Piraeus was a longed-for port. Was it not the gate of long-dreamed-of Greece?

Through the dust of a rough road, in shabby cabs, we came upon scenes of unexpected interest. Arriving the first of May, which is thirteen days later than May Day where people speak English, we saw at dawn groups of young men and maids, their arms filled with flowers, returned with laughter from the fields. Baskets of parti-colored blossoms hung on the latches of the doors of many houses,—tributes of love. At last we reached the hotel, where the best of accommodation was fairly indifferent. We sat down to a breakfast where tiny fried fish, full of bones, were served. "What shall I do about these bones?" said Mamma. "Eat them," said Minna Timmins as she crunched the fish, with her head thrown back like a satisfied lioness.

Athens welcomed us. The Brimmers had been eagerly expected by all classical scholars, and President Cleveland's letter opened diplomatic and court circles to the party. Mr. and Mrs. Fearn were the diplomatic representatives of the United States, and they at once gave dinners and receptions for us. My chief recollection of the first entertainment was meeting a middle-aged scholar whose name ended in "os," as did, it seemed to me, most of the names of Greeks. He had suffered the heavy grief and care of an insane wife until her death. In that dreary period he had translated into modern Greek what he called a Shakespearean trilogy,—Romeo and Juliet, Macbeth, and King Lear, then being given successfully in all the chief towns of Asia Minor. He had found Shakespearean humor his chief stumbling block, for like many others, he contended that every nation has its own type and shade of humor too subtle for perfect translation.

We were escorted to the Acropolis and to the excavation where archaic statues came from the earth bright with color. We found traces of red, blue and gold on the sheltered cornices of the Parthenon itself.

Seeing Greece in 1888 meant long drives and transportation on small coastwise steamers. The drive from Athens to Eleusis, skirting its blue Bay, meant to rise before dawn, and to reach one's bed, travel-stained, at midnight. For years I cherished the illusion of white-garbed philosophers walking the terraces of the Temple of Eleusis, debating on the Eleusinian mysteries. My second visit to that Temple was on a dull day in an automobile, to find a tall belching factory chimney pouring out clouds of smoke which stained the marble ruins black. Gone were the frank votive offerings of nature worship which had once marked the road to that shrine now decently concealed in the Museum at Athens.

The streets and restaurants of Athens were filled with gesticulating patrons talking of politics. In the days when St. Paul preached on Mars Hill the Greeks were wont to seek for something new. The modern Greek loves talk and political intrigue and promise of revolution. Nothing could be more picturesque than the Greek soldiers in their pleated white petticoats and gold-braided caps with long tassels. We went to a May festival in the country where the modern Greek soldiers, in their stiff petticoats and thong-corded sandals, danced man to man, to what may have been a far cry from the rhythm of the pyrrhic dances of the armies that won the Golden Fleece. We climbed halfway up Mount Hymettus, the far-famed honey of whose flowers made our early breakfast poetic. We could look at Salamis and the State of Attica, so small in area, a soil which sheltered artists and writers whose production for the world was a fountain of color. We ate our picnic luncheon at Marathon, and reveled in the inspiration of old Greece. I was told by Mr. Hitt, of Washington, that when, as a student with knapsack on his back, he traversed much of Greece on foot, he saw marbles as rarely beautiful as those from Aegina burned for lime by the natives.

On a little steamer we reached Nauplia to spend a night in small cubicle bedrooms without carpets, and Minna Timmins, homesick and longing for a sight of the man she loved and later married, talked until morning, saying that if she could only return to America, she would postpone her marriage as long as her aunt and uncle desired. In the fashion of Italian women who make an offering of their hair to the shrine at which they worship, or the lover from whom they are separated, she had chopped off her splendid dark hair on the return Nile journey. At last, Mr. and Mrs. Brimmer consented to make an earlier return to America than they had planned.

We wound our way, on the following morning, along the road where we found a heroic statue in marble, a lion almost a replica of the lion of Lucerne. It was certainly born of the same litter and it was erected in memory of the Swiss mercenaries who shed their blood for the freedom of Greece. How many thousand

Greek mercenaries have shed their blood for divers causes in quest of wage?

We were bound for Olympia and at last we landed at Patras. Mr. Bass had brought five luxurious ship-chairs from England, which we left in charge of a storehouse at the port, while we pushed on to the extensive excavations at Olympia to be enraptured with the beauty of Praxiteles' Hermes. The following day we drove back to catch the steamer, and found that a skillful servant of the Russian diplomat Bakhmeteff had stolen our chairs. In after years, I longed to tell Bakhmeteff, then wily Russian Ambassador, that he owed me the price of five comfortable chairs stolen by his varlet at Patras. As he had a tongue like a rapier, perhaps I shrank from a discussion with him,—a man who could say of his successor in America, also named Bakhmeteff, after the Russian Revolution, that he bore the same relation to him that Booker T. Washington did to George Washington.

As we reached the plaza to embark, we heard two sharp reports of a pistol, and rushing forward, found a man with a smoking pistol in his hand, and the wounded man on the ground, supported by his friends. Our dragoman shrugged his shoulders saying, "Oh, the Greeks are like that. For a few sous they shoot." The wounded man's brother carried him onto the deck of our boat, and as the steamer slowly wound its way toward his home from morning till night, his life-blood ebbed and at last ceased to flow.

The Greek soldiers have been fearless fighters, and my brother, Frank Metcalfe, the physician and traveler, told me that in the Greco-Turkish war, among the Greek wounded there was no infection. From the drinking of pure Greek wine, seasoned with the resinous gum from their mountain pines, the hardy Greek soldier, in storm or sun, healed himself.

The erosion of centuries of wind and rain have washed the red, blue and gilt from the brilliant shrines. The statue of Athena which lured the seafarer with passion up the staircase to her feet, was of gold, silver, ivory and precious stones, visible far out at sea.

We must recall that the Greek women loved to fashion their flowing robes in saffron hues, and that they were rebuked for pulling their sashes to make a waist of slender girth. Their glory was to be the deep-chested woman of the Greek. Our girls are not now condemned for small waists. They bare their backs, breasts and legs to fresh air and free movement. To be fair, one must note that the period when the young men and maidens of Sparta contended in the games nude, was the period of purity of morals and restraint in that stern state.

As I jot down these memories, I bless the German, Hammerling, who wrote "Aspasia." Aspasia watched the flower-decked white bulls led by joyous maidens to the altars in the spring and autumnal festivals. Hammerling's book vivified historic accounts of games when all war ceased and the gates of the city were thrown open. The poorest man of the populace was given a place, free of charge, to sit from sunrise till dark, enjoying the tragedies of Aeschylus or Sophocles, or the transcendent comedies of Aristophanes. The ear of even the lowest class was attuned to perfect accent and rhythm with a sensitiveness unknown to modern audiences, and they would cry out in derision if the actor was guilty of a slip.

At times, one wishes that our actors on to-day's modern stage, would open their holidays by purchasing a one-way ticket to Montauk to gather a few white pebbles and place them in their mouths, and following the tradition of the world's greatest orator, Demosthenes, address the waves until their diction was clean.

We pushed on to Epidaurus where the theater set on the side of the hill was acoustically perfect. We tried the full gamut of tones from a long cry to a whisper, standing where the actors were wont to perform, and at the remotest seat the lowest tone was clearly heard. At Epidaurus had been great hospitals and the Temple of Esculapius, who is always represented with the caduceus of Mercury intwined with serpents, signifying wisdom. He was evidently a practical healer of the sick and adviser in the lying-in hospital. From here spread the renown of the greatest physician of ancient times, Hippocrates.

In the early morning, as we were departing, a peasant brought to sell a small ring of pure gold of lovely design, with an inscription of good luck, which the British Museum has described and places its date as some time before Christ. I still treasure it.

Driving to Corinth, we arrived as night was falling. The great rock, rising sheer and black to dominate the city, overpowered one after the gaiety of the sparkling Bay. What had surprised me was to learn that the sultana raisins and dried currants that enriched our plum puddings and mince pies at Christmas were grown in this region. The Pelasgic walls, erected without mortar, interested the men of the party greatly. They did not seem remote to me from the stone walls made to clear the pastures on New England farms.

The glory of the Athens Museum, housed in the building erected through the generosity of one of her modern sons, to be realized must be seen, and we went regretfully back to Piræus to embark on the steamer which took us to Zante.

Reaching the port, we rushed to the hotel, where for one week I lay shivering with malarial fever. The party shook in their boots lest my illness should detain them over the scheduled steamer. I do recall that the buildings of the town showed the imprints of the Venetian occupancy, and I remember the large estates owned by that strain of Italians who, two hundred years before, had mixed their blood with that of the Greeks and obtained large revenues from dates, raisins and currants.

Venturing into a shop, I bought a beautiful fan with carved ivory sticks in one of which was a hidden receptacle for poison. It intrigues the imagination to think of a beautiful woman, with murder in her heart, gracefully waving the powder into the nostrils or the beaker of an old husband or a perfidious lover, which would send him from a terrestrial to, we hope, a celestial world. The fate of that fan I do not know. It was my gift to Countess Pourtalès.

Shortness of human life and the persistence of material objects have often stirred my ire. My son now owns a seal of the time of Darius which was long years ago given to me. When I first held it in my hand and thought of the crumbling of Greece, Egypt, Rome, the holy Roman Empire, and the results of the French Revolution, I flung afar the hard sardonyx beautifully carved gem with its intaglio of priests sacrificing at an altar, but anger assuaged, pride of possession triumphed, and I picked it up. Thrift may subdue indignation.

The voyage to Corfu was not long, and it was not difficult, on that theatrically beautiful island which seemed too magical to be true, to reduplicate a stretch of beach with Nausicaä and her maidens hanging out the week's wash as Ulysses found them. The olive trees which border the steep roads of the island are worthy of the brush of Doré. In the fields which they border, it seems as though Daphne might be hiding among their gnarled branches. On the highest point of the island stands the villa which the deposed William Hohenzollern chose for his holidays, commanding as it did the joyous beauty of Grecian waves and islands. Corfu's charms could not calm my restlessness, and I felt all islands must be put behind me that I might get to the soil of Europe. Every agent said not an inch of space was to be had on the steamer from Corfu to Trieste. It is wise never to recognize that one is beaten, and never to deal with a second-in-command; so I took a launch and boarded the steamer, and importuned the captain of the ship which was shortly to sail. It was not a case of beauty in distress that moved his Austrian heart, but the eloquence of a woman whose anxiety and the dins of many languages had driven to the keen edge of despair. Within an hour or two, we waved adieu from the port-hole of the captain's quarters.

Reaching Trieste, we found the town tumultuous on the feast of Corpus Christi. The Cardinal, brilliant as a Baltimore oriole, walked beneath a rich gold canopy held by priests in golden vestments. Acolytes with swinging censers made the air fragrant with frankincense and myrrh. There were bishops, prelates, monks and nuns, and the Children of Mary bearing flowers. The Blessed Virgin in jeweled mantle seemed to bless the following crowd. I could have kissed the very earth, for I knew enough household German and imperfect Italian to be sure that we were welcome, not hated. Trieste, that most picturesquely situated of towns, was a haven for rejoicing.

We took victorias and drove along the shell road of the Adriatic to the deserted palace of Maximilian and Carlotta. There could be no more romantic situation than Miramar, on whose rocky spur meticulous care still kept its beauty free from dust. In their library little keepsakes and small framed photographs of the friends they loved were on the tables as they had left them, and one might almost expect to find Maximilian writing at his desk in the sunny window, or to have the door open as they returned from walking in the park. Their last walk at Miramar was down the broad path to the white marble steps where, in gentle weather, the sea washes them and curls like a white feather. Reluctantly they went to the land of Montezuma to satisfy the ambition of Napoleon III. The heart of the whole world sympathized with their tragedy. I watched a young man and a pretty woman seeking seclusion among the shadows of the cypresses and hoped their romance might mean life, not death, as the birds were calling to love and continuance.

In the evening, we embarked for Venice, and it suits my fancy to believe that we followed the course which argosies of untold wealth took to that arrogant trading oligarchy of Venice, enriching it with the wealth of the Indies. The opaline tints of Venetian skies before daybreak found us on deck as the anchor dropped below the Giudecca or custom house, facing the columns at the entrance of the Piazza San Marco bearing the Lion of Saint Mark and the statue of Saint George, between which the traitors of the past were executed. It is always a thrill to mount the stairs to that great open-air salon of entertainment, the Piazza of St. Mark.

Up the side of the vessel came our valued gondolier, Pasquale d'Este. How heart-satisfying our relations were with him! If one becomes a patron of an honorable gondolier, he has charge and claim upon you until death. Pasquale, rarest of gondoliers, knew every church, every work of art and tradition. He was nature's nobleman.

CHAPTER SIXTEEN

VENICE

VENICE has her lovers. It is a city where stricken romance has sought shelter and never found peace. I could not be sincerely friendly with a man or woman who did not value that dying Queen of the Adriatic who in the height of Venice's glory wedded the sea with a golden ring flung by Doges from the Bucentaur.

The Grand Hotel welcomed our party. At that time it was a privilege to travel. There were no excursionists. After dinner, sitting on the balcony, Mr. Brimmer, Mr. Samuel Dixson, Mr. Dexter and Mr. Bass watched the Canal, and their talk was not idle. I remember that once that evening the concensus of their convictions was that the nearest approach to happiness was work done under conditions that promised achievement and success.

Sitting on the balcony we used to watch a glorious blonde Russian woman,—the type Paolo Veronese loved to paint. She had three yellow-haired children, hardly more than babies, but what a suite of nurses, governesses and tutors,—one an Oxford graduate! These tots were being taught to babble in three languages. We believed she was a Grand Duchess; there were so many, and they traveled in pleasant places. Even in the trains their maids brought crystal gold-mounted basins and poured water from gold ewers that they might cleanse their hands and faces, and dry their fingers on fine embroidered towels emblazoned with crests. A mint of money it took to educate their children! Eighty Grand Dukes, since the Russian Revolution, have met violent deaths, and those aristocratic Russian women who have escaped with their lives, have served as *vendeuses,* waitresses in bright-colored frocks, some in restaurants and beauty parlors, to earn a pittance. What water and blood have run underneath life's arches since 1888! It is not so many years since I gave up having a maid lug a carry-all filled with fine covers, sheets and pillows for my use in traveling.

I have spent much time in Venice, but the only visit ever paid to the Monastery which housed the archives of Venice was with our group of able American men. Like the Vatican, it contains untold as yet pages of history. The reports of Venetian Ambassadors in its period of greatness give brilliant accurate pictures of all European states. For modern investigators, it is hard to decipher the Roman texts in which these documents are inscribed. Rawdon Brown translated for the British Government, the ambassadorial data relating to England. For scholars there is a mine of golden information beneath the walls of the building that, thank heaven! are of slow-burning construction.

Old, disabled gondoliers torment one at every landing with a hook on a stick to steady a gondola as one lands. Once Venice minted the smallest copper coins. By lucky chance one came into my possession and I resolved to hand it to the bothersome beggar at San Marco landing. As I put it in his hand, he raised himself with gesture of insulted dignity and flung it away. I hastened to recover it as a curiosity, but he scampered on all-fours quick as a cricket, and fixed me with a glance of triumph.

Our time was spent in gondolas, and every morning we visited churches and palaces. On the floor of the gondola each morning was placed a canvas bag marked "ex libris." The luxury of leathern cushions filled with down banished fatigue as one sat, or if one chose, the gondola became a convenient study and writing-room. Excursions to the Lido, and the outlying islands even, with two or three men, occupied the afternoons; and we came back at sunset with our correspondence finished,—time well spent, as was that with Ruskin and W. D. Howells' enchanting "Venetian Life." What a fortunate choice the powers that were made when the Consulate in Venice was given to Howells! No one has added more interest, not even Horatio Brown, who has recorded the inner life of gondoliers and the charm of lagoons. Those who peek into Venice and act as though a gondolier were a taxi-driver, do not reckon with the unique history of an ancient Guild with whom the government of Venice has always had to reckon. One who has had the proud accommodations of the fine palatial suite at the Grand Hotel, at the end of the Annex, which overlooks the traghetto knows the gondoliers are quarrelsome. Some of them are wine bibbers, but from time to time they have battled for their civic rights with success. They are prolific fathers whose families, under marching modernity, can hardly beat back starvation during the winter.

The beauty of the dying city can capture the romance of honeymooning newlyweds and tourists, but one needs the knowledge that Molmenti gives, or that unique book, "Venise dans le dix-huitième siècle," to galvanize to life the heroic past, and the exotic fantastic society when Goldoni wrote comedies. Guardi and Longhi revealed that life and its follies in speaking paintings of Venetian high life.

One needs time and discretion to be friendly with Venice; not to be of those who hold their noses at low tide in narrow malodorous canals. One may still pass the asylums for mad men and women, hearing their cries as one sees their shadows behind the bars; or catch the voices of children lamenting and dying from pellagra, caused by insufficient salt in their diet of polenta.

We went to the Armenian Monastery where Byron stayed to learn the language of the black-bearded quiet monks whose successors now print and sell to visitors Byron's "Childe Harold." Until the still afternoon when we reached its walls, my view of oleanders was of an occasional small tree in a tub kept in the cellars during the winter by the wives of American farmers, to bloom in their door-yards the following August. Here masses of pink blossoms riotously tumbled from trees, the branches of which nearly touched the water beneath the brick walls of the Monastery garden. I recalled Elizabeth Barrett Browning's line of "Aurora Leigh,"—"reaching England with smell of oleander in her hair."

Byron's letters reveal the importunities of that man-chasing Jane Clairmont who beat her way through a tempestuous night to Byron's presence. The result of that importuning woman was the ill-fated child, Allegra, whose life fortunately was short. Byron, the Shelleys and Brownings glorified every phase of romantic passion. "A Toccata of Galuppi's," by Browning, in brief, sums up the picture of his time and its spell, of the triumph and passing of glowing blonde women.

Wagner's ghost, as he wrote the second act of "Tristan and Isolda," broods over a palace and garden on the Grand Canal.

If one went to see the sunrise, the beggars who slept under the arches of the Piazza shook their rags and awakened to hate and curse the Austrians with the fervor of Italian patriots.

What fascinating hours we spent at Murano, where Salviati, leader of the famous glass-blowers of Murano, joined us in the designing and selection of glass to be sent back to Edgeplain in Colorado. The unique liqueur glasses, each fragile as a flower, we hoped were not short-lived. No finger-bowl at that time was complete without an accompanying *rinse bouche,* for, a meal finished, people hid their mouths with their napkins, and cleansed them from the drinking glass into the finger-bowl and used, without shame, a toothpick. Are we more refined now or a trifle squeamish? A cleansed mouth after dining would be refreshing.

A great brass founder copied from a painting of Titian a fruit salver, and we proved a little tasteless in adding in its center a personal monogram. These pleasures added a touch to our journey of home-building and furnishing. Alas! home-abiding does not necessarily follow. Whatever wall one builds, the instinct to wander remains. A friend once said to me that he was "homesick." "I am sick of staying at home," said he. But in this era of Ford cars, one can take quick leave of family, house and home.

To take tea or an orangeade in the late afternoon in the Piazza of San Marco, watching the crowd and looking up to the most ancient mosaics of the jeweled façade of San Marco, refreshed us. Going to and from the Hotel to the Piazza, passing under the Bridge of Sighs, recalled inevitably Byron's lines on Palace and Prison. Nowhere do the romantic dead walk beside us more than in the *calli* of Venice, and one would hope that the noisy bells of every campanile might call us to return. Always my eyes have been wet as the gondola turned toward the crowded railway station for leaving.

I longed to go on to the Fishermen's Shrine of the Virgin, standing above the waters of the lagoon, where they pray for fisherman's luck and immunity from danger. May that Queen of the ocean survive my life! I should like my grandchildren to see her glories and my hope is founded on the fact that the piles of her foundation are of rare mahogany driven deep and in sufficient quantity that were they raised and stretched and sawn to boards, they could panel all the luxurious houses of England and of her annex, the United States.

As late as 1888 no young woman could walk in the Piazza without male attendance and even were she leaning on the arm of a male protector the gallants of the city approached saying as they walked near her "How beautiful you are! How charming!" The noble art of boxing used by husband or brother would have seemed to these men provincial and uncalled for. Perhaps such attentions were a thrill to ugly women and a trifle flattering to the most seemly and good-looking ones.

Nowhere is the mystic glamor of half-remembered poets, painters and musicians more potent than in gondola days on the breast of the quiet lagoons or wandering canals of the city.

Sometimes we bathed at the Lido. Then there was only a rude pavilion which enabled women to put on voluminous hideous bathing suits to wade a half mile to the breaking waves or to a sufficient depth of water to swim. Shelley's verses of "Julian and Naddalo" brought the shades of Byron and Shelley galloping their horses as they went down on "a narrow space of level sand" now hidden by villas and hostelries. What a contrast to the Lido of to-day, luxurious and degenerate as Sodom, vulgar with the scum and riff-raff of all races, where sprawling hairy fat men and naked women grease their own bodies and those of their companions with vaseline in an effort to attain the patine and color of a red Indian.

One is surprised how watchful and fearful the gondoliers are of the threat of storms. They well know the danger when the sky grows black, tinged with yellow and green, and seek the nearest possible shelter. Once returning from a reception at the Palazzo di Mula, we could not reach shelter until we were drenched to the skin. Hanging my best frock and corsets to dry did not restore them to pristine beauty.

We were handicapped by indifferent knowledge of languages. To enjoy fully the dinners in the evenings at the red Capello Palace of Sir Henry and Lady Layard, one needed to be polyglot. We knew them during the last decade of his full life when he sought quietude and the power of uninterrupted work after his return from Far Eastern wanderings, the experience of political life as Member of the House of Commons, and acting as Ambassador at Constantinople and Madrid. Sir Henry seemed strangely brusque and impatient for a man who had suffered the restraint of ambassadorial position. The fascination of the relation of his archæological experience in uncovering the ruins at Nineveh, read to both the man of science and the reading world at large like a fairy tale. His home was a mecca for scholars and important travelers of every race.

An occasional great aristocrat arrived at Mestre in traveling carriage and four horses guided by postilions, and came by gondola to lodge in a palace to loaf and invite his soul.

Sir Henry's house was inviting and home-like, and Lady Layard's circle did not include the resident heroes and heroines of illicit romance. He was a friend and intimate of Morelli, patriot and art critic, who had cast a quickening seed into learned research of early writers on painting and sculpture. The theory he advanced seems to me as important as that of the use of finger prints in the identification of individuals, criminals and otherwise. In the drawing of an ear, in the brush-marks of a painting, he found that the personal touch of an artist can be identified, as individual as the color of his eyes or the shape of his hands; also that one must have the emotional reaction which causes the blood of the onlooker to flow more quickly and warms cold criticism to a living influence. Sir Henry became an eminent collector of paintings of the Venetian school, many of which are masterpieces now in the National Gallery. The power of purchase is an enlightenment and educator, and to buy a spurious work of art and to pay as the Israelites say,—"through the nose," cultivates discretion and judgment. Sir Henry was supposed to have made no mistakes in the paintings he acquired of the Venetian school. It was pleasant to raise one's eyes from one's plate to look at a portrait by Giovanni Bellini against the ancient crimson brocade which covered the walls of dining- and reception-rooms. The patrician families of Venice mingled freely in the Layards' international evenings,—names which were written in the Libro d'Oro of proud Venetian pedigree,—and rubbed shoulders with aristocratic travelers of every land.

Of that society were Mr. and Mrs. Frederick Eden. They came in an effort to restore the health of the young groom who, on his honeymoon, had been thrown in the hunting field and had injured his back. In 1884, fatigued with life on the water only, he purchased a series of vineyards around which he built a high brick sea-wall. For nearly sixty years it has been called "The Garden of Eden," and for sixty years Mrs. Eden occupied a lovely palace a door or two beyond the Grand Hotel. After the death of her husband, her nieces and nephews kept her from being lonely. Mrs. Eden was connected by blood or marriage with half the great families and leading literati of England. Leaning on her sea-wall, one looked across the San Giorgio on island villages on the edge of the lagoons. On fine days, Mrs. Eden was taken in her gondola to her garden, which she made as near an English garden as climate and conditions would permit. Her tea-table would be set in the shadow of the cypresses. The political world and the latest books were discussed by the best resident society of

Venice and intelligent travelers. Her intellect had as much or more of youth than was shown by the clever young relatives who shared her attention. Her affiliations with the best Italian people were intimate and she was an honored guest everywhere.

Formerly the Venetian "season" was in the winter, and the Venetians arrived at the most lovely of eighteenth century opera houses sheltered from storm and wind by the coffin-like black *felse,* which in summer is rarely used on a gondola. Cards and dancing and late hours marked the Venetian Season. In the summer the nobility traveled or remained late in their villas in the Veneto.

Those exquisitely fashioned marionettes which are chiefly manipulated now in South America, by hands of inherited flexibility of generations of artists, who had amused the Venetian populace with their lifelike imitations, have since forsaken Venice to gain a livelihood, and Venice is shorn of their color and gaiety. It is not so many years ago that being asked to a breakfast by Edward Sheldon, the playwright, to meet Somerset Maugham in a charming house in Irving Place, I found the dining-room walls festooned with strings of marionettes, each a portrait of the character so well represented in the comedies of the eighteenth century.

Mrs. Eden needed water for her garden, and Frederick Eden sank the first artesian well driven in the Veneto. Gas raised from the layers of peat penetrated by the drill, coming to the surface, ignited and exploded. The natives crowded to the island and insisted that Sir Frederick had direct communication with Hell. The excitement rose to a pitch which finally necessitated a visit from the Cardinal in scarlet, and priests in full regalia, acolytes with holy water and smoking censers, to exorcise the devil and cleanse the caverns of Hell.

We often lunched under the trellises of the little hotel which Ruskin loved, and as we watched shipping from every port casting anchor, the thought intruded itself that superstition was as persistent as race itself. The seaworthy boats from the mainland, gaily painted with signs against the evil eye and hidden devils of the sea, as they brought lumber and fagots from distant shores, possibly carried on the tradition inherited from the crafts of the civilizing Phœnicians or the harrowing galleys of piratical Saracens. What good luncheons we ate as we watched the ever-changing scenes on the deep breast of the Giudecca!—tiny devil-fish known as *calamai*, or *calamaretti*, or *ravioli*, washed down with goblets of light Verona wine, red or white, too delicate to bear transportation by rail or ship, as we relished the perfect cheese and fruit brought from the picturesque market near the Rialto.

We left Venice, followed by the affectionate wishes of our faithful gondoliers, as they sadly put the bags into the compartment in which we should skirt the Italian Lakes to reach Lombardic Plains.

Well as I know Milan, I shrank from the beating heat of summer and the icy winds of winter sweeping from the mountains, which make for one's discomfort. At the Hotel Cavour we were welcomed as old friends, and we undertook the usual round of sight-seeing, which naturally included the Gothic Cathedral, which excites the admiration of all sightseers. Why Mr. Bass insisted, for a second time, on spending five francs to descend to the crypt of the Cathedral for a look at the shrine of San Carlo Borromeo, which he had seen in 1876, was beyond my ken. For myself, the brown husks of prelate, crowned monarch, Egyptian or Christian, have neither sex appeal nor personal magnetism.

VENICE

Most women might covet the cross of superb emeralds, given to the shrine by Maria Theresa, which hangs above the remains in that rock crystal casket where that hideous effigy reposes, in full cardinal's regalia, including gloves and ring. The Church seems able to retain the treasures of Maria Theresa when those of many monarchs have been sold to the highest bidder. Nature, left to herself, makes more fitting disposition of the dead. The beasts of untrodden wilds or the little creatures of the fields and birds of the air meet death and nature removes all trace of them.

Everyone still rushes to see Leonardo's "Last Supper." For me, I care more for his drawing of Christ's face than for that vast restored canvas. One must go to Milan to love Luini, so like and yet unlike Leonardo. Did his lady-love, of all flowers, care most for the fragrant Stephanotis which he paints so often in his portraits of fair women? Whether it be the sentiment with the power of the Church, or fear of punishment hereafter, the bloody despots of Italy, in expiation for their sins, seemed to try to fool a personal God. Sforza, the Scorpion, most cruel of rulers, built the Certosa di Pavia, than which nothing is more beautiful, except possibly, the Taj Mahal. Shah Jehan evidently brought Italians to finish the interior with precious marbles and gay *pietra dura* in the tomb he built for the mother of his fifteen children. Travelers fatigued should not deprive themselves of seeing both, the Taj Mahal and the Certosa di Pavia, at dawn, noonday, sunset and under full moon.

Speed is killing taste and the heart of beauty. A skyscraper with skeleton of steel and a facing of stone put on like an overcoat is not erected for anything but utility and to be wrecked after a short life.

What an artistic pleasure one found in Milan in the marvels of brick and terra cotta reliefs shown in hospital, convent and palace, awaking our admiration for the architects of the north. As one walks the streets of Milan and sees men of height and stature, blond of hair and blue of eye, one recalls that they must have in them the strain of the northern hordes which conquered Italy and destroyed the Roman Empire. More than the Cathedral, the ancient church of Sant' Ambrogio interested me. Its ancient altar of rare enamel, pietra and precious stones, is where the monarchs of the Holy Roman Empire were crowned with the Iron Crown of Italy. The form of the early Christian upper and lower church, rich in column and balustrade, lectern and pulpit, in the best work of the Cosmati, has the lovely bloom and patine of antiquity.

Now the Hotel Cavour has been enlarged, but it was comfortable in 1875. What hostelry in America ever weathered fifty-five years with dignity?

For me Milan has always been either too hot or too cold, and we were not sorry to board the train for Paris.

CHAPTER SEVENTEEN

PARIS

HOW glad one is to hear the guard shout "Paris! Paris!" and to see one's hand-luggage passed through the window to be examined at the Customs! Glad to find the Column Vendôme standing spite of the fact that the enthusiastic idealists under the Commune once pulled it down, joined by the artists of Paris, and the sanest of Americans, Calvin S. Bryce, who in his youth helped to level to earth this record of Napoleon's battles, with the dream possibly that with the destruction of records of royal despots and blood-stained history, it could be replaced by a perfect democracy. Calvin S. Bryce, in his maturity Senator of the United States, in his youth failed to recognize the fact that the vanity of any group of men or women reveals the truth that the brotherhood of humanity at large is still hidden around the corner of time.

Our party unpacked silks and precious stuffs woven in the looms of the Near East, intending that they should be made proper for modern use by the skill of the best dressmakers of France. Minna Timmins's selections Worth turned out in sweeping lines that arrayed her like an empress of the Orient. Modestly I pulled from my hand-bag Persian stuffs acquired in the warm gloom of the bazaars of Constantinople and Damascus, and when they were finished, I looked as well as I could.

Père Worth had a love for the richest materials that the looms of Lyons could produce, and he used them in making Court gowns to clothe exacting Americans. He once said to me, "You should wear *clair de lune* because of your eyes. Never alter a dress I make for you. It should remain to the end, perfect." His wildest flight of imagination never saw the time when a lady with a "perfect thirty-six" bust, or our girls in their slenderness, could be tastefully attired in a frock bought in a side street for nine dollars and ninety-nine cents, or that the laboring female should array her nether limbs in silk stockings to do what a maid of mine once called "me-*ni*-al" work. John Addington Symonds wrote, "Blood lust is hidden in every human soul." Certain it is that hidden in women, high or low, there is a longing for fine raiment and jewels. The dress of Paris in 1888 launched the modes of the world's latest fashion. Silk stockings today are a symbol of democracy.

We were all keen to visit studios and taste the gay life of Paris, and breathlessly climbed many stairs to see the promising work of struggling artists. Walter Gay was recognized as an artist of merit,—a bachelor of small means. We found him surrounded by his work, genially awaiting us, and Mr. Brimmer bought one of the paintings of an eighteenth century interior, which is now recognized by the world as of rare merit. He had not then married his delightful wife, Matilda Travers. Now in their town house, a splendid moated villa near Fontainebleau, Mrs. Gay can guide a small skiff in the waters where swans swim, and a draw-bridge is extant at the château entrance. His present residence gives him eighteenth century background, and he never needs leave his superb home to depict the scenes which art collectors now aspire to hang on the walls of their American homes, reflecting the height of elegant and artificial civilization which existed under Louis XIV, XV and XVI.

We lost no opportunity to see Zambelli dance. She was the queen of all Italian dancers, trained in the school at Milan. On those occasions, not one bald head was missing from the three front rows of the orchestra. From our box, they looked like rows of ostrich eggs.

To have Virot create a hat on my head was one of my vanities; I watched him in the mirror, hoping for some personal chic, even if my build was that of a pony rather than that of a graceful greyhound! And then the delightful evenings in small restaurants, frequented by gourmets, possibly served in a room where the floor was covered with sawdust, or the Café de Paris thronged by foreign visitors. No Frenchwoman went to a restaurant unaccompanied or in a décolleté frock. A discreet, becoming, high-necked frock served for the dinner or the play. Time lends luster to the nights at the Française when Croisette charmed the public in Dumas fils' "The Demi-monde." It was not written about the realm of cocottes, but of a circle of damaged fair fruit which, at first glance, was without blemish, but spotted, was inwardly rotten. One heard much talk of the Jardin de Mobile where gay girls danced the cancan and kicked off the hats of gallants. How beguilingly bright it seemed as one drove down the Champs Elysées! The sounds of revelry and the festooned lights were as enticing to good wives and daughters as to fathers and sons; but protected and respectable wives were dully sent to find, if possible, beauty sleep in their beds at an early hour, while their men came home in the gray of the morning after having enjoyed the rush of Paris night life.

Sarah Bernhardt at the Française was the *cri de tout Paris,* whether in "Phèdre," "Adrienne Lecouvreur" or "Frou-Frou." In the pleasures of experience, I reckon my passion for the theater the most absorbing, and I went to France with a reverence and a desire to weigh the values of the French theater. It came to me then, as it does today, that behind all great acting must be study, discipline and the full knowledge of the use of one's body and gesture, the proper use of the diaphragm and the resonant arch of the mouth, and the knowledge that a whispered sibilant can reach the ear of the most distant listener in an auditorium. At Mrs. Macauley's School, as I was reading a passage of a play of Shakespeare's, Dr. Leonard called out, "Frances Esther, you have swallowed a conjunction. Bring it up." To an actor who has not freed his potentialities in utterance, there must be many undigested conjunctions.

The wit and naughtiness of the little theaters of Paris,—above all, that most perfect of small theaters, Gabriel's *chef d'œuvre,* the Palais Royal, required that an American should check her modesty with her cloak in the dressing-room, to be called for at the end of the play. Their art is not casual but a talent well-trained. One must remember that Sarah Bernhardt wrote that it took her three years to learn to walk the stage.

Of course we heard Mounet-Sully in "Oedipus Rex," but I fear that all French tragedy written with the classicism of the Greek unities, I felt to be passion in a strait-jacket. Many years afterwards, sitting in a box with Winthrop Chanler, he said of Mounet-Sully, "If that man doesn't stop barking I shall leave the theater," but I have never recovered from the illusion that "Sylvain" was in truth Louis XI, and as the curtain fell on his masterly performance, having crushed the feudalism of France, he might step over the footlights, descend the grand staircase glancing at Houdon's statue of Voltaire and passing the restaurant where Napoleon played at chess to win, he might reach the Chambre des Députés and crush the young Republic of France, for in 1888 an impression was abroad that the Republic was not of long duration. But as a French Minister of Finance once said to me, the Republic was growing daily in strength, and its foundations were *"dans les sabots des paysans."*

Whether it be to interpret Bach or to sing the "Casta Diva" satisfactorily on the stage, there is the necessary discipline which cannot be attained without years of preparation and self-sacrifice. We must not forget that Chopin could not have given the full revelation of the perfection of his own creation if he had not worked diligently at scales and five-finger exercises. The road to the stars must always be over stony ground, and the youth of today wish to fly over the obstacles.

What pure delight one found in Bartet! She suggested every phase of human emotion and passion without fully depicting it, yet she shook the audience to the foundation of their souls.

One afternoon at the Baroness Rothschild's the Duchess Wagram entered, enthusiastic over an entertainment from which she had just come where Bartet had recited. The salon was crowded with women bearing the greatest titles in France, but, said she, Bartet was the greatest duchess of them all. She portrayed the graceful woman of the world. The Parisienne went to the opening of her plays to see what they felt was the last touch of an exclusive mode. Jacques Doucet was both her friend and her dressmaker. When I saw her one time in close consultation with Doucet in one of his salons in the Rue de la Paix, her personal distinction was dominating. No man in France had a greater flair than he for art and for revealing every good point in a client's face or figure. After the sale of his great eighteenth century collection, he gathered the paintings and sculpture of the modern movement. I had longed to see his house, and a well-known architect, and a curator of the Musée du Louvre, received permission to see his gallery where he was to welcome us. As we reached the house, a heavy downpour of rain made a descent from the motor difficult, but through the storm his valet and servants in grief and consternation told us he had just dropped dead.

I never found Sarah Bernhardt, despite her retention of her velvet utterance, as convincing after she separated from the Théâtre Française and developed what I called "upholstered drama," but she was a superb actress and had the courage of a lion. A riotous spender of the wealth she earned, she knew no moderation in work or love. She reckoned every distinguished man in France her friend and in her leisure, strove to model and paint, freeing talents it may be of less degree than that of her histrionic art, but she shared with other gifted artists the power of creating in more than one medium.

How pleasant it was to drive in an open victoria along the Avenue des Acacias in the Bois de Boulogne, where leaders of society as well as well-known members of the demi-monde watched one another as they slowly passed. The attitude of Paris was one of uncommon tolerance.

Leaving a fitting-room at Worth's one morning, I heard the high-pitched voice of an old, short, fat woman, with a tiny asthmatic dog in her arms, saying she had been neglected. "Who is that?" I inquired. "Oh, that is Rose Pom-pom." "And who may be Rose Pom-pom?" asked I. The *vendeuse* replied, "The most famous cocotte of the Third Empire." She was still an honored client of the Maison Worth. Rose Pom-pom and her dog were out of fashion, for there is a fashion in dogs. The late Great War has nearly exterminated the wisest of canines, the *caniche*. What has become of the lap-dogs loved long ago,—the priceless King Charles and Blenheim spaniels which Van Dyck painted, the giant mastiffs and St. Bernards? Fickle we mortals be!

The Salons were open. The artists of the mode at that time are less considered now. The Impressionists, Dégas, Monet and Renoir, have more or less shouldered them into the background. One sometimes asks what has become of the canvas and paint constituting the miles of pictures through which one walked with fatigue. They are gone like the snows of yester-year.

Rodin's statues had been rejected by Salons and Academies as being revolutionary. When as a child he had walked through the Musée du Louvre, craving brushes and paint which he was too poor to buy, he had striven to model figures from the mud of the Paris gutters.

Were it possible to evoke the spirit and the glamour of the past, Paris would give one that power. More than any people, the French use the art of living. It is reflected in every walk of life and is founded on the family which centers about the children. The doctors and churchmen who served on battlefields and in hospitals during the late War bore testimony that in the agony of suffering, the French soldier invariably called for his mother. The authority of the mother in Latin lands is reinforced by her comprehension and acceptance of human nature as it is, and in its trend comes the sense of value of the moment and pleasure in small things.

In 1888 Paris housed great chefs, and the creative cook was proud of his profession as a king of a royal throne. Food is not wasted in France. It is properly prepared and whether for viands or wine, rich and poor have a palate which demands flavor. It was always interesting to watch a man and wife come into a restaurant, making an event of a good dinner, sharing the choice of wines, the ordering of the menu and showing the intention of being entertaining to each other.

Who does not remember the dinners at the Tour d'Argent, where the great Frederic and Madame and their trusty waiters served the *spécialité de la maison,* pressed duck, each duck wearing on his leg an identification tag stating his number in sequence, tokens of years of ducks squeezed by poor old Frederic, who must have hated more and more the fowls he squeezed, for he had never tasted one.

The little shop-girl who, on a gray, damp day, snuggles with her young man under a dripping awning before a beer shop seasons her frugal repast with a little loving without self-consciousness but a desire to live her hour fully. What a gay sight to see the midinettes run from their workrooms to walk gladly with their soldier lovers unaware of criticism of the passerby. The outside world for them does not count. One night at Foyot's famous restaurant everyone at table rushed to the windows and street doors as a group of young masqued revelers, with tambourine, fife, fiddle and drum, swept dancing by, bound for a student's ball. The onlookers were in tune with the merry-makers. It needed neither money nor prestige to answer the call of youth and spring to free the joy of living. The Englishman and American are too self-conscious to give successfully and get fun at carnivals and masqued fêtes. In the heart of Paris, as in the fields and vineyards of France, the voice of Pan still calls.

Murger was dead, but his "Vie de Bohème" filled me with ardor to peek into the Latin Quarter. We climbed rickety stairs to see young sculptors. In the Latin Quarter, as elsewhere in France, the dullard and indolent have no place. Brooks Adams once told me that there never was a more mistaken statement than that the French are frivolous,—that no nation demands harder work of its men.

One afternoon we went to the Latin Quarter where students of medicine and art go in the late afternoon with their French grisettes and their sweethearts, cur dogs on leash. They seemed to me quite unaffected nice young people. Some of the art students wore black and white checked trousers, broad-brimmed felt hats and large black bows tied under their chins. They probably fancied that they might some time be as great as Rubens, and in any event it was well to look like him.

The old Paris that Meryon loved to etch was not then leveled to the ground, and the Champs Elysées housed the prosperous and aristocratic, and was not then a highway of trade, poisoned with the gas from automobiles which, together with the asphalt, has doomed the chestnut trees which were the glory of spring in Paris,—now replaced by young sycamores that can survive smoke and cramping.

Widor was organist at Saint Sulpice, and all fine ladies of musical taste hungered for an invitation to sit on the bench with him as he played,—an honor which I once shared.

As I watched the divinity students, I saw no promise of great prelates. After the Franco-German War, good wives of *concièrges* and small shop-keepers, feeling that in a black soutane a son of the people, so garbed, had as much dignity as a man of title, strove to have their boys educated for the priesthood. A scrubby lot they were to my eyes. When the government forbade all clerical processions save within the confines of the Church, Holy Days lost interest and color but it seems to me socially wise that the pious go to early mass and reserve the rest of Sunday for pleasant amusement—theaters, races, concerts and balls.

Madame Waddington, an American, née King, married the able Frenchman who became Ambassador to the Court of St. James. Her house welcomed international nobility, visiting English of rank, and royalty. The Waddingtons were friends of both Princess Alexandra and the Prince of Wales. Once when she was giving an entertainment for Prince Edward she submitted, as is a rule, lists of guests for his approval. He added the name of an American beauty who was renowned for amorous adventure, and Madame Waddington said, "Sire, she is not received in Paris." "She is a friend of the Princess Alexandra," replied the Prince, and wrote her name legibly. She came to Madame Waddington's ball, and her social status in Paris and London was assured by the loyalty of him who afterwards became Edward VII.

Living at the Hotel Vendôme, one was interested in a casual glimpse of the Prince of Wales who, for a quarter of a century before Queen Victoria's death, occupied bachelor quarters on the ground floor next door at the Hotel Bristol. Paris reveled in the pleasure of Prince Edward's incognito. The gaiety of the little theaters glowed with his praise, and over the footlights passed sparks of wit from the clever actresses who were his admiring friends. One often saw him at the races and his attire set the style in dress for the dudes of Paris.

Have women now forgotten that flannel petticoats ever existed and were once trimmed with real lace? No trousseau of a girl of the upper circle was complete without such preparation. If their clothes, like architecture, are the expression of the needs and taste of their period, a petticoat may be a high sign marking an epoch as well as a skyscraper. Times have altered. Today the female seems to have a body that needs no covering,—an adequate epidermis that repels the north wind. My brother has said that there is neither curiosity nor adventure left for a male. The shop windows and advertisements in trains have killed all romantic illusions. Of old, the trousseau of a bride of the inner circle was supposed to provide underwear which would endure until she needed a shroud. Au Montaigne Rouge in the rue St. Honoré was patronized by conservative families. At the time of a marriage, all the friends were asked to view the *chemiserie* and drawers-erie, tied up in parcels of dozens with pink and blue satin ribbons. Hand-woven linen lawn, trimmed with real lace and embroidered with monograms, had no touch of indiscretion. The frills at neck and wrists of night-dresses were dainty and virginal, —suggestive but not revealing. To the washable garments were added beautifully made silk petticoats, ruffled and brocaded. A good corset-maker was important, and the lifting of a long dress revealed white petticoats of embroidered and lace-trimmed lawn. Like the underwear, table and household linens to last a lifetime were a perquisite of the bride.

No well-born unmarried girl was expected to walk abroad unchaperoned. She was permitted the *littérature de jeune fille,* but novels, like the big theaters, were a closed book to her. Pantomimes and classical performances at the Française were her portion. I was told by a young American girl that her associates at the Convent of the Sacré Cœur wished to marry early in order to go to the little theaters. Human nature in convents rebels at restrictions and bars, and those sheltered girls were probably more knowledgeable of the facts of life than their American schoolmates. Their baths were taken while wrapped in a sheet that they might not be aware of their own nakedness. The late war struck a blow at all false modesty, for the French married and unmarried women ministered to suffering mankind without reserve.

My faith is that the arranged marriage in France, built on a foundation of the requirements of the family, provides as much or more stability and happiness than does the "rule of thumb" in the United States whereby the *coup de feu* answers the call of the unborn to marriages that do not entail either submission or sacrifice but the unspoken idea of severance, though unwritten in the marriage certificate.

John Hay once criticized to me our world which permitted a girl of seventeen to set aside all the wisdom her elders had gained by love of her, a knowledge of human nature, and personal experience, to marry willy-nilly a hastily chosen mate. Today we may echo the adage of the ancients in uttering the prayer, "God save a man from his heart's desire!" Happiness, like the perfect climate, is ten miles further along the road beyond the point man reaches.

Once I saw Rosa Bonheur at a *vernissage* during the later years of life,—a striking picture, she being the only woman in France permitted by the state to wear man's attire.

One read de Maupassant's "Contes" and discussed the rebellious brutal frankness of Zola. The dead Balzac's "Comédie Humaine" and his letters and light romance were discussed at pleasant dinners.

Painters of the school of 1840 charmed us. Bonnat and Carolus Duran at studios welcomed us. When we arrived at Duran's apartment, he—a gay, attractive little man—was strumming on a guitar to his posing model, whom he at once dismissed. Bonnat's portrait of the head of the French African Missionary Order attired in white soutane and scarlet sash, his heavy black beard meticulously depicted, took the first prize at the Salon. This giant shepherd of the unconverted black men crossed from France to Alexandria on our steamer, as commanding and noble a presence as ever paced a deck, reading his breviary. What fate awaited him? He went where a poisoned arrow might possibly end life and success.

The day has come when the common law of England for the protection of woman is no longer needed, wherein was inscribed that no woman could be deprived of shift or bed, however great her debts. Now the dainty *chemise de bébé* of the Frenchwoman which prepared her to meet any accident with decency is forgotten. Today all women have cast off their shifts and fine ladies are paid for use of their names to advertise comfortable beds,—all for the sweet cause of charity.

I used to be awakened by the clump of the heavy-footed Percheron horses of Normandy toiling towards the market with the high-wheeled carts in which were vegetables systematically and tastefully packed. Do travelers go now, at break of day, to les Halles? It was fun to see the containers filled with sea-water in which swam live fish to be chosen by a purchaser; the butchers cutting the fat of beeves and sheep into ornamental patterns; and oh! those *fraises de bois* served with coagulated cream. Some of our friends reveled in eating snails,—a dainty which I avoided. I have always had admiration and respect for the snail, whose house moves with him. The partnership between the farmer and his wife, as with the small tradesmen, in France, is such that one is not unlikely to find the woman the better man of the two. The very stones of Paris are vocal. The passing carts for market follow the streets over which the tumbril of Marie Antoinette passed to the guillotine, marked now by the lovely fountain which cannot wash away those blood-stains in the Place de la Concorde.

Alexandre Dumas' historical novels are illuminating companions for those who walk the streets of Paris, and to live with the society of historic personages he depicts, is to make one's daily acquaintances seem a trifle drab, and one is spurred to leave them to prowl in those historic streets.

One morning after a breakfast on the broad terrace of St. Germain, we seemed suddenly plunged in the heart of the eighteenth century when a field of riders, the women in *tricorne* hats, their coats bright with gold braid, answered the winding of the hunter's horn as they dashed to the chase, the antipodes of the correct style shown in England by followers of the fox.

On the day we left Colorado Springs, I had spent an hour with a lad who seemed to me ill and forlorn. Joseph S. Stevens had been cradled in luxury and sent with a trailing wing to find strength in a high altitude. His joking courage in a cold hall-bedroom was the result of sacrificing an income because of what he believed to be an unfair withholding of an allowance from his eldest sister. His mother, then the Marquise de Talleyrand, was occupying the Chateau Enghien, which her husband had purchased and furnished with the inherited knowledge of things rare and beautiful of the period of le Roi Louis XIV and his successors. He was the grandnephew of the great Talleyrand, who had not been unskilled in craft.

The Marquise was a granddaughter of Joseph Sampson, who left her untrammeled in the spending of a vast fortune. I have known few women whom I liked better. She had been a strong-bitted girl,— a rule unto herself. Radiant with health, she married Frederic Stevens. Together they built a perfect mansion on the southwest corner of Fifth Avenue and Fifty-seventh Street, where the fashionable world enjoyed superb entertainments. She was a born generous mother of four children, all of whom loved and enjoyed life in the Stevens cottage at Newport.

Talleyrand-Perigord arrived. He was divorced from his first wife, Miss Curtis of Boston. He came to pay a visit to Mr. and Mrs. Stevens, where he collapsed with typhoid fever, and was skillfully nursed back to health. He was an able fisherman in muddy waters. Finding that his hostess was mistress of her money without let or hindrance, he proceeded to distil subtle suggestions of a poisonous nature about her good husband, and to lay pipe to becoming his successor. He was a man with the art of pleasing women; burning incense of flattery, he interested by both color and trenchant wit. He gave his intelligent counsel as to the acquirement of rare art, and hypnotized an uncomplex honest woman and disrupted the harmony of a family. Eventually, after endless criticism and adverse chatter, he married Mrs. Stevens.

Soon after we reached Paris, the Marquise, who had been ill and had recently left the hospital, asked Mr. Bass and me to luncheon, sending her carriage to fetch us. Prejudice and love for the boy in Colorado were our equipment as we reached the historic chateau. Our hostess was unable to rise from the chaise-longue which had once belonged to Marie Antoinette, as she rested in a bijou of an eighteenth century boudoir. On the hearth a small fire glowed and with cordiality she welcomed us, apologizing for the necessity that would call the Duke to Paris directly after luncheon to see his aunt, and we would then be alone for her to have news of her son.

The Duke's appearance was disappointing. He was a short, lean, more or less battered blond of the Belgian type. After having been presented to us, he led the way to the dining-room and unveiled his battery of anecdote, learning and repartee. Two lovely daughters were at table, both of whom later struck deep root into the soil of France, becoming devoted wives to a Frenchman and a Polish cousin of Talleyrand. After taking leave of us, the Duke said au revoir, and we returned to the boudoir and seated ourselves for the interview with the Marquise. In full flight of earnest talk, the door opened and in came the Duke. He evidently had forgotten about his aunt. He had but one purpose,—to prevent a reconciliation with their mother, of the daughter who read him as an open book and opposed him, and the chivalrous lad in Colorado. Against his subtlety I had no weapon, and that skilled courtier fought my tactless bludgeon of truth with a rapier. To my appeal that any mother should have love for and pride in a child who faced penury from a sense of justice and right, the Duke said, "When I served as a soldier in Mexico, I lived on two sous a day." "But you managed to live and be healthy," said I. He rushed from the room to bring back a black leather box containing data of an incriminating nature against everyone but himself, but I fought him step by step. Finally he asked if he could not show me the chateau, and I accepted. As we mounted the grand staircase I said, "You are ignoble. The only voice in the United States which ever said a good word for you is that of the noble fellow you strive to starve."

The result of that afternoon was that a deceived woman let her heart give counsel, and her children accepted the income which was theirs by right. As we drove back to town Mr. Bass said, "We have found a good woman where I looked for a heartless one."

The acquaintance so begun lasted for many years. Often I enjoyed the performances from the box of the Duchess at the Opéra Comique, as well as her sumptuous hospitality at an apartment in the Place Vendôme and in the small private *hôtel* overlooking Paris in the rue Reynouard, filled with beautiful bronzes and tapestries and signed furniture of master cabinet-makers.

To a straight-thinking American woman the Duke, whom I studied for many years, was a *rara avis*. Naturally astute, with a trained intelligence founded on cold conviction, he was cruel as a Turk with the skilled psychology of a Machiavellian Casanova. He was avid for riches. The woman he won was a child in his hands. He spent royally and selected wisely. He bought a golden set of tapestries designed by Raphael, which now are inherited by her son in America. His marvelous collection of armor—none better save royal treasures—is the pride today of the Metropolitan Museum, worth four times as much as the price they paid him for it. He wrote a charming poem on the desert after a journey of exploration, which he dedicated to his wife—subtle flatterer.

At a dinner in Paris he once brought out a box containing a mandragora root. It was the perfect effigy of a man. The Duke said there was an equally perfect one in the form of a woman, worshiped as the Virgin in Palestine, and made a ribald suggestion as to the mating of his man with this woman. These roots give no sign above the sand, but when the Bedouin discovers them and pulls them forth, they give out a human cry. Polished, witty, wicked, attendant at every *répétition générale* at the theater and opera, he was a gambler at every resort where fashion thronged, and even when crippled refused to give up champagne, for he was a gourmet. He gave me the first paper-bound copy of Oscar Wilde's "Ballad of Reading Gaol," printed over the initials C. 3. 3. He loved to browse in literature of four languages; a seeker for power, he used vice in restraint that it might long give stimulus without destroying health. What woman who loved him could fail to be broken on the wheel! The propagating soil of a young country is unproductive of such refined social villainy. In my ignorance, I should have been no more shocked than I was at the natural inheritor of an ancient order of self-interest, self-indulgence and sensualism, had that scourge of princes, Aretino, or the scholar and lover, Casanova, sat with me at table.

I greatly wearied of the plays of Corneille, but those of Molière held me spellbound. In a recent printing of David

Garrick's Note-book describing his journey to France taken on his birthday, the 19th of May, 1752, his criticism on the theater of France are illuminating. It chanced that his birthday anniversary and mine are the same, only mine is a hundred years later. Eagerly he sought every phase of amusement, be it opera, ballet, classical or modern plays, and art in all its forms. Equipped with his own genius and the standard of the great period of the English stage, he "found the opera raw, the singing abominable, and the dancing so poor it would have been hissed in London." As to the action being different from what he had seen, he could not find it agreeable to them or to any nature. "The women were ugly and painted, but excellent in shape. They tread better than our English ladies. Their legs are more worth seeing than anything else about them." The footlights being of candles only, the performance was handicapped.

Good days, like bad, wear to an end, and we booked our places for a journey to London.

Mr. Brimmer took a loge at the Française the night before our departure. "Le Monde où l'On s'Amuse," was perfectly given, Robert M. McLane, our American Minister to France, was hospitable and we knew the young Secretaries. One attaché had apparently been devoted to Mr. Bass. He came every afternoon to talk with him. Beautiful flowers which came anonymously to me daily intrigued my curiosity. I think I suspected handsome young Larry Rathbone, who was married to an agreeable woman. At the theater, during the first intermission, our good-looking friend knocked on the door of the box and asked if he could speak to me. He had come to take leave and to declare an undying passion for me, though he had a perfectly good wife whom he loved. The contagion of the gallants of Paris had produced a sort of pinchbeck imitation of their gallantries. It was a damp night. We stood at the window of the foyer overlooking the Square, and I was flattered and touched by his avowal. Alas! for many years, I became aware, my adorer had used the same words and short breath of passion to every woman who lent an open ear. That romance could not have survived a Channel crossing.

CHAPTER EIGHTEEN

A LONDON SEASON

REACHING London we found spacious lodgings in the Mayfair district,—a well-equipped writing table, a fire laid ready for the match, and flowers filling all the vases. Through the open windows came the cries of the elderly flower girls, or the sellers of violets and lavender,—a contrast to the cries of the Paris venders of birdseed and cleaners of filters of the Place Vendôme.

One forgets so much more than one remembers. I do not know now by what influence Mary Grant, one of Lord Elgin's granddaughters, was asked to make a portrait bust of Mr. Bass. The London season was at its height. I went sometimes to Mary Grant's studio for Mr. Bass's sittings. She was an intimate friend of the poet laureate, Lord Alfred Tennyson, and to learn that he was the vainest and most irritable of men was an unpleasant enlightenment, but I rejoiced to know that his reading of his own verses and his wonderful songs was of unforgettable beauty.

The weather being sunny and warm, we drank endless refreshing tumblers of hock and soda. We were diligent sightseers, and a visit to Watts's studio was a stirring event. Some of his paintings and portraits thrilled me. His marriage to Ellen Terry when she was scarcely more than a child, and their marital debacle, intrigued our meeting, for to the end of his life, Ellen Terry's face haunted his mind and moved his brush. We enjoyed his hospitality, but he was then a stoop-shouldered almost aged man.

While we were entertained in Queen Victoria's conservative circle, the Marchioness of Ely, the Queen's Mistress of the Robes, included us in stately dinners. One night, on my left, sat General Gordon of the Indian Army, yellow as a lemon and splenetic. Being uninformed and desirous to please, when India was under discussion I said, "Did you speak the language?" "What language?" he barked out. "The Indian language," said I. "There are more than forty of them," he growled. I was wearing a good frock and was not an old hag. I turned away hating him and never addressed another word to him. During the evening our hostess turned to a pretty young married American woman and inquired what her life and duties were. I thought she might have replied, "Having a good time," but she, young thing, being fixed by the eye of one who looked after her own tenantry with inherited duties and valued the respectable attendance at every church service, was too petrified to answer. I fear the Marchioness of Ely found our gay American mediocre and hardly worth reckoning with.

Edward J. Phelps, of Vermont, was Minister to the Court of St. James, and Harry White, as he was affectionately called, was Secretary of Embassy. I think Harry White was a born liaison officer to promote diplomatic good will and open the doors of acquaintance with the ruling political and pleasure-loving world to his countrymen. No one ever served the United States with greater unselfishness. His finger was on the pulse of the international and London world. His young wife was born Daisy Rutherford; tall, well-proportioned, with a small, well-balanced head, she attracted admiration in whatever large or small assembly she found herself. She once told me that for one year she lived in comparative solitude and loneliness because she intended her friends should be reckoned those of England's best-known circle. Beloved by Henry White, he seconded her desire, and was a flawless and devoted husband. At tea table or dinner one found political leaders and men of letters, her clear thought, clothed with a well-fitting vocabulary spoken in a delightful voice, giving her intimate association with the leading brains of England and Europe. She scorned subterfuge and spoke the truth, and her friends included Haldane, Arthur Balfour, George Curzon, Henry James, Sir William Harcourt, Harry Cust and Alfred Lyttleton.

Sir William Harcourt had married the daughter of the historian Motley, whose distinction and breeding made her a graceful and cordial hostess to her countrymen. The House of Commons woke up when Sir William debated with merciless tongue and caught his opponent on the hip.

Lady Frances Bailey, aunt of Mary Grant, proved a genial friend. Her son, David Bailey, was courted as a fascinating bachelor. Later he married Lord Burton's daughter, and through the power of foaming ale, since he had no male descendant, Lord Burton's title, by the kindness of the Queen, was passed through the female line. "Deochfur," their ancient countryseat, needed repair, as did the Bailey family exchequer. Lady Bailey asked me much about her brother, Sir Edward Bruce, who had been British Minister in Washington. He had set the tongues of the capital wagging because of a romance with the wife of a naval officer who afterwards became the wife of the Secretary of the Navy Robeson. Lady Bailey probed into my remembrance of the record of gossip, and finally I said, "Well, it was said he had a son who did not bear his name." "Oh, I know all about that," said Lady Bailey; "that doesn't matter."

Going into Loeb's on St. James's Street one morning to order riding boots, I found Mrs. Adolf Ladenburg giving a like commission. It was shortly after her marriage, and under her arm she had "Mouky," the black and tan dachshund which was as well-known as was "dear Emily," as the world called her. She was skimming the pleasures of life with a golden spoon. She was recognized abroad and at home as a fearless rider, owning fine hunters; and men were always ready to give her a mount. She had a congenital protest against being on time. She never was. Diplomats who were to escort her to dinners where royalty were entertained tore their hair in the vain attempt to get her there to receive the guests of honor. The end was that both they and royalty forgave her tardiness. She was a marked individual. With her child-like feminine appeal, almost sexless, in her mobile face I seem to trace her French ancestor Gallatin. If she sought pleasure, she loved to give it and share it. Our friendship began because I liked her cousin, Joseph S. Stevens. She loved beauty and traveled far and wide to seek it. She did what she would and when she would without taint of scandal. When she was little Emily Stevens, and spent her week-ends at the house of Charles Eliot Norton, at Cambridge, he found no place to hang his hat as those of the beardless undergraduates who worshiped her filled the hatrack. I recall being on a yacht with her to see a Yale-Harvard boat race at New London. The father of the owner of the yacht fled in disgust because wind and tide were not reckoned with for the sailing of the yacht. It should go when "little Emily" awoke and had had her coffee, as she did not like to be disturbed by noise. At that time she had an unusual social appeal and was asked everywhere. Rome, Paris and Vienna received her cordially. She was, in her youth, one of the great hostesses of New York. She is today, I hope, my loyal friend, as I am hers.

Sunday in London, before the use of automobiles, was as cheerful as a morgue. John G. Milburn, with whom I had been dashing about London shops in a hansom, getting presents for his wife and family in Buffalo, went with Mr. Bass and me to Bournemouth for the week-end. Between the leaves of an edition of Shelley's verse there is a dry ivy leaf which we took from the grave where Mary Wollstonecraft and her daughter Mary Shelley, born Godwin, lie side by side. The thought of Mary Wollstonecraft, grand of brain and heart, betrayed and fairly crushed in the dust, sends over me today a hot flash of indignation. She was a hundred years ahead of her era, and to read her letters and of her struggle will today bring tears to any honest eye that peruses them.

We drove to Christ Church to pay tribute to Shelley's monument whereon are inscribed the lines from "Adonais" beginning, "He has out-soared the shadow of our night."

The following week we visited in a country seat not far from where William Penn once lived, and our hostess was one of the Ladies in Waiting to the Queen, and others of the same circle were house guests. There was a cabal of indignation about a man who was eventually to carry on the title of a leading ducal house. The affair was the talk of London. Being bidden by the Queen to come to Windsor, his infatuation for a foreign woman who had already made one great English match displeased the Queen. A royal carriage at Windsor was at his disposal, and he was seen driving about the country road and along the reaches of the Thames with his inamorata. The Queen's circle felt it was an insult flung in the face of Her Majesty. One heard that the sweetheart was in force and purpose as powerful as the great Russian Catherine. The tale was that she had come to England with the intention of enslaving the Prince of Wales. Failing that, her aim and mark was to win him who could become a great political leader. Eventually she married the Duke who was of a rather indolent nature though of fine intellect, and she became the directing motive power both in his public and private life. Had my knowledge of her ended there, I might have believed her a satanic creature who had hoofs and horns.

During the Queen's Second Jubilee, I was invited to the great ducal town house to a dinner of seventy covers, at the opening of Parliament, where were a group restricted in number but unrestricted in commanding power of position. I cabled Worth for a frock which should be the color of my eyes, as had been the taste of Père Worth. I was laced into the bodice, which almost burst with the strength of my pride at being included in that distinguished gathering.

The salons, being lighted with candles only, enhanced the good looks of the women. On the balcony over the double broad staircase was a powerful incandescent lamp. The Duke and Duchess received on the landing. The head of the house of Rothschild stood next me on the balcony, as eager as I to see the people coming for the evening, the dinner being over,—the Duchess of Portland, towering above other women, the Marchioness of Granby wearing her tiara upside-down at the base of the nuke of her head, instead of its framing her face in the conventional mode for tiaras, Lord Salisbury, and other Cecils. The Duchess was imposing, but the garish light revealed her make-up. As I studied the crowd passing under that cruel light, I felt that a sin on any conscience could not be hidden. My own inconsistency ruffled my self-esteem; having refused to receive an American woman who, to say the least, had a reputation no more tarnished than that of the Duchess, it seemed that my standard of behavior was determined by latitude and longitude and not by high principle. I said all this to young Phil Carroll years after at a dinner at Mrs. Winthrop Chanler's. He was little more than a boy and a son of my old friend, Governor Carroll of Carrollton. He said, "You entirely misread the circumstances. Either woman would not influence in the slightest, in brief contact, the most unsophisticated débutante. It is what they each stand for that counts,—one the fringe of a frivolous, ribald, degenerate circle; the other shines as a political and patriotic influence." Out of the mouths of babes and sucklings may come forth wisdom.

Later on, after the death of the Duke, I met his widow at Carlsbad. Her plethoric proportions tightly encased in a pale gray frock, her massive features almost enameled with white and red, her youthful brown transformation under a Réboux hat (anciently a transformation was called a wig), old and fat, shorn of power, perhaps she felt, without reading the last chapter of Ecclesiastes, "Vanity of vanities, all is vanity."

Mr. Bass and I, being invited by Mrs. W. J. Palmer to dine, went for a brief visit to "Ightem Moat." It was our delight to arrive at the portcullis and see swan plying about the moat, which was well stocked with fish. At dinner, our eyes were attracted to a painting above the chimney-piece, of Dame Dorothy in a sort of Elizabethan attire. She was supposed to have died, in some previous century, an agonizing death from having pricked her finger while sewing on Sunday. So draughty was that dining-hall that every chair at table had to be screened from drafts from everywhere and nowhere. Our spines were chilled. The ghost of this naughty lady was supposed to walk the galleries of the staircase hall. I know I felt that a woman's best friend was a hot water bottle and that to jump into bed and pull up the coverlets to shut out sight and sound was but the part of wisdom.

A gentleman who played delightfully on a Stradivarius violin was arrayed in the mode of Oscar Wilde, in velvet jacket and knee-breeches, his patent leather pumps ornamented with large steel buckles. I enjoyed the evening but I did recall a conversation with a Member of the House of Commons, American by birth and English citizen by election. He had said to me, "I no longer accept invitations to country houses. When I did, I found the best plan was to wear perforated chamois skin next my body." I could hardly see myself in a low-cut bodice, with a perforated chamois skin coming to my throat, ornamented with a pearl or sapphire necklace. I think I had said to him that I had been in despair and sitting at table looking black and blue from lack of circulation, with my toes turned under the arch of my foot, and had seen English women with pink cheeks and bright eyes adorn a gathering; and oh, those trying hours when accommodating youth, both male and female, entertained the company by singing a little after dinner!

Like all other Americans, we frequented coffee houses made famous by Boswell and Johnson, and sought the highways and byways described in Dickens's novels, and that memory of Dickens which I still hold dear is warm with romance as, seated on my father's knee in St. James Hall in Buffalo, I heard Dickens end his reading with the lines from "David Copperfield" describing the death of Steerforth: "I saw him lying with his head upon his arm, as I had often seen him lie at school." I can almost hear now Dickens's voice.

My memory of Thackeray is vague and dim. I seem to recall a small round face and large spectacles.

The first time I saw Alfred Harmsworth, with whom later for years I had interesting relations, was when he came to visit Mr. Bass, doubtless to inform himself on questions relating to lines of American railways running west from Colorado. Clear of skin, round of head, with a sonorous voice which pleased, above all when he talked of his mother, whom he believed to be the fountain of love and wisdom, I felt him to be a stormy petrel who delighted in the tempest. His questions attacked the heart of the subject without circumlocution. A boy-like merriment left gaiety even after his leave-taking. A year before his death he called me up to speak about the appointment of Wilmont Lewis, now Sir Wilmont Lewis. Later, Lord Northcliffe made him American correspondent for the London *Times*. Lewis was a beloved friend of mine, a Welshman whom I esteemed as having the most brilliant mind with which I had ever come in contact. He was called to be a member of the corps of the ablest newspaper correspondents ever gathered by any organization. Blowitz had been the leading correspondent of the *Times*. Sir Valentine Chirol and Wickham Steed were among the cleverest men in Europe as correspondents for the London *Times*.

We went for one week-end to stay with Alfred Renshaw in the lovely manor house in Kent. Renshaw was of that fine flower of England's upper middle class. It was William Pitt who recognized and rewarded the backbone of the English nation with well-deserved titles as he broke the habit of founding titles, the claim to which came from the bastards of royalty. Renshaw was a highly esteemed Queen's counsellor. With a head of closely-curled light hair, a fine figure, he bore the stamp of an athlete. He was liked in all circles. Perhaps he was the model which has given me the faith that bachelors make the best of housekeepers.

Under my pillow were hidden fragrant bunches of lavender. In the early morning my curtains were drawn, my tea brought by a tidy maid whose low-pitched voice uttered an English far superior to my own. At nine o'clock we descended for a hearty breakfast. He had an honest contempt for my ignorance as to the botanical names for flowers, for he tended his conservatory with knowledge and love. It seemed that so rarely charming a man should meet the party with whom we had been happy for five months; so he was asked to dine with us in London. The women agreed to wear dresses made from the textiles from Eastern looms found in the dusky bazaars of Damascus and Constantinople. Mrs. Brimmer clung to the richest of fabrics and lines recommended to her by Worth, as usual, as a thing he had seen her clothed in in his dreams. I thought what a delight Alfred Renshaw and Minna Timmins would have sitting next each other at table, and I expected her to arrive resplendent in scarlet and cloth of gold. Imagine my horror when the door opened and Minna entered, wearing a shabby blue silk frock which had served its full time in Africa, Greece and the coast of Asia Minor, her cropped hair straggling from an insufficient number of hairpins. She paid no heed to handsome Renshaw, turned her shoulder and almost ignored him. It was the form of her loyalty to the man she loved in the United States, which demanded that she should in nowise either adorn her person or make herself fascinatingly agreeable. The evening was not a success.

Our Minister to the Court of St. James's, Edward J. Phelps, asked us to dine, and there James G. Blaine greeted us and electrified the company during a long dinner with brilliant conversation. The following warm afternoon, he came to our lodgings for hock and soda, and he answered our impatient questioning colorfully, for we were eager and hungry for news. Conkling's death in March naturally brought forth an inquiry as to Conkling's devotion to Kate Chase Sprague, and whether it had endured. "Oh, no," said Mr. Blaine, "all illicit romances end in bitterness. Theirs wore out in recriminations and sordid quarrels about money, and they ceased to meet one another. Yet in that last delirium of Conkling's on his death-bed, he called constantly the name of her whose magic controlled him in the fullness of his manhood." In Mr. Blaine, as in all big men I have known, there was the strain of the child. His attitude towards self-cure when he had a slight ailment was the love of taking medicine the efficiency of which seemed to lie in the blackness of the dose and the unpalatableness of the taste on his tongue. Mr. Bass was, as I had always been, a loyal admirer of James G. Blaine. There have been able Speakers of the House since his day, but no Secretary of State or Speaker of the House has equaled James G. Blaine in charm.

A lifelong friend of Mr. Bass, Edward R. Bacon, Vice-President of the Baltimore and Ohio Railway, added to the gay phantasmagoria of the London season. Mr. Bass and President Cleveland had known him from his boyhood and he had seen me grow from childhood to womanhood. He cared much for externals and I used to mock at him for being a bit of a Beau Brummel, wearing a long-tailed fitted top-coat and beaver hat tipped to a rakish line, and spats, which were most unusual then and not the rage in Buffalo. He had dyspepsia and a splenetic irritation at trifles. He married a woman whose looks and social position gratified his pride. A great tragedy caused him to turn to our friendship for solace. Life had not taught him that pin-pricks and never being on time can exasperate a wife and kill her love. He had an unselfish younger brother who came from life on the Western plains where he had not seen a woman for months on end. Living in the house where a woman was continually disappointed, he tried to heal the breach of a husband who was quite unconscious that no woman's love could survive the irritation of neither being on time nor in a peaceful mood. In a sense, Edward was a faithful husband, providing elegant surroundings, priceless works of art and furniture of French eighteenth century pieces signed by their makers; but however historic may be French furniture in adorning our salons, it does not bring rest. He awoke to find that his wife loved and wished to marry his handsome young brother. He permitted divorce and their marriage followed.

In London, if anybody took note of me as I drove round and round Hyde Park in his perfectly turned out victoria, he bending over me rehearsing grievances I could have repeated backward, I am sure they thought I listened to the intensity of an impassioned lover. His collection of old silver was notable and I wearily went from one old silver shop to another while he bargained for rare specimens. Not knowing or caring for hallmarks any more than for Egyptian hieroglyphics, I could not see how the stamp of George I or Queen Anne could be a healing balm for a wounded heart and broken pride. He was kindness itself to Mr. Bass and me.

What a regal picnic he gave on a launch! Delicious food, beverages of rare vintage, well-served while we watched the boat races or skillful punters on the Thames. The life of the gay youth of England, fluttering in holiday attire in small boats in the locks or dining at Maidenhead was exhilarating. I felt myself almost a heroine of Arthurian romance as I fed the white swans floating on the river. The weather was that which heaven should bestow, a warm sun and a fresh breeze. The landscape was softened with a blue haze, and the hollows filled with purple shadows.

Edward Bacon's kindness opened every playhouse where laughter reigned. John Hare and Mrs. Kendall were playing in "Sweet Lavender." Pinero, though by birth Portuguese, was by choice an English citizen. He was past master in the writing of farces and comedies in which he introduced a touch of French naughtiness. There was much talk of the marital virtues of Mr. and Mrs. Kendall, who were never separated in their work. The Queen, for the first time, received actors by honoring the Kendalls. Joseph Chamberlain, but recently married to Mary Endicott of Salem, Massachusetts, was their enthusiastic friend and supporter. Through excessive praise of their fireside virtue, I was a little in the mood of the Greeks when they banished Aristides, wearied of hearing him called just.

Minna and Gemma Timmins were of the same small coterie of Boston girls as Mrs. Chamberlain. She had the stamp of the blonde beauty of the Peabodys which the world recognized as being as individual as was that of the ugliness of the Hapsburgs. London at once admired her, and her carefully groomed statesman-husband arrived at the House of Commons each day with a rare orchid in his buttonhole. His hobby was the cultivation of those spinster blossoms which, though cut, last fresh in water for days on end. They wait for the fertilizing insects, their lovers, which remain behind in southern jungles. Poor things! their posterity must increase by cuttings only.

Novels from Ouida's pen were then in vogue. Dreaming girls

saw their future husbands, Prince Charmings, in the mold of the glorious sinners of Ouida's heroes.

Audacious hopes of mine died at birth. I had hoped to meet Herbert Spencer, whose "First Principles" I had struggled over; possibly Darwin; and above all, Robert Browning. Browning and Du Maurier were moving easily in literary, aristocratic and theatrical circles.

Before we left Colorado, Louis Swinburne, who had been passing the winter in the Engadine, a friend of the widow of General George B. McClellan, sent me the English edition of "Diana of the Crossways." He begged me to read it as the heroine reminded him of me. A friend of mine who wrote book reviews in Buffalo begged that I read the book as the heroine reminded her of me. Several flattering men told me I was a "Meredith woman." To this day I am in ignorance of what constitutes a "Meredith woman." I had read with interest "The Egoist." Why, I cannot imagine. Neither curiosity nor personal vanity enabled me to read "Diana of the Crossways." Seeing the first pages, I felt as I did in my childhood, seeking for the subject at the end of a long German sentence. During the Pan-American Exposition in 1900, Richard Le Gallienne came to Buffalo and said I was a "Meredith woman," and sent me a copy of his book on Meredith. I gathered together all Meredith's novels, and one midnight, embarked on reading "Diana of the Crossways." Daylight came without my finding recognition of my own qualities in the book, but I soaked my mind with Meredith.

Balzac's "Comédie Humaine" was supposed to have been read by people of culture, pondered upon and fully digested. Both he and Meredith made the road difficult to the comprehension of human nature. I was vain enough to think I knew a little about the psychology of man and woman by my practical experience.

One of the memorable experiences of 1888 was hearing Joachim play, in London at St. James's Hall, Brahms' Violin Concerto from the manuscript dedicated by Brahms to Joachim.

How clearly Ellen Terry stands out against the fading background of the past! She charmed the world. The night I first saw her in "The Amber Heart," as she stepped toward the footlights, the eyes of the audience were filled with unshed tears before she had uttered a word. As she had accepted my mother's hospitality, as had Sir Henry Irving, they welcomed us as friends.

While lunching with her one day in London, she told me the story of her marriage to Watts, of her love for the father of her children, and of the tragedy of receiving, on the day of the birth of her last child, the news of the marriage of her lover. A long illness followed. What a truthful simplicity of statement! A story written in the blood of her heart! Who would not sob in listening to it, as did I! I loved her then and found her a faithful friend always. I recall her one August evening in the court of my hotel at Aix-les-Bains. We dined tête-à-tête and adjourned to the gambling tables. The croupiers were in flaming excitement. The rooms became thronged with watchers of her gay betting. Remaining deaf to the entreaties of her traveling companion, she stayed, always losing, until the tables closed. She had lost far more than she could afford. Croupiers, onlookers, gamesters and friends adored that guileless undaunted girl-woman.

I saw Sir Henry and Ellen Terry often together, and in their unaffected intimacy, his mantle of selfishness and arrogance made a dark foil to the ardent desire on her part to forward his fame rather than her own, and to please him.

Irving demanded that all furniture and décor of his stage should be of the rarest and of the period, and his textiles of the finest dye and weave. Even the slightest engraving or object in his dressing-room was rare and of artistic value. Whatever Irving's manners, he was at all times supreme master of the stage. As Shylock, when he discovers the loss of his daughter and his ducats, he reminded me of a conversation I once had on the long-short journey from Boston to Philadelphia, with the great nerve specialist, Dr. Owen Wister. He advanced the theory that the Jewish people are the most hysterical of all races. Two forms of hysteria, which he had seen rarely, had been among the "chosen people." I have seen many Shylocks. All save Irving have fallen below the intensity demanded by the scene before his despoiled house. I have wondered whether Irving knew the facts on which Owen Wister dilated, and based his interpretation on that hypothesis. Dr. Owen Wister I never saw again, but I remember that he was scientifically interested in the venom of serpents and had told me that the venom of the rattlesnake bite differed in quantity but not in quality from that of the sting of a yellow-jacket. While unpacking a basket of grapes in Virginia one summer, I was stung by a yellow-jacket and carried an arm swollen to the shoulder for weeks, which convinced me that Dr. Wister was rightly informed.

Keenly awaited were Du Maurier's illustrations in "Punch." Comyn Carr was producing an edition de luxe of "L'Art." His sister-in-law, Alma Strettel, a valued friend from Colorado days, had produced a small volume of translations from Heinrich Heine, considered the most sympathetic existing in the English tongue. She married Peter Harrison, the painter, son of Sir Frederick Harrison, and they occupied a house formerly belonging to Whistler. No longer do our young people read "Trilby" or the "dreaming true" romance of "Peter Ibbetson." The Barrymore brothers on the spoken stage, and Deems Taylor's opera have galvanized "Peter Ibbetson" into life, and the movie of "Svengali" alone recalls "Trilby."

The sons of Henry Irving and Du Maurier were in the green wood to mature to sound timber for the English stage. John Drew and Ada Rehan had a successful run in "The Taming of the Shrew," and John Drew that autumn took back the translation of "Ami des Femmes" which had been triumphantly played at the Française. Drew called it "Squire of Dames." John Drew, for me, lacked passion on the stage as a love-maker. His slender grace and style were as though he had entered the world with a fencer's foil in his hand. Beguiling he was, and the most loyal of friends.

In Ellen Terry's grace, her feet seemed to scorn the earth as, light as a feather, she crossed the stage.

"Hamlet," as played with fixed traditions of forty years, received a baptism of fire when romantic Fechter, spite of strong foreign accent, sent new red blood into the impersonation of the melancholy Dane.

Forbes-Robertson was trying out his wings for an eminent career. The two de Reszkes and Melba were singing at Covent Garden.

In the tumult and vigor on the American stage of the youth of today, one could call "Halt!" Ah, if they could but follow the example of Lawrence Barrett, inheriting the spirit with which he consecrated his existence and intellect to become a great actor! In the midst of strife and battle for the interpretation of many characters, long runs, and the box office, the axe has been put at the throat of theatric art.

What delightful evenings in the theater,—comfortable in seats where there was enough space for a man to stretch his legs,—the women in low-cut gowns, the men faultlessly attired in evening clothes!

Classical standards, our youngsters feel, make for the static beauty of flies in amber, but only by hard work can true artists reveal the telling moment when inherited discipline and the personal passion of the present moment unite to sway an audience. But even discipline will not enable a bow-legged man to play Orlando; a bow-legged woman can succeed in a character part, but in the dress of a lady she can never tread the stage with perfect grace.

We have all marveled at the story of Chopin and Liszt, who were to play in a dark room the music of Chopin for the most trained of critics to ascertain which artist was at the piano. Shut all day in his room, Chopin played Bach's well-tempered clavichord. Lo and behold! No critic could decide which was Liszt and which was Chopin, so perfectly did they play. Love Chopin if you will, but to interpret his magic requires years of stern practice on the piano.

The world cries out for leaders in all the creative arts, as well as in national life, yet our education is being founded on group study and mass education, conformity and standardization, instead of freeing individual potentiality. Mr. Bass said to me, after returning from a dinner given by a leading influential solicitor of London, "England is richer in marked individualities than America. My clear-brained host last night gave me a start when, on entering his spacious house, wild animals, skillfully stuffed, peeped from every corner and seemed ready to leap from over every high doorway. Dinner over, he showed his collection of microscopes, some of them made in China thirteen hundred years before. His scientific hobby of microscopic research rested the law-fatigued lobe of his brain." Were one fanciful, it might seem that the solicitor had opened his eyes at birth dreaming of the jungle. Chained under low skies to the management of great estates not his own, he could not seek through the telescope the infinitude of the star-emblazoned firmament, so sought the infinite in the infinitesimal which his microscope revealed.

With the verses of Matthew Arnold and Arthur Hugh Clough, and the controversies arising from the novels of that most virtuous and wife-like of sinners against narrow convention, George Eliot, the fetters of Victorian orthodoxy were weakening. With "Adam Bede" and Hardy's novels of witty dialogues, tasting of the very earth, over which the reader smiled at the peasants' talk, Darwin's "Evolution" and Buckle's "History of Civilization" generally read, society was beginning to stand on solid ground. Ibsen's psychological disturbing plays were not yet given in the London theaters, but they were knocking at every stage door of London.

Though London won our hearts, duties and pleasures awaited us at home. Sadly and gladly we sailed from Albion's shores.

We crossed Southampton water on a tender which, as we were mounting the gangway, collided with the ship. For the first time I discovered that fear could turn humanity into unreasoning beasts. I reached the head of the gangway and was starting to help my husband, when the wrist of my extended hand was struck by a cane in the hand of a strong, fairly decent-looking man. Cries of panic everywhere, and a deaf jewel-bedecked Californian woman poured forth on the helpless head of her husband, a stream of billingsgate and filth unknown to the average human being. Maggie Grant and my boy had reached safety on the upper deck.

We were allotted seats at table with the aged General Thom of the Army, and Henry E. Dixey, the graceful actor whose "Adonis" had won him fame. A kinder, more unselfish heart never beat than his. All that he could do to help amuse or aid my sick husband was done. He could laugh with one side of his face and cry with the other at the same time. He was distressed at the inartistic toupée that graced General Thom's head and could not be deterred from suggesting an able theatrical wig-maker.

Dixey was a most exciting playfellow for my son, and when he asked me to dance with him on the deck, my pride in acceptance seemed to be a panacea for seasickness.

The motion of the steamer drove me one night rushing to the deck from the dinner-table. Dixey followed me to the stern of the vessel where an afflicted spinster sat in solitary misery. There was a covered seat and Dixey settled down beside me. Suddenly we saw rushing towards us the threat of a following wave, which all seamen hate. After the danger was past, Dixey, true to the actor's desire to be starred in print, said, "What a splendid headline for the New York papers! 'The Distinguished Mrs. Bass Was Swept from the Stern of an Atlantic Steamer! The Talented Henry E. Dixey Sprang to Save Her and They Both Sank in the Stormy Sea!'"

Dixey carried a large leather portmanteau filled with the love letters of stage-struck women. Scented stationery with crest and monogram, or lined foolscap sheets,—all honored the charm of the most graceful man on the American stage. The kindness of Henry Dixey, his stories and merry quips, won our hearts and called us again and again to the spell of his unequaled dancing in the New York theater.

CHAPTER NINETEEN

THE CLOSING OF A BOOK

THE traveler returns with the same heart that beat when he sailed away. The Stars and Stripes greeting one as the steamer passes through New York Harbor, straining eyes for the sight of welcoming friends, tightens the heartstrings and tears are near to falling. We were housed in St. James Hotel on Broadway for a night or two before leaving for Buffalo to have a sight of my mother and brothers.

Coming in to see me, my friend Jane Cary Rumsey's greeting was, "Are you not thankful to be in Buffalo?" I, yearning for the starry high firmament of the altitude of five thousand feet, replied, "Oh, it seems as though the sky would hit me on the head here!" Scornfully she cried, "You were born here, were you not? Do not be affected." Yet John G. Milburn, with whom I conferred, and who had joined Edward O. Wolcott's law firm in Denver, felt that we both had upon us the brand of the sun calling us back.

On North Street lived with her step-father, the well-known citizen Edwin T. Evans, Edwine Blake. She accepted our invitation to return to Edgeplain with us. One of the few times I ever broke the Tenth Commandment was when I watched her sleeping, stretched on the sofa of my drawing-room. Her perfect nose and delicate skin of mingled pink and white aroused envy of youth and beauty. Her little name was "Dwine,"—so she was called by those who loved her.

Edward O. Wolcott joined us midway between Chicago and Denver, alert and full of talk about his campaign for election to the United States Senate in the Colorado State Legislature the coming winter. Naturally he commanded the backing and power of the Denver and Rio Grande Railway, and the national Republican leaders were well aware of his legal capacity and persuasive speech, and desirous for his success. His henchman was Archie Stevenson, who in the Chicago National Convention in 1916 proposed Theodore Roosevelt's name, though Charles Evans Hughes won the candidacy. The sporting fraternity to a man were Edward Wolcott's friends. One agreeable supporter was Jake Sanders, a retired rich gambler who, through Edward Wolcott's influence, became National Committeeman. He patronized Mr. Wolcott's tailor and would have lain down his life for Mr. Wolcott. The sporting crowd I knew more or less. I smile as I think of what is called a "bucket-shop gambler" who, seeing me hastening, late for the train to Colorado Springs, helped me to reach the platform of the last car, thrusting into my hands books and periodicals which he had doubtless bought at the newsstand for his personal delectation. He said, "There is light literature to manure your mind."

To all trainmen, engineers, firemen, brakemen and conductors, our faces were familiar and they gave us warm greetings.

Edward Wolcott's campaign was full of vilifying lies and some disagreeable truth-telling. He became United States Senator. In the late autumn he had sent me the tiniest of toy pug dogs, sweet-smelling and affectionate. Coming to Edgeplain for a gay dinner in celebration of his victory, as he went to the spare room to go to bed, he found "Posy," the pug, had deposited a litter of puglets in the center of his blue satin eider-down coverlet. No doubt she was political minded and thus presaged a wish for rich fertility in his future career.

We found our home spick and span and our neighbors glad to see us. Colorado Springs was changing hourly, and what a cosmopolitan group occupied the houses facing south on the college reservation! A. E. Touzalin lived across the street. He had been Vice-President of the Chicago, Burlington and Quincy Railroad, close friend and associate of Charles W. Perkins. How many hours I spent with him in the saddle as we skirted the foothills! I had acquired a fine Kentucky thoroughbred, sired by the prepotent stallion "Longfellow," so from "Hiawatha" I chose the name "Wabun" (East Wind). A light rein and a stern knee-grip were needed, for that beast could see a feather miles away, and unexpectedly whirl like a dervish on the smallest of hoofs,—a born dancer. When depression assailed me, Joe Stevens used to say to me, "Go for a ride on Wabun. That will take up your mind." When I think of gentleness and intuitive sympathy, I remember A. E. Touzalin's face. Small in stature, homely of face, of defective vision, he radiated potent charm. Born in the West Indies, of French blood, he differed from American men. He came to Colorado to restore failing health. He had never wholly recovered from the loss, thirteen years before, of a cherished wife whose lustrous hair had rippled from the crown of her head to touch the ground. The friendship of Mr. and Mrs. Perkins, and her unfailing comprehension, had been to him like the shadow of a great rock in a weary land. His only daughter, Ellen, presided over his house at fifteen years of age and won my admiration. Not beautiful, but radiant with mounting color and abundant warm brown hair, a large mouth filled with flashing teeth, she was born understanding men,—an ageless knowledge

LYMAN METCALFE BASS AT EDGEPLAIN

EDGEPLAIN

THE CLOSING OF A BOOK

of human nature. When she went to Boston to school, the Forbeses and Perkinses opened to her every social portal. Later she married George Nicholson, who indulged her with every luxury, and she bore him sons and daughters. He died, and she, as a widow, dipped into intelligent travel and residence in our national capital, as well as in foreign lands. She seemed to have a thirst for beautiful things and clever people. The Boston pundits and Cambridge undergraduates responded to her spell. She now lives in England, her children married there, and she is the widow of England's brave Admiral, Lord Hood who, during the battle of Jutland, commanded the flagship *Invincible* of the Third Cruiser Squadron. Bringing his ships into action was worthy of the tradition of his great naval ancestors. The turret of the *Invincible* was struck, an explosion, followed by the blowing up of the magazine, the ship broke in half and sank, and England sustained a serious loss when the distinguished Admiral Horace Hood went down with his ship. Fortunately Ellen Touzalin bore him a son to carry on his name.

We found Charles Perkins, of New York, valued member of the Union Club, had rented the house next door to Edgeplain. His wife, sparkling with good nature, her dimpling countenance radiating ease of living and kindness of heart, added to our pleasure. There were three handsome daughters,—Elise, Fannie, who still lives in California, the widow of Henry Jay Chapman, and half-grown Mary, called "Baby," now married to Waldron Kintzing Post. Pride and love for all her progeny had Mrs. Perkins, but the crowning glory of her motherhood was stalwart, handsome, loyal Bob Perkins. No son of Manhattan was ever closer to the heart of his townsmen. His genial encouragement of young men, as well as his service as a chief of the Red Cross in

Italy during the late war, was notably effective. In his early manhood, wherever smart society moved, his presence was in demand. Charles Perkins was accustomed to have nightly supper at ten o'clock. He braised venison with port wine in a chafing-dish, and he taught me his art of making a Welsh rarebit à la Union Club. In the period when ale and wine were not considered a sin against the Holy Ghost, as his disciple I was often held as a *cordon bleu.* Mrs. Perkins had the wisdom of a perfect wife and mother. No matter how often her husband told the same story, she laughed as though it were fresh from the mint. She never failed to say, as she tasted venison or rarebit, "Charlie, I think this is the most delicious dish I ever tasted." To believe daughters are intelligent and beautiful, is a leg-up to their becoming so.

John Ingalls, a brawny Scotch gentleman, built near us a tasteful residence where his wife, Lizzie Day of New York, became a prized friend. She could be found daily at tea time embroidering or knitting. Her fastidious warm nature and tenderness for those who suffered, filled the community with hope for her recovery. Nearly every house in town sheltered a woman unwearied in the care of a stricken member of her family. Nobody ever mentioned the fact. When John Ingalls gave up his business and devoted his days and nights to the woman he adored, the community talked constantly of his virtues. I feared the ladies might erect a monument in his honor. To stay with her came her sister, Mrs. Hall McCormick of Chicago, and Susan Day and her brother, George Day. He was afterwards smashed on the polo field at Meadowbrook, and invalided for many months. Of subtle charm and broad culture, I was proud of his friendship. He induced me to read Anster's translation of Goethe's "Faust" and the earliest novels of Paul Bourget.

Edgeplain surged with youth and my son had a governess, Edith Ferris, later head of a girls' school in Paris. What that boy needed was eleven brothers to lick him into shape. He had a good horse, and rode my horses as well. A better horseman than anyone in town, he shot straight and I think told the truth. It was an atmosphere which made him feel he was cock of the roost. Boarding-school taught him modesty.

No longer the white-covered wagons crawl southward with "Pike's Peak or Bust" or "Westward the Star of Empire Takes Its Way" rudely painted on the canvas. The young bloods of leading Eastern parentage drove that road in high carts with tandem teams, and Griswold from New York tooled his four-in-hand on excursions in a Brewster coach drawn by a well-matched four-in-hand.

Within a few days, I have read that to welcome the year 1932, a huge bonfire flamed on the crest of Pike's Peak. It would have been death in 1888 to follow the narrow trail through the snows to the summit of that mountain. Motor roads and snow-ploughs easily permit a great hope for banished depression to blaze east and west from the top of the Great Divide.

Countess Pourtalès had rented a house on Pike's Peak Avenue. Mrs. Braggiotti, née Chadwick, one of the best family brands of Boston, came West with her son Francis, seeking his health. She had married a man who was a Harvard graduate, though a son of the mixed race of Italian nobles who, a century or two earlier, had settled in Syria. He was a clever but extremely ugly man. She thought sometimes his face resembled Jesus Christ, and others, Napoleon I. She liked to sleep all day and wake all night. Her unconscious wit and gaiety spurred merriment at the foot of the Rockies, as it did wherever she found herself. Once she said, as James Pourtalès offered her a mint julep, "Why, I seem to be drinking a meadow!" And a man mentioning the state of Iowa, she cried, "Why, when I went to school they called it Ohio!" She once said to me that she could do without things but she could not economize. Her knowledge of geography ended with Europe, not reaching further west than New York City. When her son wrote her he was stopping with the savages in Omaha, she thought he was in danger of death from Indians. Once when she came to pay me a visit at Edgeplain, I saw all traffic stopped in the street. Drivers of butcher and grocery carts were escorting a figure whose head was hidden by a scarlet umbrella. I rushed down the stairs and found her sunk upon a seat in the entrance hall. She had been met by my slobbering mastiff. Wagging his tail, he would have welcomed a burglar with offering his paw for a friendly shake. She feared hydrophobia. A more sparkling child-woman never lived. She worshiped her son Isidore Braggiotti, who had a voice like Caruso's and a power of mimicry which would have given him high place in any theater. To-day he has countless friends in Florence, Boston, California and New York.

Rich young dudes built houses on Pike's Peak Avenue. Mrs. Goddard, sister of Lewis Cass Ledyard of New York, made a cosy corner for Eastern homesick lads. Her son, Harry Goddard, is now an able district judge in New York City.

A young man named Sneeden constructed a bachelor house with a large ball-room. He gave a ball to open it, and when Dwine Blake and I entered, a wave of admiration stirred the guests who said she looked as though she had stepped down from the frieze of the Parthenon. There was a sizable vacant stone house near the campus, and I gave there a ball in her honor. The empty house was decorated with branches of bull-pine and every colored rag or garment I could get. Fred Sterner, architect of New York, entered saying as he glanced about, "Oh, how fine are these decorations *à la fourchette!*" An orchestra from Denver played until it was time to go home for breakfast.

Clara Wilder of Rochester, who lived in a house packed with brothers, male relatives and other friends, had large brown eyes with a come-hither look, and the boys followed her like hounds an anise seed bag. That night when Herbert Timmins was presented he said, "I call you Jane because you are my best friend"—a queer way to begin a flirtation which was still-born. General Palmer furnished Dwine a docile well-schooled horse to ride.

Joe Stevens, suffering from fever, came to stay with me to be nursed. At first I gave him my best French toilet water to bathe his face and hands. He forthwith refused to use unscented water until he was well.

A checked Scotch plaid cape of mine was borrowed for warmth and to sit upon by all philandering couples. Sympathetic, humorous Will Otis, and his wild, red-headed brother Tot, from Cleveland, made for gaiety at Edgeplain. Those delightful little Crosby girls were petted by everyone. Nina, the elder, married lovable, beguiling Jim Eustis, and after his death, became Princess Polignac, now a leader of the Parisian world.

Mrs. John Milburn came from Denver to find the merry riot somewhat wearisome, but John G. Milburn lapped up the adulation and fun of the youthful group as a cat would cream.

We had a hired man, red-cheeked, robust, handsome, who did odd jobs about the place and was sociable. He got uproariously drunk, and it was found he had stolen. It became necessary to send for the police and give him a lodging for the night in the village jail. The following morning, Mr. Bass went to see him and paid twenty-seven dollars and fifty cents to bail him out. How condescendingly gleesome were our merry-making friends at Mr. Bass's weakness! Years may have taught them that the judgment of a universal mind, the quality of whose mercy is not strained, helped and not punished. *Sans peur et sans reproche* were those sunny days.

As spring, 1889, was near, we made our usual exodus for New York. Clara Wilder went with us. Boarding the train at Denver, we found that the privilege which we took as our prerogative, namely, the drawing-room from Denver to Chicago, was in possession of the Marquis and Marchioness of Stafford, afterwards Duke and Duchess of Sutherland. The Duchess was the youngest sister of the Countess of Warwick, and her sisters and half-sisters were children of the youngest of mothers, the Countess Roslyn.

We watched her breathlessly. Tall and slender as a reed, golden hair simply knotted, a skin translucent as the heart of an ocean shell,—no greater loveliness was ever given to woman. The Duke, having seen her when, at sixteen years of age, she came from the school room to share dessert with a large house party at Roslyn Castle, fell in love with her. Very shortly after, they were married, and after the birth of her son, they left for a journey around the world. She could not have been more than eighteen years of age on that return journey to ship for England. In her tweed skirt and white silk shirtwaist, she looked younger, at first sight, than a sub-débutante.

We made pleasant acquaintance with them, and the first night, as the husband and wife retired to their compartment, the curtain on the glass door was up. Under the bright light I saw her put her arms about her husband's neck, and I felt the throb of romance. However, before the end of the journey, I sensed he was cold and unperceptive. In later years, as she ripened to womanhood, as Millie, Duchess of Sutherland, with London at her feet at Stafford House, now the London City Museum, I knew her. Once she came to Paris. Ethel Barrymore was with me and we all went for a bright evening to one of the small theaters at Montmartre. Ethel Barrymore, in her early girlhood, made her headquarters at Stafford House, for the Duchess of Sutherland was a loyal and effectionate friend to her.

It is never wise to go back, and so, until the end, for me Colorado reflects the roseate hue and sun of bright, glad morning.

Minna Timmins once wrote me, "One must never speak of pain and sorrow,—only of joy." I shall not lift the curtain of the three months preceding Mr. Bass's death at the Buckingham Hotel, May tenth, 1889. From the night after he died, for three months, my mind was washed clean of all record. Grover Cleveland came, in all sincerity of friendship, to see his lifelong friend, and Dr. William Draper said of Lyman K. Bass, "His courtesy and consideration survived his consciousness." I pay a proud tribute to the father of my son. Never by word, thought or deed could I find in him a stain of pettiness. For himself, with full lucidity of splendid intellect, he forgave my weaknesses, never censuring his fellow-man. He walked in nobleness. I saw him face death three times with quiet courage. Seated one warm afternoon by the stream in South Cheyenne Canyon, Colorado, having read a portion of Fiske's "Cosmic Philosophy," I asked if he believed in an individual future life beyond the grave. "I neither believe nor disbelieve," said he. "The evidence is against it. In any event, the best we can do on earth would be the best we could do to gain heaven."

His son can never find a deeper philosophy nor follow a greater example.

"... we do not quite forget,
Nor quite remember, till the last days seem
The waving memory of a lovely dream."

INDEX

Abdul Hamid II, Sultan, 202-3
Abydos, temple of, 173-4
Academy of Music, Buffalo, 20
Academy of Music, New York City, 33
Acropolis, the, Athens, 209
Adams, Brooks, 236
Adams, Mr. and Mrs. Thatcher, 60, 61
Ægean Sea, the, 200
Agassiz, 103, 114
Aix les Bains, 40
Alden, John, vi
Aldrich, Mr. and Mrs. Thomas Bailey, 53
Alexander the Great, sarcophagus of, 203
Alexandra, Princess, 237, 238
Alexis, Grand Duke, 39, 40
American Academy at Rome, 142
Anderson, Mary, 20
Arnold, Matthew, 266
Arthur, Alan, 157
Arthur, Chester A., 157
Asia Minor, 191 ff.
Assouan, 177 ff.
Assouan Dam, the, 180
Astor, Mrs., 148
Astor, Mrs. Jack, 153
Astor, Viscount, 65
Astor, Waldorf, 65
Athens, 208 ff.

Babcock, General Orville E., 46
Bacon, Edward R., 258-60
Bailey, David, 250
Bailey, Lady Frances, 250
Bakhmeteff, Russian diplomat, 211
Baldwin, Charles, 105
Balzac's "Comédie Humaine," 240, 261
Bandits, Mexican, 126
Barrett, Lawrence, 31, 264
Barrymore, Ethel, 102, 277
Bartet, 233

Bass, John, the ancestor, marries daughter of John Alden, vi
Bass, Lyman K., 4, 39, 50, 53, 54, 66, 72, 180, 182, 186, 207, 208, 211, 217, 226, 243, 244, 248, 256, 258, 265, 276; friendship with Grover Cleveland, 41; marriage, 43; in Congress, 46-7; ill health, 65, 67, 70, 77, 78, 158; General Counsel for Denver and Rio Grande Railroad, 84, 91, 125; portrait of, by Rice, 151; death of, 157, 277; character and outlook of, 277
Bass, Metcalfe Lyman, 67, 68, 69, 73, 74, 158, 174-5, 214, 273
Bass, Susan, 182, 203
Bath, Steuben County, N. Y., 14
Bayard, Senator and Mrs. Thomas F., 45
Beach, Fred, 28-9
Beaman, Charles, 135
Beckwith, Carroll, 151
Beirut, 192-4
Belknap, General William W., 44, 46-7
Belknap, Mrs. William W., 46, 47
Bell, Dr., 78, 84, 131
Belmont, August, Sr., 29, 30, 31
Belmont, Mrs. August, 30
Belmont, August, the second, 24
Benedict, Commodore, 141
Benedict, Helen, 141
Bernhardt, Sarah, 231, 232, 234
Bierstadt, Albert, 25, 26
Bingham, Lady, 29
Bismarck, 107
Bismarck, Herbert, 107
Bismarck, William, 107
Bissell, Wilson S., 41
Blackburn, Representative and Mrs. Joseph, 46
Blaine, James G., 4, 42, 45, 46, 49, 103, 108, 139, 257, 258
Blaine, Mrs. James G., 45, 139

279

INDEX

Blair, Woodbury, 48
Blake, Edwine, 268-9, 274-5
Blashfield, Edwin, 177
Bliss, Reverend Mr., of Beirut, 192, 194
Blowitz, Henri de, 256
Blunt, Sir Wilfrid and Lady, 167
Bologna, 60
Bonheur, Rosa, 240
Bonnat, Leon, 240
Booth, Edwin, 31, 32, 146
Braggiotti, Mrs., 273-4
Braggiotti, Isidore, 274
Brimmer, Mr. and Mrs. Martin, 132, 133-4, 196, 208, 210, 230, 246, 257
Brisbane, Albert, 150, 151
Brisbane, Arthur, 150
Bristow, Benjamin H., 43, 47
Bristow, Mrs. Benjamin H., 47
Bristow, Nannie, 100
Broadmoor, Colorado Springs, 105
Broncho, the wild, blood of ancient war horses in, 22
Brooklyn Museum, 23
Brown, Horatio, 219
Brown, Rawdon, 218
Browning, Elizabeth Barrett, 178, 220
Browning, Robert, 220, 261
Bruce, Sir Edward, 250
Bryce, Calvin S., 229
Bryce, Mrs. Calvin S., 152
Bubastis, temple of, 188
Buchan, John, vii
Buckle's "History of Civilization," 266
Budge, Sir Ernest, 186, 187, 190
Buffalo, N. Y., memories of, 3 ff., 15 ff., 34-5, 38-9
Buffalo Club, the, 22
Bunker Hill, battle of, Metcalfe ancestor killed at, v
Burden, Mrs. Douglas, 25
Burden, Mrs. Jay, 146
Burton, Sir Richard, 200
Byron, Lord, 220, 221, 222

Cadwallader, John, of New York, 66
Cadwallader, John, of Philadelphia, 66
Cairo, Egypt, 158-71
Cairo, Ills., 8, 9
Calvé, 152
Cameron, Senator Donald, 65, 66
Cameron, Lizzie, 65-6
Cameron, Simon, 65
Canal boat traveling, 16

Canfield's gambling house, 155
Cantacuzene, Princess, 65
Capri, 57-8
Carlotta, wife of Emperor Maximilian, 63, 215-16
Carmencita, 151
Carr, Comyn, 263
Carroll, Governor, of Carrollton, 254
Carroll, Phil, 254
Cary, Dr. Charles, 24
Cary, Evelyn Rumsey, 23
Cary, George, 24
Cary, Julia Love, 23, 24
Cary, Phoebe and Alice, 19
Cary, Dr. Walter, 23, 24
Castelar, Spanish president, 58
Cavour, 56
Centennial Exhibition of 1876, at Philadelphia, 67
Certosa di Pavia, the, 227
Chamberlain, Joseph, 260
Chandler, Zachariah, 48
Chanler, Elizabeth, 144
Chanler, Winthrop, 139, 232
Chanler, Mrs. Winthrop, 254
Chapman, John Jay, 144, 185
Cheyenne Mountain, 90, 115, 122
Chinese, qualities of the high-class, 92
Chirol, Sir Valentine, 256
Choate, Joseph, 135
Chopin, 233, 265
Churchman, Mrs. William, 110
Civil War, the, 19
Clairmont, Jane, 183, 184, 220
Clemens, Mr. and Mrs. Samuel, 35
Cleveland, Grover, 39, 41, 141, 164, 208, 258, 277
Cobra, the, 159
Cochran, Bourke, 108
Cohasset, Mass., 116
Cologne, 62
Colorado, 69 ff.
Colorado Springs, 70, 76, 85 ff., 132, 270 ff.
"Comédie Humaine," Balzac's, 240, 261
Conant, Mr., 70, 71
Conkling, Roscoe S., 42, 48, 49, 182-3, 258
Conkling, Mrs. Roscoe S., 49
Constantinople, 201 ff.
Coppell, George R., 126
Copts, massacre of, 171
Corfu, 214-15
Corinth, 213

INDEX

Corneille, 245
Cornell, Douglas, 20
Cornell, Katharine, 20
Coward, Mrs. Timothy, 25
Cox, Bishop, 54
Cox, Sunset, 201, 202
Cram, Henry, 147
Crawford, Marion, 117
Croisette, the actress, 231
Crosby, Nina, 275
Crystal-gazing, 27
Cunningham, Edward, 116
Cunningham, Mrs. Edward, 120
Cushman, Charlotte, 21
Custer, General George A., 19
Custer, Mrs. George A., 19–20

D'Acosta brothers, the, 122
Damascus, 194–6
Dana, Charles A., 148–9
Dana, Mrs. Charles A., 148
Dana, Eunice, 149
Dances of the 'seventies, 39
Darwin, Charles, 261, 266
Davis, Judge Bancroft, 66
Day, George, 272
Day, Susan, 272
Dégas, 235
de Lesseps, Ferdinand, 187
Delmonico's, 32
Denderah, temple of, 174
Dennison, Jane, 73, 75
Dennison, Mrs. William, 49
Denver, Colo., 125
Denver and Rio Grande Railway, 84, 91, 125, 126
Depew, Chauncey M., 43
De Reszkes, the, 152, 264
Dervishes, 167
Dexter, Arthur, 103
Dexter, Mr., 217
Diaz, Porfirio, 125, 126
Dickens, Charles, 255
Dickinson, Emily, 114
Dickson, Samuel, 122, 217
Dixey, Henry, 21, 267
d'Orémieux, Monsieur and Madame, 28
Doucet, Jacques, 233
Draper, Eben, 100
Draper, Dr. George, 150
Draper, Paul, 149
Draper, Ruth, 149
Draper, Dr. William, 149, 277

Draper, Mrs. Dr. William, 149, 152
Drew, John, 264
Duels, abolition of, 29
Duff Gordon, Lady, 177–8
Dumas, Alexandre, 241
Du Maurier, George, 261, 263
Dunham, Etta, 144
Dunham, James, 144
Duran, Carolus, 240
Duse, Eleanora, 102, 118

Eden, Mr. and Mrs. Frederick, 224–5
"Edgeplain," 91, 110, 119–20, 122, 157, 269, 273
Edmunds, Senator George F., 44
Egypt, 158 ff.; American excavation in, 177
Eleusis, temple of, 209
Eliot, George, 266
Elizabeth, Empress of Austria, 154
Ely, Marchioness of, 249
Endicott, Mary, 260
Ephesus, 196, 197
Epidaurus, 213
Erie Canal, 16
Esculapius, 213
Ethel, Agnes, 20–1, 102
Eugénie, Empress, 104, 106, 187
Eustis, Jim, 275
Evarts, Senator William M., 43, 135

Fagnani, Joseph, 33
Fargo, William G., 34
Farnbühler, Count von, 107
Fearn, Mr. and Mrs., Athens, 208
Fechter, the actor, 264
Ferris, Edith, 273
Field, Kate, 127
Fillmore, Millard, 41
Fire department of early days in Buffalo, 16–17
Fish, Miss Edith, 45
Fish, Hamilton, 43–4
Fish, Mrs. Hamilton, 44, 45, 47
Florence, 59
Folsom, Frances, 41
Folsom, Oscar, 41
Forbes, W. Cameron, 121
Forbes, John, 120
Forbes-Robertson, 264
Forrest, Edwin, 21
Fountain Abbey, 50
Fowler, Mrs. Robert L., Jr., 147
Fox sisters, the, 27

INDEX

Fra Angelico, 59
Frémont, John C., 69
Fuller, Mrs., 25

Ganson, John, 25
Garden of the Gods, the, 69–70
Gardiner, Jack, 116
Gardiner, Mrs. Jack, 116–19, 134, 196
Garfield, James A., 49
Garrick, David, 245–6
Garston, Mrs., 123
Gay, Mr. and Mrs. Walter, 230
Gebhard, Freddie, 157
Genoa, 52
Gibbons, Cardinal, 66–7
Gilder, Richard Watson, 142, 143
Gillespie, Mrs., relative of Benjamin Franklin, 66
Glumbowitz, Silesia, 104, 105–6, 107, 109, 110, 111
Goddard, Mrs. Daniel, 115–16
Goddard, Harry, 274
Gold and silver in Colorado, 93
Goodyear, Conger, 22
Grain, transporting of, in early days, 16
Granby, Marchioness of, 253
Grant, Mrs. Fred, 44, 65
Grant, Mary, 248
Grant, Ulysses S., 42, 44, 46, 66, 91–3, 167
Grant, Mrs. Ulysses S., 44, 47, 49, 66
Grant, Ulysses, Jr., 48, 65
Greece, 208–14
Green, General Francis V., 45
Greenough, the sculptor, 208
Grenfell, Sir William, Sirdar of Egypt, 165, 185
Griswold, Frank Gray, 147

Hale, Senator Eugene, 46
Hamilton, Gail, 45
Hammerling, 212
Hamp, Mrs., 90
Harcourt, Sir William, 103, 250
Harden, Maximilian, 107
Hardy, Thomas, 266
Hare, John, 260
Harem, visit to an Egyptian, 168–9
Harmsworth, Alfred, 256
Harriman, Mrs. E. H., 32
Harrison, Sir Frederick, 263
Harrison, Peter, 263
Harvest Festival of St. Geronimo at Taos, New Mexico, 94–6

Hastings, Thomas, 141
Hatzfeldt, Fürst, 109
Hatzfeldt, Princess, 109
Havana, 135–8
Hay, John, 66, 240
Hearn, Lafcadio, 92, 134
Heidelberg, 62
Heine, Heinrich, 263
Helen of Troy, 102, 185
Herrick, Mrs. Peggy, 120–1
Hewitt, Mr. and Mrs. Abram S., 62
Hieroglyphics, Mayan and Egyptian, 144–5
Higginson, Henry, 119
Higginson, Thomas Wentworth, 114
Hippocrates, 213
Historical Museum, Buffalo, 24
Hoffman, Malvina, 32
Hoffman, Richard, 32
Hohenlohe, Cardinal, 55
Holland, 62–3
Holmes, Judge, 134
Hood, Admiral, Lord, 271
Hooper, Mrs. William, 120
Hopi Indians, snake dance of, 198–9
Horseracing with sleighs in Buffalo, 15–16
Howells, William D., 219
Howland, Mrs. Samuel, 30, 167
Hoyt, Elizabeth Colgate, 66
Hughes, Charles Evans, 269
Humbert, Prince, 55, 57
Hunt, Governor, of Colorado Territory, 126, 129
Hunt, Helen, x, 71, 78, 113–16, 143
Hunt, William, the painter, 134

Ibsen, 266
Impressionists, the, 235
Ingalls, Mr. and Mrs. John, 272
Ingersoll, Robert G., 193
Irving, Sir Henry, 21, 262–3

Janauschek, Madame, 21
Jefferson, Joseph, 21
Jewell, Marshall, 48
Jewett, Admiral, 48
Joachim, 262
Jones, Robert Edward, 13
Joppa, 192
Josefy, the pianist, 121
Juarez, 63–4
Jutland, battle of, 271

INDEX

Karnak, ruins of, 174
Kemble, Frances, 10, 21
Kendall, Mr. and Mrs., 260
Kimball, Heber, Mormon Elder, 128
Kirkpatrick, General, 20

Ladenburg, Mrs. Adolf, 251
La Farge, Christopher, 141
La Farge, Grant, 140
La Farge, John, 4, 119, 140-1, 142, 143
Lamborne, Colonel and Mrs., 94, 95, 130
Langdon, Mr., Mrs. Clemens' brother, 36
Langtry, Lily, 154
Lansing, Mr., missionary in Cairo, 170-1
Lansing, William, 71
Layard, Sir Henry and Lady, 223-4
Le Gallienne, Richard, xiii, 261
Lehmann, Lilli, 152
Leonard, Dr., of Columbia University, 7, 33, 232
Leonardo, 227
Lewis, Sir Wilmont, 256
Lincoln, Abraham, 13-14
Lindberg, Col. Charles A., 25
Lindsay, Ronald, 66
Liszt, 55, 121-2, 265
Lockwood, Florence, 140-1, 148
Lodge, Henry Cabot, 134
London in 1888, 248-66
Love, Miss Maria, 23, 38
Lovejoy, City Surveyor of Buffalo, 4
Lovering, George, 38
Lowell, Amy, 154
Lowell, Percival, 134
Lucca, 42
Luini, 227

McClellan, George B., 43
McClellan, Mrs. George B., 43
McCormick, Mrs. Hall, 272
McKim, Charles F., 142
McKim, Mead & White, 4
McLane, Robert M., Minister to France, 246
McLean, Mr. and Mrs. Edward, 94
McVeagh, Franklin, 68
Macauley, Mrs., school of, 7, 18, 28, 31-4, 232
Madison Square Garden, 142
Manitou Park, Colo., 78 ff.
Manitou Springs, Colo., 69

Marcy, General and Mrs. R. B., 43
Margarita, Queen, of Italy, 54
Maria Theresa, 227
Marie Antoinette, 123, 241, 243
Marionettes, 225
Markets of early days, 10
Markham, Pauline, 32
Marriage, the French arranged, 239
Maspero, Gaston C. C., 144, 185
Matthews, J. N.. 42
Maugham, Somerset, 225
Maupassant, Guy de, 240
Maximilian, Emperor, 63, 215-16
Mayan and Egyptian hieroglyphics, 144-5
Mead, William R., 142
Melba, 152, 264
Meredith, George, 261
Merode, Cleo, 63
Merry del Val, Cardinal, 144
Meryon, Charles, 237
Mesmerism, 27
Metcalfe, Dr. Frank, 181, 211
Metcalfe, James S., 68
Metcalfe, Thomas, v-vi
Metcalfe, Mr., the author's father, 4, 6, 8, 14, 20, 27, 41, 42, 64, 119
Metcalfe, Mrs., the author's mother, 4, 5, 6, 7, 11, 14, 41, 42, 180, 181, 186, 187, 190, 208
Metcalfes of Yorkshire, the, vi
Metropolitan Museum of Art, 17, 33, 177, 245
Metropolitan Opera House, New York, the opera at, 151-4
Metternich, Princess, 106
Mexican National Railway, 125-6
Meyers, Otto, 125
Milan, 226-8
Milburn, Devereux, 21
Milburn, George, 21
Milburn, John G., 22, 122, 152, 252, 268, 275
Milburn, Mrs. John G., 275
Millet, Jean François, 134
Minstrels, negro, 21
Molière, 245
Molmenti, 219
Moltke, Count, 107
Monet, 235
Monterey, Calif., 131, 132
Morgan, J. Pierpont, 142, 177
Morley, John, 123
Mormonism, 26

INDEX

Mormons, polygamy among, and its suppression, 127–9
Morris, William, 67
Morton, General Oliver P., 49
Mounet-Sully, 232
Movius, Edward, 51
Munthe, Dr., 57
Murger, Henry, 236
Museum of Modern Art, New York City, 22
Mussulmans, religion and habits of, 160–1, 162; fanaticism of, 170–1

Naples, 57–9
Napoleon I, 164
Napoleon III, 24, 187, 216
Neilson, Adelaide, 21
Newport, 155–7
New Year's calling, 17
New York City, police of, xi; in the 'seventies, 28, 30, 32–3; in the 'eighties, 140 ff.
Niagara Falls, 15
Niblo's Garden, New York City, 18, 33
Nicholson, George, 271
Nile River, journey up the, 172 ff.
North Cheyenne Canyon, 123–4
Northcliffe, Lord, 256
Norton, Charles Eliot, 251

Oakman, Mrs., 183
Oelrichs, Herman, 24
Olmsted, Frederick Law, 24
Olympia, 211
Ouida's novels, 260–1

Paderewski, 152
Pæstum, 59
Palmer, Mrs. Potter, 44
Palmer, General William J., 78, 84, 88, 124, 125, 126, 131–2, 157, 275
Palmer, Queen (Mrs. William J.), 88, 99, 126, 254
Paris, 64; in 1888, 229–47
Parrish, Anne, 86
Parrish, Maxfield, 86
Parrish, Steven, 86
Parrish, Tom, 85, 86
Parthenon, the, Athens, 209
Paul, Mrs., of Philadelphia, 65
Pazolini, 56
Pearce, Mayor, of Boston, 53
Perkins, Bob, 271–2

Perkins, Charles, 121
Perkins, Mr. and Mrs. Charles, of New York, 271–2
Perkins, Mr. and Mrs. Charles W., 120, 270
Perkins, Elise, 271
Perkins, Fanny, 271
Perkins, Mary, 121, 271
Perry, Admiral Matthew C., 30
Phelps, Edward J., Minister to England, 249, 257
Philadelphia, Centennial Exhibition of 1876 at, 67
Philæ, temple of, 180
Phrenology, 27
Pike's Peak, 69, 119, 273
Pinero, Arthur W., 260
Piræus, 208
Pisa, 59
Pitt, William, 256
Pius IX, Pope, 53, 54
Plançon, 152
Police force, New York City, xi
Polignac, Princess, 275
Polo, 21, 24
Polygamy, Mormon, and its suppression, 127–9
Pompeii, 58–9
Porter, Mrs. Augustus, 25
Porter, Fort, on Niagara River, gathering place of Buffalo fashion, 37–8
Portland, Duchess of, 253
Post, Waldron Kintzing, 271
Potter, Maria, 143
Pourtalès, Berthe, 102–11
Pourtalès, Count, 102–3, 114
Pourtalès, Count Jacques, 110
Pourtalès, Count James, 104 ff., 109, 110–11, 274
Pourtalès, Count Otto, 74, 75–6
Pourtalès, Countess (Princess Putpus), 106, 273
Pratt, Mrs. Orin, Mormon woman, story of, 127–8
Prescott, William H., the historian, 133
Prospectors, 93
Pueblo Indians, 95–6
Pupin, Prof. Michael, 198

Railroad projects in Colorado, 125–6, 129
Rand Building, Buffalo, 3
Récamier, Madame, 104
Rehan, Ada, 264

INDEX

Religious sects, creation of new, after Civil War, 26
Remenyi, Hungarian violinist, 121–2
Renoir, 235
Renshaw, Alfred, 256–7
Rice, William, 151
Richardson, Abby Sage, 77
Richmond, Dean, 16
Risley, Hanson A., 98
Ristori, 32
Robeson, George M., Secretary of the Navy, 250
Robeson, Mrs. George M., 48
Robespierre, 123
Rodin, 235
Rogers, Admiral, 48
Rogers, Fanny, 68
Rogers, Robert Cameron, 68
Rogers, Mr. and Mrs. Sherman S., 41, 130
Rome, 53 ff.
Roosevelt, Theodore, 269
Roosevelt, Mrs. West, 28
Rossetti, Dante Gabriel, 67
Rostand, xi
Rothschild, Baron Alphonse de, 48
Rothschild, Baroness, 154, 233
Rothschild, the banking house of, 29
Rubinstein, 152
Rumsey, Aaron, 3
Rumsey, Bert, 24
Rumsey, Bronson, 22–3
Rumsey, Charles Cary, 23
Rumsey, Jane Cary, 268
Rumsey, Lawrence, 24
Rumsey, Mary Harriman, 23
Ruskin, John, 219, 226
Rutherford, Winthrop, 156

St. Gaudens, Augustus, 142, 143
St. James Hall, Buffalo, burning of, 17
Salisbury, Lord, 253
Salt Lake City, 125, 126, 128
Sampson, Joseph, 242
Sanders, Jake, 269
Sargent, John, 144, 146, 147, 151
Sargent, Professor, of Boston, 148
Scarabeus, the, 175
Schliemann, Heinrich, 185, 191
Schumann-Heink, 152, 153
Sedgwick, Mrs. Lily, 68
Seidl, Anton, 151
Sequoias, giant, of California, 132
Seward, Olive Risley, 98

Seward, William T., 98
Seymour, Horatio, 49
Shaw, Bernard, 199
Sheldon, Edward, 225
Shelley, 59, 222, 252
Shepheard's Hotel, Cairo, 160
Sheridan, General Philip H., 34
Sherman, General William T., 65
Silsbee, Captain, of Salem, Mass., 183–4
Simplon Pass, the, 60, 61
Smith, Joseph, 26, 127–8
Smoking in early days, 17
Snake dance of the Hopi Indians, 198–9
Sothern, E. A., 21
Spencer, Herbert, 261
Spiritualistic mediums, 27
Sprague, Kate Chase, 42, 258
Stafford, Marquis and Marchioness of, 276
Stafford-Northcote, Sir, 45
Stanhope, Claude, 89
Stanton, Edwin M., 149
Steed, Wickham, 256
Stevens, Frederic, 242
Stevens, Joseph S., 242, 243, 244, 251, 275
Stevenson, Archie, 269
Straus, Mr. and Mrs. Oscar S., 202
Strettel, Alma, 263
Strong, Marian, 25
Sumner, Senator and Mrs. Charles, 43
Surratt, Mrs., 14
Sutherland, Duke and Duchess of, 276–7
Swinburne, Dr., of Albany, 130
Swinburne, Louis J., 122–3, 261
Symonds, John Addington, 230

Taj Mahal, the, 227
Talleyrand, Marquise de, 242–4
Talleyrand-Perigord, Duke de, 242–5
Tanta, Egypt, visit to and phallic revelry at, 186–90
Taos, New Mexico, 94–6
Taylor, Deems, 263
Taylor, General Dick, 19
Taylor, Mrs. Josephine, 152
Tennyson, Alfred, 248
Ternina, 152
Terry, Ellen, 21, 102, 248, 262, 264
Tesla, Nicola, 197–8
Thayer, Mrs. Bayard, 118

INDEX

Thebes, 174–5
Thom, General, 267
Thomas, General George H., 65
Thomas, Theodore, 33
Thornton, Sir Edward and Lady, 66
Timmins, Gemma, 175, 183, 186, 260
Timmins, Herbert, 132, 133, 275
Timmins, Mrs. Herbert, 133
Timmins, Minna, 133, 144, 175, 183, 184–5, 186, 201, 208, 210, 229, 257, 260, 277
Timon, Bishop, of Buffalo, 53, 54
Tod, Kennedy, 143
Touzalin, A. E., 270
Touzalin, Ellen, 270–1
Trachenburg, 109
Tracy, Frank, 21
Traveling in early days, 16
Trieste, 215
Turenne, Count de, 48
Turks and Greeks, contrast of characteristics of, 205
Twain, Mark, 35, 36, 37
Twombly, Ruth, 146
Tyre and Sidon, 198

Vanderbilt, Commodore, 28, 145
Vanderbilt, Mrs. Cornelius, 145
Vanderbilt, George, 146
Vanderbilt, Mr. and Mrs. William H., 145
Vanderbilts, the, 145–6
Van Rensselaer, Mrs. Schuyler, 150
Venice, 60; in 1888, 217–26
Verdi, 52
Veronese, Paolo, 217
Victor Emmanuel, King, 56, 57
Victoria, Queen, 252, 253, 260

Waddington, Madame, 237–8
Wadsworth sisters, the, 24–5
Wagner, Richard, 220
Wagram, Duchess, 233
Wales, Edward, Prince of, 237–8
Wall, Berry, 157
Wallace, General Lew, 201
Wallack, Lester, 33
Walpole, Horace, 125
Walsh, "Bonanza," 93–4
Warren, Whitney, 142
Washburne, Elihu B., Ambassador to Paris, 50

Washington, social and political life in the 'seventies, 43 ff., 65–6
Watson, Gertrude, 22
Watson, S. V. R., 13, 22
Watson, Mrs. S. V. R., 22, 38
Watts, George F., 248, 262
Webster, Daniel, 120
Wellesley, Mr. and Mrs. Arthur, 89
Wells, Jane, 39
Wetmore, Senator and Mrs., 104
White, Mr. and Mrs. Harry, 249–50
White, Horace, 25
White, Stanford, 141, 142, 143, 151
White, Sir William and Lady, 206, 207
Whitman, Mrs., 134
Whitney, Gertrude Vanderbilt, 146
Widor, organist at Saint Sulpice, Paris, 237
Wilde, Oscar, 245
Wilder, Clara, 275, 276
William II, German Emperor, 107, 214
Wilson, Francis, 21
Winchester Cathedral, 50
Winthrop, Bronson, 147
Winthrop, Egerton, 146–7
Wister, Dr. Owen, 263
Witherspoon, Rev. Orlando, 12
Wolcott, Edward O., 135, 138, 192, 268, 269
Wolcott, Frances M., girlhood home in Buffalo and early memories, 3 ff., 15 ff.; school days in New York, 28 ff.; marriage to Lyman K. Bass, 43; life in Washington, 43–9, 65–8; European tour in 1875, 50–64; birth of son, 67; in Colorado, 68 ff., 85 ff.; in Egypt, Asia Minor and Europe, 158 ff.; return to America, 266–7, 268; death of Mr. Bass, 157, 277
Wolcott, Mrs. Roger, 133
Wolcott, Rev. Samuel, 192–3
Wolf, Baron, 107
Wollstonecraft, Mary, 252
Wood, General Leonard, 136
Woodhull, Virginia, 26
Worth Père, and Jean, of Paris, 104, 229–30

Young, Brigham, 26, 126, 129

Zambelli, the dancer, 231
Zola, Emile, 240

Printed in the United States
39300LVS00003B/34